Decks

Meredith® Books
Des Moines, Iowa

Stanley Complete Decks
Editor: Larry Johnston
Photo Researcher: Harijs Priekulis
Copy Chief: Terri Fredrickson
Publishing Operations Manager: Karen Schirm
Edit and Design Production Coordinator: Mary Lee Gavin
Editorial and Design Assistants: Renee E. McAtee,
    Kairee Windsor
Marketing Product Managers: Aparna Pande, Isaac Petersen,
    Gina Rickert, Stephen Rogers, Brent Wiersma, Tyler Woods
Book Production Managers: Pam Kvitne,
    Marjorie J. Schenkelberg, Rick von Holdt, Mark Weaver
Contributing Copy Editor: Ira Lacher
Technical editor, The Stanley Works: Mike Maznio
Contributing Proofreaders: Susan Brown, Sue Fetters,
    David Krause
Indexer: Donald Glassman

**Additional Editorial Contributions from
    Art Rep Services**
Director: Chip Nadeau
Writer: Martin Miller
Designer: LK Design
Illustrator: Dave Brandon
Photographer: Mike Dvorak
Technical Director: Mike Schonhardt

Meredith® Books
Executive Director, Editorial: Gregory H. Kayko
Executive Director, Design: Matt Strelecki
Executive Editor/Group Manager: Larry Erickson
Senior Associate Design Director: Tom Wegner

Publisher and Editor in Chief: James D. Blume
Editorial Director: Linda Raglan Cunningham
Executive Director, Marketing: Jeffrey B. Myers
Executive Director, New Business Development: Todd M. Davis
Executive Director, Sales: Ken Zagor
Director, Operations: George A. Susral
Director, Production: Douglas M. Johnston
Business Director: Jim Leonard

Vice President and General Manager: Douglas J. Guendel

Meredith Publishing Group
President: Jack Griffin
Senior Vice President: Bob Mate

Meredith Corporation
Chairman and Chief Executive Officer: William T. Kerr
President and Chief Operating Officer: Stephen M. Lacy

In Memoriam: E.T. Meredith III (1933-2003)

Thanks to
New Image Deck Construction, Waconia, Minnesota
John and Karen LaFond
Sass Construction, Eden Prairie, Minnesota
Lampert Yards
Thomas Homes
Monarch Homes
Deckburst
CertainTeed Corp.
Cover photo location: Mr. & Mrs. Einar Frobom

All of us at Meredith® Books are dedicated to providing you
with the information and ideas you need to enhance your home
and garden. We welcome your comments and suggestions
about this book. Write to us at:
    Meredith Corporation
    Meredith Books
    1716 Locust St.
    Des Moines, IA 50309–3023

If you would like more information on other Stanley products,
call 1-800-STANLEY or visit us at: www.stanleyworks.com
Stanley® and the notched rectangle around the Stanley name
are registered trademarks of The Stanley Works and
subsidiaries.

If you would like to purchase any of our home improvement,
cooking, crafts, gardening, or home decorating and design
books, check wherever quality books are sold. Or visit us at:
merredithbooks.com

Note to the Readers: Due to differing conditions, tools,
and individual skills, Meredith Corporation assumes no
responsibility for any damages, injuries suffered, or losses
incurred as a result of following the information published
in this book. Before beginning any project, review the
instructions carefully, and if any doubts or questions remain,
consult local experts or authorities. Because codes and
regulations vary greatly, you always should check with
authorities to ensure that your project complies with all
applicable local codes and regulations. Always read and
observe all of the safety precautions provided by
manufacturers of any tools, equipment, or supplies,
and follow all accepted safety procedures.

CONTENTS

CONTENTS

HOW TO USE THIS BOOK

If you're thinking about adding a deck to your home but have never built one before, this book is the best place you could start. Greatly expanded from the first edition, *Stanley Complete Decks* contains all the information you'll need to plan, design, and build the deck you've dreamed of. Here you'll find all the information you need to create an outdoor living space that increases the comfort and enjoyment of your home and does so within your budget.

Building a deck is straightforward. It requires only average carpentry skills and basic tools. Building your deck will prove more enjoyable and the results will be more satisfying if you take time before you start to learn as much as you can about the project. Adding a deck is not just a matter of tacking a wooden platform to the back of the house. The best decks combine architectural style with your family's needs and desires to create a space that fits best into both the climate and landscape.

That's where the first two chapters come in. In those pages you'll find ideas to help you pick the right location and develop a functional, beautiful design. There's also a preview of three deck plans, which are detailed later in the book. Even if you've already decided how you want your deck to look, you might find some new design ideas to incorporate. The chapter includes a host of photos to help you visualize the ideal deck; consider them a design library that can help you decide which stylistic and functional elements you want for your deck.

Building a deck without a plan can result in disappointment—a deck that's too small or that is uncomfortable or unusable during some times of the day. Lack of planning can also affect the safety and longevity of your deck. The chapter on drawing plans shows you how to distill your research and study into a plan for a perfect deck.

The chapters covering tools and materials show which tools are essential and which are helpful, along with tips for selecting materials for your deck project. You'll find advice on everything from buying lumber to selecting framing fasteners, information critical to the structural integrity of your deck as well as its appearance.

For a clear, concise look at all the tasks required for building a basic deck, read through chapter 5, "A Quick Guide to Deck Building." This chapter provides a step-by-step explanation of everything you need to put up your structure, from forming the footings to building stairs and railings.

The next three chapters show how to build a freestanding deck, a deck on a sloped site, and a multilevel deck. You can build one of these projects as-is or adapt it to fit your deck vision. Read through these chapters for tips that will make your work easier. After that you'll find information about building or adding elements to your deck that will increase its usefulness. And the chapter on finishing and repairing shows you how to protect the results of your hard work and to keep your deck in top shape.

If you're new to carpentry or your skills are just a little rusty, you can bring yourself up to speed with the information in the last chapter, "Mastering Basic Skills." This basic course in carpentry includes everything from how to take measurements to how to use power tools. Even if you know basic carpentry, you'll find this chapter a useful reference as you work.

What if...?

No two projects are alike, so you may run into situations unlike those shown in the instructions. When you encounter a difference, check the lower half of the page for boxes that provide more information.

Boxes labeled "What If… ?" help you apply techniques to specific situations. You'll also find "Stanley Pro Tip," "Refresher Course," and "Safety First" boxes. These items contain tips and advice, quick recaps of applicable techniques and methods shown elsewhere in the book, and information that will help you work safely.

Know your limits

Understanding your physical limits and time constraints will go a long way toward making your work enjoyable and safe.

Plan your time carefully—make a list of the stages of your work. Check the "Prestart Checklist" at the beginning of each project to get an idea of how much time it will take, and allow a little extra if you're new to do-it-yourself projects. Take frequent breaks, and stop working when you get tired; fatigue is a common cause of mistakes and accidents.

SAFETY FIRST
Keeping the work site safe

Working with power tools, standing on ladders, and building any kind of structure with wood can pose safety hazards. Keep yourself safe with the following steps:
■ Set goals, and allow enough time to complete them. Take rest breaks. Fatigue and frustration quickly lead to unsafe practices, mistakes, and accidents.
■ Make the workplace comfortable. Keep tools organized and close at hand. Invest in a good tool belt or bucket belt and put each tool back in the same place after using it. Not having to look for a tool saves time and reduces frustration.
■ Wear a respirator or high-quality dust mask when sawing or engaging in any activity that produces airborne dust.

■ Eye protection is a must when sawing or chiseling any material. Get the kind of safety glasses with protection on the sides.
■ Save your knees and hands—wear knee pads and get into the habit of wearing gloves when working. Gloves will not only protect your hands from abrasions and cuts, they'll also give you a better grip on hand tools and materials. Take them off when using your tablesaw or mitersaw.
■ Make sure you have all the materials and tools you need on hand before you start any phase of a project. Running to the home center or hardware store in the middle of a task takes you from the work and can increase your frustration.

CHOOSING A SITE AND STYLE

Decks have become a fixture in the American landscape—and it's no wonder. A deck can make your home more spacious, more comfortable, and more valuable—at a fraction of the cost of any other home addition. Decks let you expand your living space to the outdoors, providing a place for activities you might not otherwise be able to enjoy. A well-planned deck enhances the landscaping around your house and can even become the focus of a yard.

The word "deck" might make you think of a wooden platform at its most basic, about 8×10 feet, sticking out from the back of the house. This chapter will show you how that pallet-like platform, along with the bare, ground-level concrete-slab patio, is merely a starting point for today's outdoor living spaces. A deck today can certainly be as simple a structure as will meet your needs. It also can become an elaborate architectural creation that is as important a part of your home as the living room. What distinguishes the modern deck from its earlier counterparts is that it's not just a platform. Instead it is an expression of its owner's lifestyle and an extension of the landscape in which it stands. In short, today's deck has a purpose as well as a personality.

Achieving unity of design, livability, and harmony with the landscape is what this chapter is about. All deck planning starts with one question: How will you use your deck? Once you and your family have answered this question, decisions about where to place the deck, how large it needs to be, and how it should look will fall into place. Think about all the ways you might enjoy your deck, including new things you might want to try.

Whether you plan to use your deck for quiet dinners for two, family barbecues, outdoor parties, recreation, sitting and contemplating the landscape—or all of these activities—you'll enjoy each one more when the deck design takes that use into account.

Start with a good plan, then add the right materials, sound construction techniques, and basic carpentry skills, and you can build a deck that will become a beautiful addition to your home.

All successful deck plans begin with one proposition: How will you and your family use your outdoor space?

CHAPTER PREVIEW

Planning with a purpose
page 8

Assessing your site
page 10

Getting to and from your deck
page 14

What size?
page 16

What shape?
page 18

STANLEY PRO TIP

Add value to your home

The National Home Builders Association estimates you can recover about 75 percent of the cost of deck construction when you sell your home. The exact return depends on which part of the country you live in and home resale values in your neighborhood. The cost of the deck plus the market value of your house generally should not exceed the value of any home in your neighborhood by more than 20 percent.

An inviting deck like this is both enjoyable and a valuable addition to your home.

PLANNING WITH A PURPOSE

Deck design begins with a look at your lifestyle. You'll want your deck to invite you into it, and the best way to create that space is to start making lists. Get the family together and gather everyone's opinions. Start with a wish list—put down everything without regard to practicality or cost. Then pare the list back to what you can afford, what you have room for, and what you have time to build.

Entertaining

If entertaining makes the final cut on your list, consider the number of guests you'll routinely invite. Small groups may not require much more space or furnishings than your family would need. But large gatherings need seating, cooking, and dining areas. Decide where you'll put the sit-down-dinner table and a buffet table for informal gatherings. And if you need a barbecue, you'll probably want to include a small sink as part of the space devoted to outdoor cooking.

Getting away from it all

If you need a special place to sip your morning coffee or just to relax with a good book or nothing but the landscape, plan an area with a little privacy. Simple furnishings, a hammock or outdoor recliner, plus some plants for screening out the rest of the neighborhood can quickly make an outdoor retreat. And if you need space for both privacy and parties, consider a narrow, unused side yard for your private deck and a large open area for entertaining. Unify the spaces with a wraparound design. Don't have enough room (or funds) for both? Then bring in benches or portable seating. You can move them around to create different-size areas as you need them.

Child's play

Decks can be perfect for children's play, especially if you give them wide stairs or descending platforms for their playgrounds.

You can't put the jungle gym on the deck, but you should make sure that the deck has a spot from which you can keep an eye on children playing in the yard.

Build in some flexibility so your deck can grow as the kids get older. A space that starts out as a sandbox can easily be transformed into a small platform with the addition of a few joists and decking. Plan your space so you can phase in such improvements in the future.

Gardening

Plants are something decks just can't get enough of. Planters, windowboxes, and flower pots will not only beautify the space, they'll also provide the perfect hobby garden for anyone whose green thumb appears only on weekends. The avid horticultural hobbyist can incorporate cold frames— even greenhouses—into the design. Build your own containers from the same material as your decking or railings, or purchase commercial units whose style fits your deck design.

Bringing back an old deck

If your house came with a deck that makes you feel like staying inside, it doesn't mean you have to tear it down and start over. Try improving it instead.

Unused decks usually suffer from practical or aesthetic problems. For example, if cooking space is cramped or guests are sitting sideways, it's a sure sign you need more room. Often just a small platform addition built from the same lumber will fix the problem and improve the looks of your landscape. Finish the new material so it blends with the old (see page 214).

Mix materials when practical. A ground-level flagstone or brick surface makes a great extension for an existing redwood platform deck. And if there's no room next to the deck, build a detached area farther from the house and unify the two spaces with a crushed-stone path. Lay decking on sleepers to cover an old slab patio.

Always try to build on what you have. Instead of trying to fit a fire pit into an old cramped design, extend the deck out into the yard to accommodate the new feature.

A deck doesn't have to be attached to the house—or anything. A freestanding deck can make a great spot for getaways, especially if you build it away from the busy life of the house and surround it with garden plants and greenery. Depending on location and your inclination, a deck like this could be planned as a sun deck or a shady haven.

If you want a spa or hot tub, allow plenty of access so the tub doesn't interfere with other deck activities. Spas, pools, and hot tubs are major focal points as well as primary centers of activity. This spa adds an extra dimension to outdoor living and relaxing, and its raised platform separates it visually from other areas on the deck.

Entertaining sometimes requires plenty of space for large groups. But what if you want a private spot too? Here's where a multilevel deck can give you the best of both worlds. Build your smaller lounging deck off an upper-story room, then add stairs to a larger lower-level deck outside the family room.

Decks are great for cookouts, whether you simply wheel out a portable barbecue or turn one area into an elaborate outdoor kitchen. Plan your outdoor space so it gives you plenty of room and also fits into the natural features of the landscape.

STANLEY PRO TIP

Checklist for deck planning

Good deck planning means taking an inventory of a number of factors. Here are some of the things you should keep in mind.

■ **Traffic flow:** If your deck will be built between the house and other backyard destinations—a utility shed or play area—connect them with 3-foot walkways.

■ **Views:** Orient the deck—and the furnishings—to make the most of a pleasing view. Don't hide the yard behind planters and decorative elements.

■ **Sun, shade, and wind:** Nature can turn an otherwise perfect location into a miserable spot. Note the patterns of the sun and shade, and provide shade where nature doesn't. You can move lightweight furniture as the sun moves or you can make your own shade by building an arbor or overhead structure. A lattice fence or a hedge will buffer the wind and reduce street noise, increase your privacy, and hide unsightly views (see page 32.).

■ **Storage:** Make a list of equipment you need to stow away, and plan storage that's easy to get to. You'd be surprised at how much you could put in a small shed attached to the wall of the house.

ASSESSING YOUR SITE

Landscape features—the terrain, existing vegetation, views, and climate—have a large effect on the design of your deck and where you build it. Before you draw final plans, look around your property to see if anything might require changes in your deck's design or location.

Terrain
The contour is the most significant feature of your landscape. No site is perfectly level, but many are generally flat, and that will help keep deck construction uncomplicated. A slope, especially one that falls off sharply, might mean you have to grade the soil or build a retaining wall.

Hillsides—as well as banks, ravines, and swales—can offer more design opportunities than you might think. Because decks are supported by posts, they are the best structures to build on slopes, allowing you to capitalize on other characteristics of the terrain. For example, land sloping away from a high spot can create magnificent views. Land that slants uphill from a deck site can provide natural privacy and shelter from the wind.

If you have to level the soil for a below-the-slope deck location, either cut it to form a flat area, or fill in a low spot, or both.

Both methods will create a surface of unstable soil that will settle unevenly and can stress a ground-level deck, weakening its structure. You'll need to tamp and firm the loose surface before installing such a design. Use footings, not piers, to support the posts, and dig the holes deep enough so the footings are in firm soil.

If the remaining soil in the slope is unstable, build a retaining wall to keep it from washing onto your deck surface. A retaining wall will also increase the sense of enclosure on a deck nestled into a hillside.

Soil
Soil composition and compaction, characteristics that can affect your site and how you prepare it, vary widely.

Loose, sandy loam absorbs water and drains quickly but erodes easily. Local codes may require posts set in concrete footings.

Silted soil is also easy to dig and compact, and posts should be set in concrete.

Sloped sites present a host of design opportunities. Stepping a deck down the slope in tiers establishes platforms for multiple uses—like a series of cascading grade-level decks. A single deck cantilevered over the top of a slope can provide spectacular views.

A verdant slope rolling down to a small deck creates a sense of shelter and privacy. Groundcovers can add color but more important, they'll keep the soil in place. Cushions turn the low retaining wall into bench seats.

Clay is dense and sheds water, which can create runoff problems. You may need to install drainage lines with storm sewers or catch basins.

Sun, shade, wind, and rain
Paying attention to weather patterns can mean the difference between a deck that's pleasant and inviting and one that stands unused. For example, a deck placed where the sun beats down without mercy will not be comfortable. Harsh winds will likewise limit the use of the deck. Become familiar with the way the elements affect your site and plan accordingly.

As the sun passes overhead, the amount of heat and light will vary at different times of the day and year. The sun's movement causes shadows—and shade—to shift throughout the day. Because working with nature is more efficient than working against it, you'll want to place your deck so sun and shade patterns correspond to times when you'll use it.

What to do with the dirt?

Landscapers often use the soil removed from grading to level other parts of the work site—a technique called cut-and-fill. Cut-and-fill eliminates the expense of disposing of excess soil, as well as the cost of purchasing fill dirt.

Cut-and-fill works best, of course, when the amount of soil removed equals the amount needed in fill areas. But if you still have excess from the deck site, use it in your landscape—in planting beds, raised or flush with the rest of the lawn.

Because you'll probably remove more than just topsoil, not all of the excavated dirt will be suitable for planting beds. Instead, make berms with it—low mounds of earth in a landscape. But don't spread excess soil around trees, even temporarily. Just a few extra inches of dirt over tree roots can suffocate feeder roots and kill the tree.

Working with nature always produces more enjoyable and attractive results than working against it. Trees and shrubs offer natural shade and screening, which keeps costs down because you don't have to build overhead structures or fences. And if one deck isn't enough, set several small decks throughout your landscape and link them with boardwalks or loose-stone paths.

When you're planning your deck, you might think of trees, rocks, large boulders, or slopes as obstacles. Instead, put them into the plan. Incorporating an opening for a tree requires only a few more pieces of framing lumber and little effort. The results can be stunning. Building this deck around the tree close to the house makes good use of the site.

THE SUN'S MOVEMENT
Choosing your site for shade

A north-side deck, in almost constant shade, can be too cool for comfort. Locating a large section of the deck beyond the shadow of the house can produce both shady and sunny areas. Consider a detached deck for comfort in a year-round cool climate.

A deck with a southern exposure receives sunlight most of the day, but from different angles as the seasons change. Summer sun is high, but winter sunlight comes in low. A lattice-covered pergola will filter the summer sun but allow full sun in the winter.

Sunlight warms an east-side deck in the morning, but this side of the house will be shaded sooner than others. That's great for morning coffee but can make evening hours unpleasantly cool in mild climates. Here, too, a detached deck can provide a solution.

A west-side deck starts the day in the shade, but by early afternoon, can become too hot to use. Here's where a wraparound can come to the rescue, offering you a chance to follow (or avoid) the harsh sun. Natural or man-made shade can also make such a site comfortable.

ASSESSING YOUR SITE (continued)

Watch how the sun moves across your property at various times of the day during warm months. Drive stakes in the yard so you can keep track of moving shade patterns. Make notes and use them when you put your plans on paper (see pages 48–55).

Note wind patterns in your yard the same way, and if possible put your deck in a spot that's sheltered from strong prevailing winds. Build a slatted fence or plant a windbreak—you'll transform a strong wind into a gentle breeze. To protect yourself from the rain, install solid roofing over a part of your deck.

Microclimates

If you've noticed that the temperature on a deck feels different from the air out in the yard, you've experienced the effects of a microclimate. Microclimates are small areas within a site that exhibit "weather" patterns different from the general area.

Microclimates result from a number of factors—materials used, the location of a structure or area, and terrain.

Different materials, for example, absorb and reflect different amounts of heat from the sun. They also reflect different degrees of light. Unstained light-color decking will reflect more heat and light than a dark wood. Such a surface might feel comfortably warm, but harsh and glaring.

A dark wood like Ipe won't reflect harsh sunlight, but it will absorb heat, which can make the surface uncomfortable underfoot during the day. The stored heat, however, will radiate back during the cool of the evening, and can extend the use of your deck after sunset.

A hilltop deck will feel warmer on a calm day than one at the bottom of an incline because cooler air flows downhill. What's more, if you trap the cold air at the bottom of a hill with retaining walls, fences, or house walls, you might make your deck quite cool in the evening.

Walls and fences also can create microclimates. Where you put a wall or fence and how you build it can increase or decrease the force of the wind. Solid structures won't reduce winds. That's because they create low-pressure pockets that pull the wind into the very area you want protected. The wind swirls over the top and drops back down—with equal force—at a distance roughly equal to the height of the fence.

Louvered or board-on-board fences offer a good compromise. They are closed enough to provide privacy, but open enough to let filtered wind through.

If your proposed site is already shaded during the times you'll use the deck, that makes decisions about location less complicated. But even if you don't have much flexibility in where you put the deck, you can alter the environment.

If you need additional shade, you can make some. Add trees and other plants to shade a site that gets too much afternoon sun. A pergola can filter hot sunlight. So can a roll-out awning, which you can retract when it's not needed.

Let roses or vines climb up an arbor to create a private shaded spot for outdoor reading—without blocking the breeze. Vines climbing up a lattice wall can cool off a site that gets hot in the late afternoon. Or you could try a compromise—a location that features partial shade and partial sunlight during the hours of greatest deck use.

Picture-perfect plans

Carry your camera along and take lots of photographs when you assess your site. Photographs call attention to details you may have missed because you see them every day.

For example, you may have forgotten that the neighbors can see right into your living room window. The camera will remind you that you need to correct this in your deck plans. You may have gotten used to how unattractive your utility shed is. A photo will tell you that you need a lattice screen.

Photos are especially helpful when you begin putting your plans on paper. Your site analysis will be a record of the characteristics of the landscape that need attention. Use the camera to help you keep track of the ideas you want to include on this drawing.

If nature hasn't provided shade for your deck site, you can make your own. Pergolas filter the sun and enhance the appearance of your deck. At a minimum, a table umbrella can make a quick and inexpensive shady spot on a sunny deck. Plan for the future too—a small tree planted now will add shade when it grows to its mature size.

Mature trees are always a blessing on a deck site, but don't let their age and size fool you—even large trees can be easily damaged by construction activities. Take extra care when digging and building around them. Minimize grade changes and avoid adding soil under the perimeter of the leaves. Even a thin layer of soil can suffocate delicate feeder roots.

Here's a site that could have been a good candidate for a patio, because it would have required only minimal grading. It's hard to imagine, however, any design fitting this spot as well as this deck. Its low profile seems to grow right from the ground up, and its integration with the landscape is enhanced by the simple lines of the pergola, the green lounge chairs and umbrellas, and the transitional shrubs around the perimeter.

It's usually a good idea to remove the sod under the deck and replace it with landscape fabric and gravel. Grade the site to drain away from the house. To improve drainage from a damp site, dig a perimeter trench around the deck and fill it with gravel. In extreme cases, add a perforated drainpipe in the trench and run it to a dry well or catch basin.

Fix foundation drainage first

If you have water in your basement, don't build a deck until you've determined the cause and fixed the problem. The problem may simply be that the ground slopes toward the foundation of your home instead of away from it. Here's an easy solution:

First, slope the soil next to the foundation away from the house at least 4 feet. You may have to bring in new soil to make a slope of this width. Next, lay down landscape fabric to minimize weeds. Once you've set the deck posts, cover the fabric with rock or wood chips.

Faulty or inadequate gutters and downspouts may also be the culprits. Check the joints in the gutters and the outlets where the downspouts connect to them. Seal any joints that are letting water through. Often adding an extension to the downspout—or even just a splash block—will cure the problem.

GETTING TO AND FROM YOUR DECK

No matter how many luxuries you build into your deck, you're not likely to use it if you can't see it from the inside, if it's difficult to get to, or if its uses aren't similar to those of the adjacent interior room.

In design terms, these factors are called access and compatibility, and they can spell the difference between a deck that enhances your home and one that rarely gets any use.

Visual access

A deck you can see from inside your home—one with visual access—extends an invitation to enjoy the space.

To create effective visual access, locate the deck where you can see it through windows or doors, either existing ones or new units you have installed to provide a new view.

You don't need to see the whole deck to want to get out and enjoy it. Often just a glimpse will make a more effective invitation than a complete view.

Improving access

Improving access is often all it takes to turn an underused deck into a popular destination. If you don't use your current deck as much as you thought you would, it might be because the design has too much (or too little) visual access, or that you can't get to it easily.

For example, if you feel you're on display while meditating on the deck, the site probably allows too much visual access. Look for ways to shield the area by adding a fence, shrubs, or an overhead structure. Areas for private use require limited visual access. Areas for public use can afford to be more open to outside views.

Inconvenient physical access from interior rooms can also reduce the use of your deck. If you feel that getting to your deck from inside is a journey full of obstacles or circuitous, try rearranging the interior furniture. If the deck furnishings are in the middle of a natural pathway, rearrange them, too, and if there's no room to move them around, add a platform deck to expand the space.

When landscaping your deck include ways to entice guests outdoors by making the destination attractive. Incorporating accents that you can see from the inside—carefully placed container gardens, a change in the decking pattern, or a decorative insert in a railing section visible through a window—will make your deck more enticing. Ideally at least some of the deck should be visible from more than one room, but the most complete view of the deck should be from the room that adjoins it.

When you're considering ways to improve visual access to your deck, remember to look down. Using similar (or the same) flooring materials or similar colors or textures on both the interior floor and decking will visually link the two spaces and make a smooth transition.

Physical access

Physical access refers to the route from inside your home to the deck—and it should be easy. The path to the deck, even if visual, should be open from the rooms that adjoin it and free of obstructions.

Make a sketch of the existing routes people follow when walking through your home. You may need to make alterations that will ease movement to the deck. For example, adding the deck on the far side of your kitchen may make your cooking area a busy throughway. Moving a door, adding one, or rearranging interior furnishings will often solve such traffic jams.

Plan the entry so you don't have to step too far up or down when you walk onto the deck—make the deck surface as close as possible to the level of the interior floor.

If the deck has to be significantly lower than the doorway, add a landing or an entry deck so you won't have to step down as you pass through the door. A landing gives you the opportunity to get your bearings as you move from indoors to outdoors. If a landing is out of the question, build steps. Make the steps wider than the doorway to create an illusion of spaciousness. Make each tread (the part you step on) at least 12 inches deep and keep the rise (the distance you step up) low so the stairs are easier to go up and down.

Inside out, outside in, the best transitions will seem seamless. Fresh air, an idyllic view, and an inviting swing are only steps away from this living room. Double doors with full-length glazing, whether open or closed, make the deck seem part of the room.

Compatibility

You're likely to use your deck more often when the general purpose of both the indoor and outdoor spaces is similar. So the success of your deck may depend on its nearest indoor room.

For example, a small deck for coffee and the morning paper will feel just right outside your bedroom. This would be a poor location, however, for a large party space.

For outdoor dining put the deck close to the kitchen, even if you will have a self-contained outdoor cooking space. Build in storage for the trash so you don't have to transport it back into the house. Establish entertainment areas close to the living room, family room, or dining room, and maximize access with doorways from other rooms where you would entertain guests. Add exterior paths and walkways so guests can get to and from your deck without going through the house.

For private areas look for ways to limit access—shield your deck behind hedges or fencing. You also can build tall railings with balusters close together.

On a nice morning, stepping right out of the bedroom onto a sunny deck with a wide-angle view can make the day seem like a new beginning. Here a single door would have done nicely— there's not enough traffic from a bedroom to make wider access absolutely necessary. But the double doors enhance visual access; they open up the vista and let it come inside. The invitation to step out onto this deck is hard to resist.

Wide doors, large windows, and unobstructed views are elements that can make your deck always seem inviting. In addition to easy access, its location makes it a natural extension of the dining area.

STANLEY PRO TIP

Make the right connections

To avoid traffic jams, make sure the main door to the deck is wide enough to allow easy passage and to offer an inviting view from inside the house. French doors, atrium doors, and sliding doors are especially suitable for connecting the inside and outside.

Take a compatibility inventory of your home. Sketch a floor plan and label the use of each room as active (entertaining, for example) or passive (reading). You may have rooms that warrant both labels, but one type of activity usually predominates. Match up active deck areas with active interior rooms, and passive deck spaces with passive rooms. Deck space for kids' play is better outside a family room, playroom, or den. Deck space for reading will feel more comfortable adjacent to a bedroom or living room.

While you're at it, analyze the way that family members and guests move through your home. Sketch in the windows and doors of the rooms on your inventory and draw arrows that show the usual traffic routes. If there's furniture in the way, rearrange it to open up the view and physical paths to the outdoors.

WHAT SIZE?

How large should your deck be? Although there are many design guidelines, the primary one is to make your deck large enough to accommodate the activities on your final planning list.

Start with a sketch of your deck and assign each activity to a different part of the deck. Allow ample space for the activity itself, traffic flow through and around the area, and outdoor furniture, which tends to be a little larger than indoor furniture.

If you find that your original plans aren't large enough, expand the deck or look for ways to make spaces do double duty. Perhaps one corner of the family dining space can function as a secluded retreat. Often just moving a chair can make a small part of a larger area feel more secluded.

Give areas with different functions their own identities. Separate them visually and physically with planters, trellises, benches, or a change in decking pattern. Structural changes make even stronger distinctions. A T-shape deck or tiers connected with stairs will allow spaces to be clearly identified for different activities.

If you want to dine outside, you just need enough space for a table and chairs. Railings that are below eye level for people seated at the table make the space seem larger. Spaces between railing elements give a more open look too.

STANLEY PRO TIP: **Try out the site**

To find out if your proposed deck is large enough, rope off the area (or mark it with chalk or upside-down spray paint) and move in the furniture and equipment you'll have on the deck—tables and chairs, barbecue grill, lounges and recliners.

If you haven't purchased the furniture yet, use interior furnishings and add about a foot more space for each item. Figure about 2 feet square for each outdoor chair, plus about a foot or two to push it back from a table.

Once you've decided that the deck is equal to its functions, step back and consider its scale. It should look proportionate to the house and grounds. Small decks usually do not pose a problem (they're less likely to be built next to a huge house). More common is the lavish deck that overpowers a modest home. Your budget and lot size may provide the most help in solving this problem. Start with a design that fits the uses you envision and then scale back to fit the limits of your budget and terrain. When you finalize the size of the deck, draw the plan on paper (see page 50).

Large gatherings and entertaining call for open spaces and room for plenty of chairs and other seating. Even on a low deck, which might not require one, a railing gives the open space some definition.

Multiple levels and built-in planters help define areas for different uses on this deck. The lower level steps down to the lawn and garden. Identifying areas this way makes a larger deck seem larger or can help break up the expanse of a large deck.

Narrow decks can seem to offer limited space for seating and for defining clear areas of use. A long bench not only solves the seating problem, it also creates an opportunity for separating spaces. The table, the plant stand, and the potted plants establish different use areas.

STANLEY PRO TIP: **Fitting function to footage**

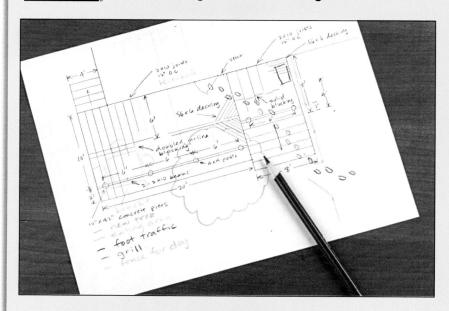

Many decks have plenty of square footage but feel cramped. That's because they weren't planned with traffic and activity in mind. Use these general guidelines to avoid this problem.

■ For a **dining area** for four people, you'll need about 10×10 feet. For six to eight, make it 12×12 feet.

■ To accommodate a typical **round table** with six chairs, provide a circular area with a diameter of at least 9 feet.

■ A **rectangular table** should have an area 5 to 6 feet wider and longer than the table.

■ A simple **cooking area** with a grill and a small table usually needs an area about 6 feet square. Provide more room if there will be a counter, island, or large table.

■ For a single **reclining chair**, allow an area 4×7 feet. For two reclining chairs, allow 7×7 feet.

■ A **conversation area** for three to six people will require a 10×10-foot space.

■ **Pathways** from the door to the stairs and between activity areas must be 3½ to 4 feet wide at all points.

WHAT SHAPE?

A deck can be almost any shape. Once you've determined how you will use your deck, turn your attention to the other factors that can affect its shape—the terrain and landscaping of your property and your proximity to neighbors.

Deck designs can be imaginative, but the overall form generally falls into one of the categories shown on these pages.

Ground-level decks are the least complicated deck forms. They are typically found on flat yards, but they'll work on sloped ground too. The ground-hugging architecture fits perfectly with single-level homes and may not require railings (check your local codes to make sure). Ground-level decks make pleasant entryways, breakfast spots, and outdoor mud rooms. On sloped ground, two or more ground-level decks with different shapes or decking patterns can create a pleasing effect.

Ground-level decks can be supported by post-and-pier foundations, continuous footings, or sleepers over an existing concrete slab. For a deck that appears to float, extend the edges beyond the posts.

Raised decks are the most common form, usually built at the first- or second-floor level. A second-story deck provides access to upper-level rooms not otherwise open to the outdoors. A high deck also can solve landscape problems caused by steep terrain. Posts for a tall deck can be faced with trim or skirted to make them appear more graceful.

Raised decks usually have one level attached to the house with a ledger and supported by piers and posts along the perimeter. The area underneath the deck can be easily hidden with plantings or skirting, either lath or solid panels. Safety concerns increase with elevated decks, which must have railings.

Multilevel designs overcome difficulties presented by rolling or terraced landscapes. Sections can be different sizes and shapes, built at different heights to follow the landscape. They can step down a hill in stages, providing different views along the way. Multilevel decks naturally establish separate areas for different uses.

Construction is complex and requires precise planning. Posts usually support each level, and stairs and railings require careful layout.

Wraparound decks are built along more than one side of a house and often used where a household wants multiple entries to different rooms in the home. They provide an easy answer for families that need spots for private gathering and parties on the same structure. Usually L-shape, wraparound decks are the perfect solution for locations that receive varying amounts of strong sunlight at different times of the day.

Multiple decks may be the best way to tie together uneven backyard terrain and provide spaces for a variety of activities. The several small decks linked together, above, make good use of the site and, because of their varying sizes and shapes, add interest to what otherwise might have been an uneventful pathway. Multiple small structures often cost less to build than a complex single deck and make less impact on the landscape.

Building codes

Your budget and intended uses for a deck are not the only factors that affect design. Building codes, zoning ordinances, deed restrictions, and easements—things you don't have any control over—are also major considerations in determining how and where you can build your deck.

■ **Building codes.** Almost all communities enact building codes to ensure the safety of construction. Some cities may treat decks as permanent structures, with regulations for footing depths, materials, and fence heights. Check with your building department before you build, and submit your plans for approval.

■ **Zoning ordinances.** These provisions govern the use of property and the placement of structures. They can establish minimum setbacks from property lines and the maximum size of your deck. In recent years many cities have become strict about deck surfaces because large areas of hardscape interfere with the natural flow of runoff.

■ **Deed restrictions.** Some communities have deed restrictions to control architectural style. You may find restraints on the style of deck you can build and the materials you can build it with.

■ **Easements and rights-of-way.** These rules guarantee access by utilities to their service lines and may affect where you build your deck. If, for example, a utility company has a line running through your yard you might not be able to build any part of a deck above it. It is possible, however, that a sand-set deck, which allows quick access to utilities below, might be allowed.

Ask your utilities to mark the path of lines through your property. Most will do this for free; you usually can make just one call to a central agency for all utilities.

STANLEY PRO TIP

Stay out of the dark

An upper-level deck can plunge first-floor interior rooms into gloomy darkness. If you foresee these shadows in your plans, try slimming down your design. A narrow footprint (about 8 feet or so) can offer plenty of room on the deck but casts less shade below.

Help with design
Don't be afraid to ask questions. Many home centers retain professional designers on staff.

DESIGNING YOUR DECK WITH STYLE

Style is in the details. Every part of your deck, from the type of structural lumber you employ to the material you use and the patterns of the decking, railings, and the configuration of stairs, contributes to the style of your deck.

The style of your deck is important because it can affect your long-term enjoyment of it and all of the hard work you're going to put into it. If the style of your deck appeals to you and reflects your personality, you'll be likely to use it more often and enjoy it more.

Style by theme
One of the best ways to come to terms with style is to organize your landscape plan around a theme, making the deck an integral part of that plan.

Perhaps you'll want a classic symmetrical look that features straight lines and right angles. If so, a ground-level deck with rectangular planting beds on each side might just be perfect. Augment the effect with a closely clipped border of shrubs.

If an informal design is more your style, your design can incorporate curves or framing that suggests them. You might lay small stones or wood chips on a path from the garage to the deck and curve the outlines of your planting beds to enhance this casual feeling and appearance.

Regional designs pick up the palette of local colors, climate, culture, and textures, so let what nature does in your local landscape lead you. Native plants and materials will look at home in their surroundings. Regional designs also make good budget sense—local plants and materials are less expensive and generally require less care and maintenance.

Elements from different regions often mix well with one another. A single bonsai tree won't transform your deck into a Japanese garden, but it will provide a harmonious Oriental contrast to a Southwestern theme.

Heritage
Go contemporary—cool, serene, and comfortable—with bold shapes and colors, sleek lines, and unusual combinations. Build your framing to support alternating sections of diamond and chevron decking patterns, and repeat the patterns in the siding of your outdoor kitchen. Zigzag your deck over a series of gentle slopes, and make the pattern even more dramatic with perimeter seating that matches the contours or angles.

Create harmony
No matter what style you choose for your landscape—even the most eclectic—combine its elements into a unified whole.

Create a sense of continuity with your house by using similar materials, colors, shapes, and patterns in your deck design.

A ground-level platform deck whose length runs parallel to a one-story ranch home creates a harmony of horizontal lines. Place the length of the deck perpendicular to the house, and the harmony begins to unravel.

A deck full of angles will fit right in with a West Coast modular home. Those same angles might look jarring on the back of a three-story Victorian, ornate with filigree and bric-a-brac. On the other hand, they might work with an American foursquare, whose style is more neutral.

The lines of the house don't have to be the only determinants. Look for design clues in the curves, angles, and free-form shapes of property lines, swimming pools, garden beds, or slopes.

Painted roof pillars and white deck furniture enhance the seaside-resort style of this deck as it spills down to the beach.

Sharp corners, cantilevered platforms, and steel railings give this deck a contemporary, urban look in a rural setting—a good example of how you can create a distinctive style of your own.

Your sense of harmony should extend to accents and furnishings. Use small, carefully placed elements to provide contrast of color, shape, and texture. Gardens, edgings, walls, colored concrete, stone, tiles, bricks, logs, gates, furnishings, lights, and decorative pieces all add pleasing and lively accents.

Select furnishings that support the dominant design. Fortunately there is a style of deck furniture to fit almost every taste and budget, from sleek, contemporary pieces to classic cedar, or charming, old-fashioned wicker.

If your deck is large or encompasses several smaller sections, position small groups of furnishings and decorative elements so they won't clutter your central area. Place your main deck furniture around focal points to give them greater definition.

How will you know when the design you've created is harmonious? It will look soothing, not jarring. It will present itself as a cohesive blend more than a clutter of parts, and its general impression will be inviting and comfortable.

Containers filled with plants quickly, inexpensively, and effectively personalize a deck. They provide color, variety, and texture—all of which you can move around when your creative urge dictates a different arrangement. Containers with plants provide a colorful break between the wood decking and the siding on the house. Hanging baskets add eye-level splashes of color.

A decorative gusset and lapped skirting add a classic touch to this deck. Such details increase the strength of the structure and add richness to the design.

Attractive railings and a skirt that matches the house keep this deck from looking like a hastily built add-on. Wide stairs on any deck offer easy access to the surrounding yard.

STANLEY PRO TIP

Finding your style

Look around your neighborhood and note things you like about the houses and yards. You may find more cohesiveness than you have noticed before. Make notes and sketches of things you like and file them in a manila folder. Clip photos from magazines for further inspiration.

When you're working on your final design, spread your notes and clippings on a table so you can see everything at once. Discard what doesn't appeal to you and keep the rest. You'll notice a general theme in the images left on the table. Use the elements of that style in your deck design.

ADD STYLE WITH DECKING PATTERNS

Although decking is commonly fastened parallel to the length of the deck, perpendicular to the joists, it doesn't always have to be done that way.

Decking and the pattern it creates can contribute to the style of your deck. Even the simplest platform deck can get a big infusion of style from an unusual decking pattern. Choosing patterns should be an essential part of your planning. Use the instructions for making a plan view (see page 54) for more about sketching in the possibilities.

The possibilities of pattern

Decking patterns fall into three categories.
■ Parallel decking runs perpendicular to the joists and parallel to the longest face of the house. This pattern is the least complicated to install, results in less waste, and is the least expensive. To make this simple pattern more visually active, scatter the butted ends randomly over the deck.
■ Diagonal decking runs across the deck surface and joists at a 45-degree angle. Installing this pattern will take only slightly more time than a parallel pattern, but you'll waste more wood because diagonal cuts at both ends of the boards consume more lumber than straight cuts.

■ Geometric patterns encompass a wide range of alternatives, among them chevron, parquet, diamond, and herringbone. Geometric patterns often combine aspects of parallel and mitered styles into modular units. Any of these patterns will require additional framing and will create more waste than simpler styles (see page 124).

Whatever pattern you choose, draw it to scale when you put your plans on paper. This is the only way to be sure you'll have complete grids and patterns at the edges.

Picking a pattern

The possibilities for creating decking patterns are almost endless. A few general

Diagonal deck boards with divider strips dress up this deck surface and make it more interesting than planks parallel to the edge. Diagonal decking also is an excellent method for denoting different areas on a deck.

Intermixed diagonal and parallel decking enhance the visual interest of the ramps and decks and delineate sections.

principles will help you pick a pattern.

■ Minimize the length of a long deck and make it seem wider by installing the decking perpendicular to the length of the deck. This will require joists that run parallel to the length of the deck.

■ Give your deck a finished look with a border around the edge (see page 170, bottom). Adding a border will increase your construction time slightly, but it's an easy way to give the deck a professional touch.

■ The smaller the space, the simpler the pattern. On small decks, complexity can look confusing and busy.

■ Diagonal patterns look best if they reflect a similar line elsewhere in the landscape— an angle of the house or outdoor structure, for example, or the lines made by corresponding planting beds.

■ Intricate patterns require high-grade lumber—they accentuate rather than hide defects. Use premium-grade lumber for geometric designs. If your budget won't allow that, paint the surface to hide the defects and keep the pattern.

Wide boards divide the larger surface of this deck into quadrants—a useful pattern for separating one space from another. Varying the size of the boards produces subtle changes in the decking style.

Modular decking patterns require additional framing to permit nailing the ends of the boards in each section. The extra work and cost is worth it, breaking up an expanse of decking and giving the deck a rhythm.

Just the right accent can set the style for a deck. Tapered decking creates a sunburst that highlights the river view from this deck. Repeating patterns of arcs and circles—the general outline of the deck, the bases of planting pots and the statue, and the center of the deck design— all reinforce each other.

Framing the subject

Complex and intricate decking patterns require careful planning, both on the surface and for the framing beneath. The ends of each board must always rest directly on the full thickness of a joist or blocking—short sections of 2× stock cut to fit between the joists.

Modular units require framing that supports both the ends and the interior of each section. Typically this means that blocking must be installed at regular intervals. (See page 197 for more information about decking patterns.)

STYLING WITH RAILINGS

Railings set the stage. More than any other element of deck design, railings express its personality. Because they have so much impact on the style of your deck, it's important that you design your railings so they appear as a harmonious aspect of your overall landscape theme.

Start by considering the character of your house, whether its style is formal or casual, its lines primarily horizontal or vertical. Pick up these characteristics in your railing design. Study the trim for design cues. An older home with a cornice at the roof line will be complemented with a similar cornice incorporated into the top rail. A more modern home might call for tubular steel, plexiglass, or formal post caps.

Consider also the practicality of your design. Will you want to set food and drinks on the railing? Will close baluster spacing make it seem too confining?

To help you avoid construction errors, design your railings at the same time you design the rest of the deck. The dimensions of the railings can affect where you sink the posts, for example, as well as how you fasten them.

A variety of infill patterns—diagonal lattice in the upper frame and alternating wide and narrow baluster slats—curved lines, extended posts, decorative caps, and an arch that frames a colorful floral display all combine to make a distinctive railing. Such a design is appealing to the eye and enhances the overall style of the deck.

In limited spaces, everything has to work just a little harder—but the extra effort shouldn't show. A wide cap rail not only adds solidity to a design, it also makes the space more flexible, providing a surface for guests to set plates and glasses on during parties. The rail effectively functions as a table when there's not enough room for additional furnishings.

The key to style is simplicity. You can get it with a design touch that's no more complicated than adding short bars to the balusters in the center of a railing section.

Welded and painted black pipe makes a functional railing with an airy, open look. The horizontal lines of the railing and upper balcony echo the basically horizontal lines of the siding, linking the deck to the architecture of the house.

Rustic logs add a woodland touch to this railing. Diagonal crosspieces help stabilize the structure and keep the design from looking too heavy, which could overwhelm the deck and furniture. Tight joints make a sturdy, long-lasting railing. Logs need to be well-seasoned before assembly so they won't shrink.

SAFETY FIRST
Codes for railings

Although railings are key elements in deck design, their primary purpose is safety. That means local building codes may govern their design and construction.

Most codes require a railing on a deck that is 24 or more inches above the ground. Baluster spacing is commonly specified as 4 to 6 inches, and the space between rails, 4 to 6 feet.

Before you commit your plans to paper, consult your building department to make sure your design conforms to local codes.

Keep it simple
It you are not sure how to design your railing, stick with a simple plan. Simplicity is almost always goofproof.

Railings—talking about them on their own terms

If you are new to the business of deck building, familiarize yourself with the name of each part. That way you'll avoid confusion when designing the deck and ordering material.

Posts, either resting on footings or attached to the deck, are the structural members that support the railing.

Rails are the horizontal members fastened between the posts. There are usually a top rail and a bottom rail, and sometimes a **cap rail**, which may be wider and is fastened to the top rail. Additional rails may be included for design and style.

Balusters are vertical members installed between the rails.

Like all good railings, this one calls attention to itself with simple techniques. Trimmed posts, extended to create space between the cap rail and the top rail, are an effective design detail.

FURNITURE AND SEATING

Choosing the furnishings for your deck should be an integral part of your planning. A deck without furnishings isn't very inviting; furniture and accessories enliven a deck, adding to its charm and making it more attractive. They have a remarkable influence on how you feel about the deck, and thus how often you use it.

Furnishings and your lifestyle

Your first thought about deck furniture will probably be, "What should it look like?" It's easier to answer that question by making sure the furniture you choose reflects the purposes of the space. For example, chairs and tables for a dining area are certain to be different from chairs and tables for a lounging area. Pick colors and styles that fit into the overall design scheme of your deck and its environment.

Be practical, too, when choosing furnishings for outdoor use. Choose durable materials that offer year-round usability. Your deck furnishings should be weatherproof, durable, and easy to move around. If possible they should be made with removable cushions for quick cleaning. If you won't use your deck in the winter, design an outside storage area so you can conveniently protect furniture cushions out of the elements.

Seating—freestanding or built-in?

Seating on your deck will fall into one of two categories.

Freestanding seating—rockers, chairs, lounges, and dining sets with cushions, come in more design styles than built-in units. Freestanding furnishings also can make the use of your deck more flexible— you can move them around to change the nature of the space.

If you design your deck for entertaining large groups of people, keep some folding canvas chairs handy for overflow crowds. Design your storage area so it's large enough to keep the chairs out of the way when you don't need them.

Built-in seating isn't portable, but it offers a few advantages that freestanding furniture doesn't: It takes up less space and, cleverly designed, can also serve as storage.

Attached benches are the most basic form of built-in seating, but planters, retaining walls, and freestanding walls can fill in as benches if you construct their top surfaces wide enough.

Stairs are an often overlooked opportunity for built-in seating. In a crowded setting, if stair treads are wide and deep enough, your guests will sit on them. Build your stairs at least 4 feet wide if you want them to serve as seating. Sturdy handrails are a must for walking safety, but also can act as grab bars to help people stand up.

The best way to pick furnishings is to choose their style as you're designing your deck—not after the plans are drawn. All of the patterns in this design—including the slat-backed chairs and planked tabletop—are variations on the theme of straight forms and parallel lines. Color and orientation of the elements contribute to the success of this style.

STANLEY PRO TIP

Sizing up the furniture

Getting the outdoor furniture scaled to its space sometimes calls for a little strategy. In small deck areas, use round tables— they take up less space than square or rectangular ones.

In larger spaces set up conversation areas with groupings of tables and chairs or lounges and side tables. Include a serving cart and leave plenty of room to walk around the furniture.

The rule of 18

You can be sure that built-in seating areas will be comfortable if you make them 18 inches deep and 18 inches above the deck surface.

Built-in seating can add dramatic architectural details to a deck. Curved surfaces take up more room than structures with straight lines, but the design effect can more than make up for the loss of space.

It's hard to beat a porch swing for relaxing. Besides, the lines of a swing will complement almost any deck style. You can hang the swing from a pair of posts topped with a beam, an arbor or gazebo on the deck, or an overhead structure. A swing also can add color to a deck, offsetting the expanse of natural wood. Neutral colors will help the swing blend in.

When you're planning your deck, include steps whenever you can— and make them both wide and deep. Wide steps are certain to serve as additional seating for any gathering. Built-in benches help unify the deck and patio spaces that might otherwise look disconnected.

Comfort and contemporary are not mutually exclusive terms. They can go hand in hand, as in this colorful combination of painted planks and aluminum rails. Hinge the bench seat or add doors to the base to provide convenient storage.

ADD PERSONALITY WITH ACCENTS

Decorations are usually thought of as things that belong in interior rooms. After all, nature provides the outdoor ambience.

But if you think of your deck as a room that just happens to be outdoors, it becomes natural to want to decorate it too.

Look for nesting places

Once you've built your deck, take a moment to relax in a comfortable chair and look around. Without intentionally making plans, notice where your gaze rests. Those are the places that could use decorative details, the nests for accent pieces. Pick one focal point per seating area. If you run out of deck space for decorative items, hang things on the wall.

Group similar objects to establish a theme. Folk art, antique hand-painted signs, or pottery pieces invite comparison, draw attention, and take on greater importance when displayed together.

Groups act as a single focal point. If you put groups of items too close together, though, they'll fight each other for attention. The best spots for displaying accents are those that offer a neutral background—walls, fences, and green plants.

Items that don't qualify as a collection can still establish a theme. Even if the objects are different, if they have similar shapes, colors, or textures, those similarities will help unify the space.

Space items far enough apart that each one gets its chance to show off. On the deck, wooden boxes of different heights make good display stands. A coat of linseed oil and mineral spirits (half and half) will accent the wood tones, richen the color, and help protect the wood from the elements.

Attach small shelves to the wall at different heights. Scattering the shelves on the wall rather than clustering them avoids clutter and helps create a larger display. If your deck is linear and formal, you can hang these shelves on the same horizontal or vertical planes. Offset the tops and edges of the shelves.

And don't forget the flowers, and especially the pots they grow in. Plain, plastic warehouse pots will detract from the overall appearance of your design scheme. Discount retailers carry a wide variety of inexpensive containers made to match almost any decorative style.

Plants are the perfect accents. Here they dress up a plain, uninteresting corner; in fact, they practically make it disappear. Choose plants that provide combinations of colors and foliage with different textures.

Lots of accessories make this deck a cheerful and welcoming place where friends gather to have fun. Accents can strike a main theme that you can carry throughout the entire deck design or they can be an eclectic collection of disparate objects. What unites the whole scene is how you use accents to fill unoccupied spaces.

Anything antique, such as an old church pew, can spice up a deck by adding an unusual architectural accent. The weathered surface of the wood and the grays of the concrete urn and the decking would be unattractive in themselves, but the neutral scheme provides a good backdrop for the touches of greenery.

A painted pattern on the decking defines an area the way a rug does inside the house. Placing the pattern at an angle to the decking makes it more eye-catching, and the muted tones keep the design from being overpowering. Where the deck is sheltered, you could even use a sisal mat or similar floor covering to accent an area.

Some furnishings are accents too. Several small tables with chairs make casual resting and dining spots around the pool and punctuate the space.

Fancy this...

Don't worry about a right or wrong way to display personal details in your deck. There aren't any rules—only suggestions.

■ Mobiles and wind chimes not only catch the breeze, they also add a vertical dimension to the predominantly horizontal planes of the deck. Wind chimes also bring charm to the space with their tinkling sounds.

■ Seashells or other small objects can be more appealing when they appear half hidden behind the sides of shadow boxes.

■ If there's an accent you can't live without, but there's no obvious way to display or support it, lean it against a flower pot on the decking.

■ Mount driftwood on a blank wall and train vines to drape its contours.

■ Paint railing or fence posts in a theme of alternating colors.

■ Take a piece of battered barn wood and paint it into your own colorful circus clown. The contrast between the neutral color of the weathered wood, its rough texture, and the paint will make this sculpture even more interesting. On a smaller scale, hang a similar small figure from the rafters of an overhead.

■ Stand a weather vane in a flowerpot to draw attention to the seasonal color of complementary blooms. Create a sculpted array with metal flowers arranged in rows. They make a neat foil rising behind containers planted with the real thing.

■ Consider replacing your metal or vinyl-clad storm door with a well-made wooden screen door. Home centers carry them in a variety of styles with plain and decorative panels.

■ Hanging old silverware or other unexpected objects from an arbor can make a delightful display. This kind of display works best if the objects are small. Sparkly objects will make random light patterns on the deck.

■ Add color with home-sewn pillows covered with colorful patterns in acrylic awning fabrics. Acrylics won't fade like cotton duck fabric, and hold up forever in the weather. Use synthetic fillers to stuff the pillows.

LANDSCAPING YOUR DECK

One of the best ways to integrate your deck with the other elements in your landscape is with plants—both garden beds beside or around the deck and plants that adorn the deck itself.

If you haven't yet built your deck but you do have garden beds in place, locate the deck to catch the best views of the plantings. If you don't have garden beds, plan their location, contours, and contents so their beauty brings an additional benefit to being out on your deck. Then use planted containers to pull the garden up the deck, right to the doorway of your home.

Container gardens are more than merely decorative. They can be a most useful tool in making your deck seem like a natural outgrowth of the landscape, not merely an architectural add-on. They are especially practical on sites (or with budgets) that prohibit complex and intriguing deck designs. Plants will turn even the most basic deck into a work of art you can use.

Plants also solve problems. Flowering beds with a rear shrub border and tall plants can hide the unattractive empty space beneath the deck. A hedge can screen out an unattractive view. Potted trees offer shade and privacy, as well as fruit. Large planters help establish traffic patterns.

When you're ready to integrate plants into your landscape design, first decide where they should go. Use your design sketches (see page 53) to tell you where you need shade, privacy, and shelter. Then pick plants that do the job.

Making the beds

Before you decide what to plant, shape the bed first. Experiment by laying out a garden hose to create pleasing outlines. Curved lines—even bordering a square deck—generally make a more interesting landscape than straight lines. Mark the contour on the lawn with upside-down spray paint, roll up the hose, and dig the bed into the soil.

Plant in tiers, with the shortest species in front, and gradually increase the height of the plantings toward the rear of the bed. Plants right next to the deck should be no higher than eye level when you're seated, unless you're using them to screen out a view or increase your privacy.

Making use of trees and shrubs

Trees are the environmental workhorses of the natural world. They cast shade, reduce erosion, and help clean the air. Shrubs make excellent transitions between larger elements—other trees, sheds, or decks, for example. They're a great substitute for trees where trees won't fit.

Trees and shrubs are either deciduous (they lose their leaves in the winter) or evergreen (they keep their leaves), but these are not the only criteria for selection.

Consider their mature sizes and characteristics. The sapling you buy today may root into your foundation in 10 years, or what you thought was a low-maintenance addition to your landscape might drop seeds, twigs, and blossoms that call for constant cleanup. Remember that a cute little shrub by your deck might prove to be an unwelcome guest when it is fully grown.

Research your choices and plant species that will adapt to your climate and the soil and drainage characteristics of your yard.

Plenty of planters and pots provide lush seasonal landscaping that softens the edges and corners of this deck. Pick colors carefully so you have a variety coming into view throughout the year.

Plantings along the side of this elevated deck help anchor the structure in the yard. Garden beds effectively hide the unattractive space under the deck. Planters add texture and color to the railing.

Groundcovers

Low plants that hug the ground reduce erosion and can act as a living palette for other plantings. Wide, sweeping beds curving around a deck define areas without dividing the space into smaller parts. Where grass won't grow, a groundcover will—and it won't need mowing.

Container gardens

Container gardens are the colorful actors of deck landscaping. You can grow just about any kind of plant in a container, even when you're faced with hot, dry weather or lack of space. Besides, they allow you to quickly change the scene when you tire of the current one.

When you start planning your deck's planting scheme, sit on the benches and chairs, and look carefully at the views. Check the view from the adjoining room. Wherever you see distractions, such as power lines or the neighbor's storage shed, block them out with a container. Wherever you need more privacy, plant a plant. Tall species can add perceived height without making the deck seem isolated.

Look for empty corners, blank walls, unattractive structures, and unruly plants on the property line. Dress up these areas with container-grown plants. And if you need to provide some unity to a large deck, plant the same kind of plant in more than one place. The repetition of color and texture will pull the spaces together.

Boxes and baskets

Window boxes and hanging baskets are the perfect containers when you want to create a composition on a small scale.

Generally speaking, all the plants in a window box or basket should have the same nutritional requirements and the same needs for sunlight or shade. That will keep their care to a minimum, but it doesn't mean you have to plant all the same variety.

To make things interesting, combine plants that have similar colors with plants that have different and contrasting textures. Fine-textured species, such as baby's breath, make contrasting companions for species whose foliage is spiky, such as rosemary. Upright forms, such as coneflowers, make a good backdrop for low-growing or trailing flowers.

Window boxes and baskets offer perfect habitats for edible plants too—lettuces, herbs, and edible flowers create an outdoor salad in a basket, just ready for the picking.

Build your window boxes as deep as your design allows—but don't make them obstacles to the natural traffic flow across your deck. Deep window boxes are healthier for your plants, but a sharp corner that you need to avoid on the way into the house will prove annoying. Ten to 12 inches of soil allows room for adequate root growth.

If you're building your own boxes, drill at least two holes in the bottom for drainage and insert a sheet of rigid foam insulation inside the front before filling it with soil. The foam will keep roots cool and reduce soil-moisture evaporation. Then, before planting, mix water-retaining polymers in the soil. The pellets swell when wet and hold moisture. Check the container for the proper proportion of pellets to soil.

Water window boxes daily or if needed, twice a day during hot weather. How do you know when the plants need watering? Poke your finger into the soil about ½ inch deep. If soil feels dry to the touch, it's time to water.

A short course in plant buying

Plants for your deck will be close to you, not in a garden far across the yard. So follow a different strategy when you buy plants for deck containers.

■ Buy plants that are at their best in the season when you'll use your deck. Flower beds are big enough to accommodate a variety that will last throughout the seasons. Containers aren't.

■ Choose low-maintenance varieties, those that don't demand deadheading and other botanical chores.

■ Select species whose mature sizes will not overwhelm their surroundings and won't need a lot of pruning to keep them that way.

■ Include fragrance on your list of criteria. Some flowers may be too fragrant to be close.

■ Give your plants an environment in which they'll thrive—check the USDA plant hardiness zone map at a nursery and buy plants suited to your zone.

■ Balance flowers and foliage. An overwhelming display of blossoms can be just that. You'll show off your choices more dramatically against a backdrop of foliage. Vary the texture of the plants—the shape and size of their leaves—and their colors, too.

■ Find your favorites first. Then build the rest of your choices with plants that provide attractive complements or contrasts.

■ Add color with plants. Woods commonly used to build decks—pressure-treated lumber, cedar, cypress, and redwood—all turn to various shades of gray if left untreated, providing an excellent neutral backdrop for plants. The natural brown tones of stained wood also offer a pleasant contrast to the greens and other colors of container gardens.

Pots and planters highlight different levels on this deck and break the horizontal lines. They also mark the steps.

CREATING PRIVACY AND ENCLOSURE

Without something to define the edges, a deck can leave you feeling exposed and uncomfortable. You'll feel more at home sitting on a deck that offers at least a small amount of privacy and enclosure, enough to make the space around you seem secure.

Planning for privacy

Plan for privacy first. Can your neighbors see your every move? Is your deck open to view from the public sidewalk or street? If so, you need to make your deck private.

The solution may be as simple as building your deck on the least-exposed side of the house or tucking it into an exterior corner. No matter where you plan to build it, stand on your proposed deck site several times during the day and evening; if you don't feel a sense of security, add a privacy fence, wall, or trees and shrubs to your plans. While you're checking the site, make a list of unsightly views you want to hide.

Screening

Screening adds privacy or blocks out an unsightly view and comes in many forms.

Which form you use depends on how you plan to use each area on your deck.

Cozy spots for reading, conversation, sunbathing, or meditation call for plenty of privacy. Pools and spas need privacy and a windbreak. Walls, high fences, or dense evergreen plantings are good choices for screening these places.

Areas for parties, large family gatherings, or children's play can be more open. Partial screens are adequate for these needs; latticework, low fence panels with open infill, airy trees, or seat walls are all good choices. They will also hide garbage cans, air-conditioners, the dog run, a heat pump, your neighbor's open garage, or parked cars. Train a vine to grow into the screen; the foliage ultimately will hide the screen and make it seem part of the landscape.

No matter what kind of screening you pick, make sure you locate it strategically. Study the location and the angle from which you see an unsightly object, then place screens to hide them. The closer the screen is to the object, the better it hides it.

The same goes for a privacy screen— the closer it is to the deck, the more privacy

it offers. Few decks need screening around the entire perimeter. Before you encircle your deck with a privacy hedge, find places where other people can see you. Then block the most revealing views first so you can enhance your privacy without barricading yourself in. Friendly, more open screening, such as lattice, picket, and ornamental iron fencing, often is all you need.

Defining space

Space usually doesn't feel like it exists until something encloses it. Defining space— visually separating one area from another— is an important aspect of deck planning.

You usually need some physical object to separate an intimate dining area from larger entertainment areas, for example. Otherwise you might feel like you're sitting out in a public place when you're trying to have a quiet family dinner, even if you are screened from public view.

Built-in or freestanding benches, raised planters, or even a change in decking pattern can distinguish private space from party space. These and other structures suggest walls or borders, so they set apart

 PRO TIP

The outdoor comfort scale

To keep the scale of your outdoor ceiling at a comfortable level, use these design tips.

Even if you think that your lowest tree branches at 15 to 20 feet off the ground are not too high, that height might make people at a dining table feel uncomfortable. Fix a problem such as this by setting up a table with an umbrella.

In general, deck space that's intended for intimate activities such as family dining, reflection, or solitary reading should have some kind of cover 10 to 12 feet above the deck surface. Party space will feel just right with ceilings up to 20 feet high.

How much of the deck you should cover? In general, shelter at least a third of the deck's surface area.

A screen house turns a portion of this deck into an outdoor sitting room. The screened walls create a sense of privacy and enclosure and allow breezes through while keeping annoying insects out. A structure like this can often mean the difference between a deck that gets used and one that sits idle.

areas without completely enclosing them. They're useful when you need to separate two areas that have related purposes.

Low hedges and small trees can serve the same purpose in the larger landscape, to visually separate the deck from the yard for instance. Such implied walls separate areas but don't entirely isolate them. They block visual and actual movement, not the view, so they direct traffic and define space without making you feel hemmed in.

Designing with materials

Choosing screening materials is an opportunity to bring in additional design elements. Select materials that go with the style of your home and landscape.

Brick or stone—solid and imposing—work well with stately classic or traditional architecture. Interlocking blocks, designed for retaining walls, look at home in most landscape styles. You can combine materials to bring more variety to your design and to create unusual or unique screens. Dress up a plain fence with an evergreen hedge or roses, for example, for a screen that's ornamental and impenetrable. Or enlarge upon a Southwestern design scheme by building low walls with adobe blocks and planting evergreens.

Overheads

Overhead space, or the lack of it, has a great impact on our comfort—both indoors and out. For example, a vaulted indoor ceiling can be visually awe-inspiring but also a bit overwhelming. Low ceilings can make you feel confined. The same holds true outdoors. Many outdoor areas need some kind of physical limit—but just in the right amount—in order for us to feel comfortable. How much of an overhead ceiling you'll need in your outdoor room will depend on how you plan to use it.

For example, space designated for entertaining large groups will feel more comfortable if left open or with a high overhead structure. Private spaces, such as those you'll use for dining, talking, or relaxing, will feel more cozy with some kind of limit overhead. And just as you can imply the presence of a wall with plants and low structures, you can suggest a ceiling too.

Train a vine across the back of the house about 8 feet above the deck and you'll find even this simple addition brings a sense of security to the corner you want for you and your Sunday paper.

You can of course come up with more elaborate solutions. You can build an overhead structure—a two- or four-post arbor, a pergola, or a canopy. You can even install a retractable awning.

Such a structure will increase your sense of enclosure. It also provides protection from the elements and is a design feature that can turn an average-looking deck into a unique addition to your backyard.

Overheads with slatted roofs will put shade on the deck when and where you want it. With some careful planning and a thorough site analysis (see pages 50–51), you can control the amount of shade provided throughout the day.

No matter what kind of overhead you build, make sure it's an integral part of the design, not an add-on. Repeating a detail of your house—a molding or post style, pitch of the roof, accent color, or building material—will link the structure to your home.

Railings set apart areas on this deck, and defined space feels enclosed. Even such minimal objects as the decorative hanging can impart a sense of overhead comfort.

Lattice works wonders when it comes to breaking up large expanses of wall or fencing. A portal makes the gabled end seem less confining.

Open rafters overhead can shade and enclose a deck without completely covering it.

Limit heavy screening

Without forethought, screening can quickly turn into a stockade. Build walls, high fences, and dense hedges only where you need maximum screening.

CREATING PRIVACY AND ENCLOSURE (continued)

An abbreviated fence can hide unattractive views or enhance privacy without being overpowering and making your deck look barricaded.

The side of a house, whether it's yours or a neighbor's, is where unattractive utility equipment usually lives. A vine-covered trellis will screen out the unsightly view without making you feel cooped up.

If you're looking for a place for a private retreat, look under a raised deck. If the deck is tall enough, you'll find plenty of room and opportunities for creative access.

Lattice panels incorporated into the railing on this urban deck provide a buffer against the brick wall. The closeness of the wall, which is the side of the neighboring house, creates a subtle intrusion. Also the very mass of the wall and its solid red brick color would make it the major focal point for people on the deck. The lattice panels overcome both problems.

STANLEY PRO TIP

Wall and fence heights

Before you build a wall or erect a fence, you should have a clear idea of what you want it to do. The adage "form follows function" has no better application than choosing the height of a wall or fence.

If you need a structure for security, a windbreak, or for total screening, you can make it 6 to 8 feet high. But structures intended solely to separate spaces can be as low as 6 inches or as high as 3 feet.

Fences and walls in general should be either well above or well below eye level. A wall or fence that cuts your view in half is an annoyance that keeps you constantly ducking or stretching to try to see what's on the other side.

An uncovered roof with open rafters provides dappled shade and creates a sense of overhead enclosure for this deck.

Looking for a light touch for your deck cover? Acrylic awning fabric shades this sitting area and diffuses light throughout.

PLANNING AMENITIES

Amenities increase the comfort and convenience of your deck and make it more inviting.

Plan your amenities based on how you want to use the deck. At a minimum, consider outdoor lighting. Adding lights costs little, but it extends the use of your deck into the nighttime hours, increases its safety, and makes your house more secure, even when you're not using the deck.

Lighting

Lighting a deck takes a little planning, but installation is straightforward. If you choose a low-voltage lighting system, installation is downright easy. Line-voltage lighting costs more, but installation is well within the skills of the average do-it-yourselfer.

Before you install any system, it helps to understand some lighting principles. Outdoor lights come in a multitude of fixtures, each made for its own purpose.

Concealed fixtures focus attention on an object or area. Typically they cast their bright light a long distance. Place them so the bulbs aren't visible from any angle.

Decorative fixtures cast diffused light. Freestanding pillars push into the ground, and units made for mounting attach to posts or other deck surfaces. Because they're styled to be part of a design scheme, choose fixtures that fit your style.

Your outdoor lighting will be more useful and will add to the beauty of your landscape if you rely on a variety of lighting strategies.

Uplighting draws attention to an object by casting light up from its base. Position the fixture in front of the object so that the beam shines away from viewing areas and grazes trees or artwork, highlighting their shapes.

Downlighting casts indirect light—it's good for steps, paths, floors, and tabletops. Mount the fixtures on trees with conduit and hardware designed so it won't harm them, or fasten fixtures to overhead rafters. Keep the fixtures out of sight and aim them to light your yard, not your neighbor's. Thread wires through the center of hollow columns or a groove routed in the post on overheads.

Path lights illuminate a walkway, linking your deck and other parts of the yard. They're made to order for lighting short flights of steps or to mark points of entry.

Outdoor kitchen

It's a simple fact of life that food tastes better when you cook it outdoors. Properly designed and equipped—even with just a basic propane grill and a prep sink—an outdoor kitchen can be easy and fun to use.

Putting a basic outdoor kitchen on your deck might require minor modifications, but the small investment of time and funds will return much increased enjoyment. You also can plan a more lavish installation, complete with a high-end gas range, rotisserie, food storage areas, and a refrigerator.

No matter what kind of kitchen you're planning, what matters most is where you put it. The best location offers a combination of convenience (close to the indoor kitchen) and safety (far away or insulated from combustible material).

Place a portable grill close to the indoor kitchen, at the edge of the deck and out from under overhangs and overheads. Construct a built-in grill with fireproof materials that conform to local building codes. Whether portable or built-in, keep your kitchen out of the main traffic route and make sure it doesn't block the views. You'll want enough room for preparing and serving food and for storing utensils. If you're short of space, tuck cooking items into a bench or screened cabinet. Make a portable grill more attractive by hiding it—large potted plants on platforms with casters make clever roll-around screening.

Look for outdoor-grade permanent equipment that's made to meet building codes and withstand all weather conditions. Waterproof countertops made of marble, metal, or tile will prove to be a worthwhile investment. And if you build the countertop with an 18-inch overhang, you'll have a bar or buffet.

Storage

Planning adequate storage is part art, part science. Like all deck design, storage starts with a list of everything you might conceivably keep on the deck: garbage cans, firewood, furniture covers, pet supplies, hoses, chair cushions, garden tools, and barbecue utensils. All this stuff needs a home. Without it, your deck will quickly turn into a large storage platform, and you won't use it as you planned.

You have opportunities to create storage space both topside and below the deck.

Setting aside part of your deck for an outdoor kitchen, whether basic or extravagant, offers many opportunities for relaxing with your family or entertaining. Appliances made for outdoor use can be built into a cooking area that adds another kitchen to your house.

On the deck surface, vertical cabinets made from the same cedar, redwood, or the lumber as your decking make attractive and functional accents. Sketch out the size of the cabinet before you build it, making it large enough for the items it will house. Then adjust the proportions so they are pleasing to the eye. When you have the size right, design a framed door with an infill pattern that complements the overall style of your landscape theme.

Deck boxes, either handmade or commercial, are also popular storage places—and they'll double as seating. Buy freestanding benches with lids—or build them into the perimeter of your deck. Paint a child's toybox with exterior paint and use it as an outdoor coffee table and a place to keep chair cushions. Keep pet supplies and birdseed in watertight tins, decorated with painted designs of your choice. A decorated mailbox makes a dry place for storing hand tools and garden gloves, and provides an unusual accent. Stand a baker's rack in front of a blank wall for storing empty flowerpots, baskets, and watering cans.

The space under the deck poses different problems and offers different opportunities.

You can put a complete storage area and workshop or planting shed under a second-story deck. Lower decks will restrict your space, but don't have to eliminate it. A space at least 4 feet high will allow access to lawn mowers, fertilizers, large plastic tubs with tops, garbage cans on wheels, and other moveable containers, as well as portable or folding deck furniture. Hide everything out of sight with hinged lattice or solid panels.

Joists on the least visible side of the deck can make a good spot for storing yard tools. Mount hooks or handle holders on the joists and hang shovels, rakes, and hoes. Protect the spot—and make it more attractive—with a small 24-inch overhang. Or go one step further and attach a backpack shed to the joists and posts.

Water feature

If you want to add some magic to your deck, you can make it sparkle with a water feature. A simple birdbath might be all you need, or a small container water garden. With a little hunting you can find attractive commercial freestanding fountains or wall-mounted units that bring the gentle sound

of moving water to your deck. And most of these features are easy on your budget.

Even an elaborate deck pond can be relatively inexpensive. For example, incorporate an open rectangle into your decking plans. Plan the framing to support the edges of the decking (see page 196), then set a plastic basin in the opening, resting it on suitable supports. Hide the edges of the basin by extending the decking over it. Add a recirculating pump and pots with water plants, and you have created an oasis on the deck.

A preformed, rigid pond liner will create an even larger pool. Beef up your framing plans so the structure will support the weight of the water, or set the liner on a grade-level concrete pad. In either case camouflage the edges of the liner with landscape timbers or rocks.

Stagnant water breeds mosquitoes, bacteria, and algae and also collects silt and debris, so install a submersible pump to recirculate water over a waterfall or through a fountainhead for aeration. Set the pump on a stone or brick on the bottom of the pond to minimize clogging, and skim the surface periodically to remove debris.

Lights make a deck seem almost magical after dark. You can install lighting fixtures to provide uniform lighting or to create dramatic areas of light and shadow.

Lights that let you enjoy the deck after dark also can add a touch of style during the day. You can find light fixtures that will match any deck design.

Voltage: line or low?

Outdoor lighting systems are powered either by line voltage (the 120-volt AC power in your house), or low voltage (which uses power reduced by a transformer to 12 volts of direct current). Installing a line-voltage system is easy enough for homeowners with experience in doing electrical work, or you can hire a licensed electrician to do the wiring.

Most outdoor line-voltage systems require a permit and approval from a building inspector. Most low-voltage systems don't.

You'll need line voltage for outdoor appliances. Installation requires conduit, fittings, junction boxes, receptacles, fixtures, and wire. Low-voltage systems require few accessories.

Several kinds of fixtures are made for both systems, but line-voltage systems generally offer more options.

PLANNING AMENITIES *(continued)*

Spas, hot tubs, and pools

A spa, hot tub, or soaking pool is a popular deck addition, but installing one requires careful planning. It's better to select the pool first. This way, you can design the deck to accommodate the pool.

The best approach often is to set the pool on a grade-level concrete pad and build the deck around it, letting the rim of the pool stand slightly above the deck surface.

The pool will probably need electrical, water, and drain connections. These should be concealed for aesthetics and to prevent damage, but need to be accessible for maintenance. An outdoor pool will have to meet local code requirements, so have your plan checked before you spend money.

Fireplaces, fire pits, and chimineas

Fire—whether in a fireplace, a fire pit, or chiminea—constitutes the ultimate focal point in both indoor and outdoor settings. Nothing matches the comforting glow of an outdoor fire, and including a place for fire in your deck plans is easy.

Of all your options, fireplaces will prove the most labor intensive and expensive. They require a strengthened frame and a safe location. If you prefer, include a rotisserie and a brick-lined warming oven in the plan, and use your fireplace for cooking and keeping food hot.

As an alternative, freestanding gas and wood-fired fire pits have become widely available for installation on decks. Lined with firebricks and surrounded by a wide, fire-resistant coping, such as stone, their open flames resemble campfires. Provide plenty of floor space on all sides of the pit to keep people a safe distance from the flames. Keep an extinguisher handy, as well as a cover to smother flames that grow too large. The cover also helps contain sparks, which might blow out of the pit after the party is over.

Chimineas are portable enclosures for fire that look like ceramic potbellied stoves. They originated in Mexico and have become increasingly popular around the U.S. Place a chiminea on a metal stand or firebrick platform to keep the deck from overheating. Chimineas are not designed for cooking or winter weather. Store them indoors when temperatures fall below freezing.

A deck is an ideal place for a spa. Install it with a raised platform (left) or set it into the deck surface (right), and plan for plenty of privacy. Spas, hot tubs, and pools require careful planning and are almost certain to fall under local building code requirements. Check with your building department before finalizing your scaled drawings.

Gathering around a fire is a time-honored outdoor ritual. With a fire pit or fireplace on the deck, you can just sit by the fire if you want or have a family wiener roast. You can design and build your own (but check your building codes first) or purchase commercial units.

Incorporating a water garden or a pond into your deck creates a conversation piece and establishes a distinctive style. You can build a pond right into the deck surface by framing an opening and dropping in a preformed plastic pond shell.

Decking spans this garden pond to make a tranquil spot that calls to mind a bridge across a woodland stream. Water features seemingly isolate your deck from the outside world, bringing calm to an urban environment and blocking out the din of busy city life.

STANLEY PRO TIP: **Lining up the utilities**

Before building your deck, plan the location of the utilities. Once the deck is up, it will be more difficult to add water and gas lines. Run utilities underground to maximize safety and minimize clutter. Plot the runs on paper and rough them in before you dig footings.

A water feature will require installation of a pair of 2-inch schedule-40 PVC pipes under the deck site. Draw them in your plans so they run like tunnels under the deck—from one end to the other. Run the electrical cables and smaller pipes for water through the sleeves. The sleeves protect wires and pipes and allow them to be removed for repair or replacement without digging up the deck. You can run added utilities through the sleeve too. Any water leaking from a line break flows through the sleeve and out of the site instead of seeping into the soil under it. Run power and water lines through separate sleeves.

Spa installations are more complex, requiring both running water and a drainpipe. Spas, ponds, fountains, and waterfall pumps also require electrical outlets with ground-fault circuit interrupters (GFCIs). Lighting systems require electric lines. For an outdoor kitchen, consider a permanent natural gas line for a gas grill instead of a propane tank. The orifices for gas and propane appliances are different—make sure you have your grill fitted with the right ones.

Install an exterior phone jack, even if you use portable phones indoors. You'll eventually want to carry on conversations off the deck surface, and the indoor phone signal might not reach that far. To bring television to the deck, you'll need an electric outlet and cable or satellite connection. It's relatively easy to run speaker wires from your stereo system out to weatherproof speakers on the deck.

After the youngsters outgrow this sandbox, you can convert the space to a pond, a planter, a fire pit, or some other use. Planning now for the future will save time and money later.

GALLERY OF DECK DESIGNS

If you don't want to design your own deck or just want a simple design you can build quickly, you can take several approaches. You can buy a deck kit, complete with hardware and precut lumber, from one of several retail and Internet outlets. Or you can choose any of the three basic deck designs shown on the following pages. Any of these decks can go just about anywhere, and they'll give you a solid, aesthetically pleasing structure that will meet building code requirements in most localities (but check to make sure).

Building a deck from a kit or published plans doesn't mean you have to end up with a cookie-cutter structure. You can customize any standard design with thoughtful landscaping, stylish furnishings, and carefully chosen decorations, details, and accents. Or you can go one step further and alter a predrawn plan to make it yours. Move the stairs, for example, to a location that better fits your site. Make 45-degree corners where the plan calls for squares. Or replace the railing with a custom design or one of the choices shown on pages 200–201. If you alter a plan, however, keep safety and the structural integrity of your deck in mind.

Modifying a deck plan

Enlarging a plan will require longer joists, additional decking, and possibly additional posts and longer beams. All of these changes can result in increased spans, so be sure to recalculate the size of the new framing members where safety demands it (page 68).

Decreasing the size of a plan is less complicated. Shorten the joists, the beams, or both, and reduce the spacing between the posts. Decreasing the dimensions of a deck will generally result in shorter deck boards. You can usually stick with existing spans, unless the aesthetics of your site require a change.

Altering the shape of a deck is easiest if you think in terms of adding one rectangle to another, for example, creating an L- or T-shape structure from a basic boxed frame. Plan the main platform first, then the additional leg as a separate deck to be joined to it.

Raise or lower the height of a deck by changing the height of the posts, but be sure to check your local building codes. Taller posts may need to be 6×6s instead of 4×4s, for example. Bracing may be required beyond certain heights, and footings may need to meet certain specifications. Altering the spacing of posts to accommodate utility lines or variations in the terrain calls for careful attention to beam spans.

Other modifications—skirting, railings, and decking patterns—may require alteration of framing members also.

Any deck built from predrawn plans can be customized by carefully selecting landscape elements.

CHAPTER PREVIEW

Freestanding deck with planters and benches
page 42

Deck on a sloped site with railing and stairs
page 44

Two-level deck with wide stairs and a pergola
page 46

FREESTANDING DECK WITH PLANTERS AND BENCHES

Triple 2× beams allow for a 3-foot cantilever at both ends and reduce the number of piers needed—a savings in back-breaking posthole digging.

DECK ON A SLOPED SITE WITH RAILING AND STAIRS

This simple railing treatment is attractive and does not require difficult joints.

To simplify construction, upper-level framing rests on lower-level framing.

Deep cantilever makes deck appear to "float."

Cutting off the corner creates an interesting feature and conserves space in a shallow lot. The stairs sit on a concrete pad with piers that anchor it to the surface of a sloped lot.

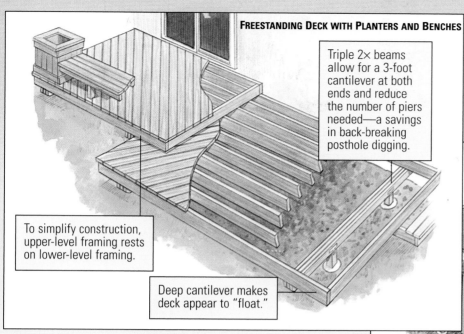

A privacy screen combined with an overhead structure blocks the view into a near neighbor's yard and offers shade and space for hanging plants.

TWO-LEVEL DECK WITH WIDE STAIRS AND A PERGOLA

This 6-foot-wide stairway climbs a gentle 6½ inches of rise for every 14 inches of run.

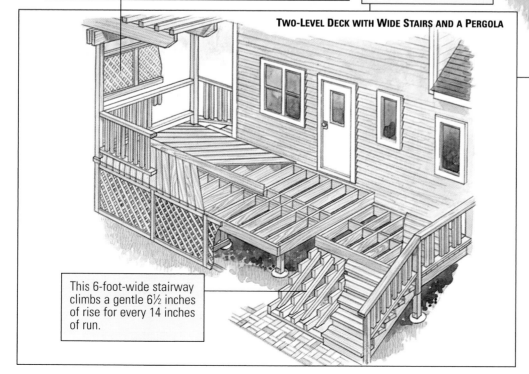

FREESTANDING DECK WITH PLANTERS AND BENCHES

A simple, straightforward deck like this one complements almost any home. A built-in bench, planters, and diagonal decking add style to the basic rectangular deck. Instructions for building it begin on page 106.

Low cost, easy to build
Several techniques make this design easy to build. The joists overhang the beam, so the posts and beam do not have to be precisely positioned. The hefty beam needs fewer piers—a real worksaver because digging and setting piers can be the most laborious stage of deck building.

The large beam also permits a 3-foot cantilever. That's a good feature for new homes where the backfill soil along the foundation has not yet settled: Building codes often require piers to be set as deep as 8 feet in such soil. The longer cantilever places piers farther away from the backfill, so they need not be as deep. The deck is rectangular, so joists can be cut the same length. Angled decking adds visual appeal and requires only a bit more care than straight decking to install.

This deck uses inexpensive pressure-treated lumber for all its parts. Treated wood resists rot and can be stained to look like cedar or redwood.

Getting the size right
The upper level, minus the benches and planters, is 10×12 feet, allowing plenty of room for a grill, a food prep table, and a pathway. The lower level is roughly 14 feet square, a good size for a dining area. If you vary the design, check page 16 to make sure you provide enough space for seating and activities as well as a lane for traffic.

Massive beams made of three 2×10s rest on 6×6 posts, which in turn rest on 12-inch-diameter footings. These larger-than-usual elements allow the beam to overhang the footings by 3 feet. On most sites a beam made of double 2×8s resting on 4×4s and 10-inch footings would suffice.

Cleats attached to the planters support a bench made of 2×4 pieces. Middle support posts are made of 4×4s; the bench top is ⁵⁄₄×6 decking.

The planter is made of ⁵⁄₄×6 decking held together with cleats. Trim is made of ripped decking. A shelf inside holds the plant container.

This two-level deck eases the transition from the kitchen/family room to the yard. A simple step fits under the deeply cantilevered deck. The entire deck is made from pressure-treated lumber.

DECK ON A SLOPED SITE WITH RAILING AND STAIRS

This is a basic rectangular deck with two twists: It's built on a sloped site and has an angle cut across one corner for a stairway. Both lead to some challenging framing work. Instructions begin on page 130.

Size and shape

This deck is 14×24 feet, providing ample room for a food preparation area, a dining area, and a lounge chair or two. The rectangular shape allows several options for positioning outdoor furniture.

The structure

The deck is attached to the house with a ledger board. Installing a ledger reduces the number of footings, posts, and beams required, saving time and work. A ledger installed at the beginning of construction also provides a handy reference point when laying out the deck.

However, installing a ledger board creates its own challenges (see pages 80–81).

Concrete footings support 4×4 posts, which in turn support beams made of doubled 2×10s. A long beam supports most of the deck. A shorter beam, placed at an angle, is needed for the cutoff corner.

The framing is mostly 2×10 joists attached with joist hangers. The angled corner is not difficult to make.

Stairs and railing

This popular railing design uses standard dimensional lumber: 4×4 posts, 2×2 balusters, 2×4 rails, and a top cap of decking. The only difficult joint is where top cap pieces meet at a corner, requiring a mitered cut.

The stairway descends about 4 feet. Detailed instructions for planning and building stairs are on pages 100–103.

The beam is made of doubled 2×10s and rests on top of posts. Special hardware anchors each post to its footing and the beam to the post.

A divider strip on the nearly 24×14-foot deck allows for the use of two 12-foot decking pieces instead of longer, more expensive pieces. Other than at this strip, no joints were necessary in the decking.

This railing is one of the most common designs, using 4×4 posts, 2×4 top and bottom rails, 2×2 balusters, and a 2×6 top cap. Newels attached directly above each post add a decorative touch.

Built to cope with a steep slope on a shallow backyard, this deck features a stairway that angles off one corner. The simple but appealing railing treatment blends with the traditional-style house.

TWO-LEVEL DECK WITH WIDE STAIRS AND A PERGOLA

This two-level deck takes ideas from the two previous decks and adds several custom features. It will take longer to build than the other designs, but none of the elements requires advanced woodworking skills. Instructions begin on page 158.

Angled decking

On the upper level, the angled decking adds a custom look that is easy to achieve. Decking pieces run at 45-degree angles to a center strip. If the angled pieces were to butt against each other, the joints would have to be perfect. But the center strip allows the deck to look great without requiring perfect cuts.

As long as the center strip is positioned accurately, most of the decking pieces will be exactly the same size, so they can be cut rapidly.

Spacious stairs

The stairs are 8 feet wide and 14 inches deep. The spacious size allows the stairs to double as seating, which comes in especially handy when you are entertaining large groups. The landing at the bottom of the stairs, made of patio pavers on a sand bed, creates a graceful transition from deck to yard.

Railing and pergola

This railing design uses more components than the design shown on pages 154–157, but it is not difficult to build. The posts and railing sections can be prefabricated to produce a neater final product.

The pergola, with slats overhead, provides space for hanging plants and a privacy screen. Like the skirt around the base of the deck, the screen is made from vinyl lattice.

Supported by posts made of 2×4s and 1×4s, a balustrade made of 2×2 balusters and 2×4 rails spans from post to post. ⁵⁄₄×6 decking is used for the rail cap. The balusters have alternating spacing of 1½ and 3½ inches.

To assure a solid railing, posts are lag-bolted to the header and outside joists. Vinyl lattice skirting, trimmed with pressure-treated 1×4s, covers the area beneath the deck. Corner posts use three 2×4s and one 1×4.

The pergola is an attention-grabbing feature that is surprisingly simple to build. Four 4×4 posts support 2×8 beams and 2×6 rafters, which are topped off with 2×2s. Lattice sections span between the posts.

This deck features two levels, wide entry stairs, a chevron decking pattern, lattice skirting, and an overhead pergola, but is still fundamentally easy to construct.

DRAWING PLANS

You can produce professional-looking deck plans even if you're not a professional draftsman. A pad of graph paper (use a ¼-inch grid), a pencil or two, a good eraser, a ruler, and perhaps an architect's scale are the only tools you'll need.

Start with rough drawings that show the basic contours of the deck. Then move on to scale drawings. Create a final drawing that details board placement. Ask your local building department about its specific requirements for plans.

Satisfying the inspector

The building department may have sample plans that you can use as guides for your own drawings. Most departments do not demand architect-quality plans, but do want to see where all the pieces fit. Inspectors don't like to squint over unclear drawings, and they may want to see a complete list of all materials.

Produce at least one plan view (how the deck looks from overhead) and one elevation (how it looks from the front and side). Include separate, enlarged detail drawings for all the parts that are complicated or unusual.

Plans save time and money

Though it may seem tedious, draw every framing piece; this shows exactly how many boards of which sizes you'll need.

With a complete set of drawings in hand, you won't have to estimate materials; you can count the exact number of boards and hardware pieces you will need. Buy several extra pieces of each size lumber, in case some are defective or damaged.

Detailed drawings also can help you spot ways to save money on materials. For example, if a plan calls for joists that are 12 feet 2 inches long, you will need to buy 14-foot boards and waste nearly 2 feet of each piece. By shortening the deck a few inches, you can buy less expensive 12-foot joists.

Drawing careful plans enables you to solve problems before you start building—it's better to waste pencil lead than costly lumber and your valuable time. The more detailed and precise you make the drawings, the more likely you are to catch design flaws that would slow the building project. For example, draw in outdoor receptacle boxes, faucets, or dryer vents that protrude from the side of the house; knowing that you may need to work around them when you attach the ledger will save time and minimize frustration in the middle of the project.

When it comes to building a safe, attractive deck, nothing can replace a good set of plans.

CHAPTER PREVIEW

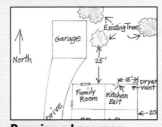

Drawing a base map and site analysis
page 50

From bubble plans to master plan
page 52

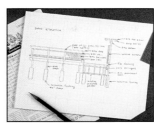

Plan views and elevations
page 54

All plans start with sketches—usually a lot of them. As you get closer to your final design, you will find yourself incorporating the best of your preliminary ideas into one cohesive design.

The planning steps in this chapter are similar to steps a pro follows. Your approach may not require the level of detail shown. However, following these steps will improve your chances of building a deck that will meet all your needs.

DRAWING A BASE MAP AND SITE ANALYSIS

Putting plans on paper requires some discipline—planning works best if you take one thing at a time.

All good deck plans start with a base map, which is simply a scaled drawing of your property. You can zip through this step by locating your plat map—it's probably among the papers you filed when you bought your house. You may also find a plat map at your county clerk's office. If you can find one, take it to a copy shop and ask for a 1-to-10 enlargement that will put the image on 24×36-inch paper.

If you can't find a plat map, go out to your yard with a 100-foot steel tape measure, a sketch pad, and someone to help you, then start measuring and sketching your yard. Here's what a base map should include:

■ Dimensions of your property and location of property lines.
■ Outline and dimensions of the house and its position relative to property lines.
■ Exact locations of exterior electrical outlets, dryer vents, and water supply— anything that protrudes from the side of the house where you plan to locate the deck.

■ Locations and dimensions of all exterior windows and doors, including distance from the ground and which room they go into. Show them all, not just those on the deck side; you may change your mind about the deck location.
■ Positions and dimensions of any outbuildings, such as garages and storage sheds, and other major landscape features, including large trees, playground equipment, and planting beds.
■ Dimensions of roof overhangs and locations of downspouts.
■ Locations and dimensions of existing walls, fences, stairs, walks, and driveways.

By gathering this detailed information you'll have everything you need to know right at hand when you plan your deck.

Making a site analysis

Once you have a record of existing elements in your landscape, note what's right and what's wrong with it. Tape a piece of tracing paper over your site plan and trace the major elements of the site. Gather up the notes and the sketches you made when you conducted an inventory of your site (pages 10–13) and transfer the findings to the tracing paper. (Leave your site plan untouched—you might need it later.)

A site analysis is a bird's-eye view of conditions in your yard, both the things you like and those you would like to change.

Note the prevailing winds; you don't want your deck in a wind tunnel, so you may need to move it or build windbreaks.

Draw arrows to indicate predominant drainage patterns so you can avoid putting your deck on swampy soil. If the best location is in a runoff area, you may have to build a drainage system to divert the water.

Indicate where the shade falls and where the sun is strongest during the part of the day you plan to use your deck most.

Make note of neighbors' views. You may need to plan for privacy. Also note the things you want to shield from your view.

You don't need to indicate solutions for each of these situations; that's a step you will address later.

Remember to include the elements you consider assets—pleasant views, the direction of cooling breezes, or natural areas that you could link to your deck for outdoor walks and recreation.

Computer deck programs

Many home centers and lumberyards offer computer planning software and employ staff who know how to work them. Bring in a rough drawing with dimensions (height, width, and length) and ask for help. If you're computer savvy yourself, browse the Internet for similar planning software.

Most programs produce several drawings—a plan view, an elevation, and a perspective view. Many also will produce a list of lumber and materials.

Some of these programs have limitations, however, displaying only a few railing styles and lacking the capacity to plan an overhead structure or planter. Unusual or odd-shape designs may also outstrip the power of some programs. So might structural requirements that differ from typical building codes. Most professional deck contractors draw their plans by hand. It's quicker and more flexible.

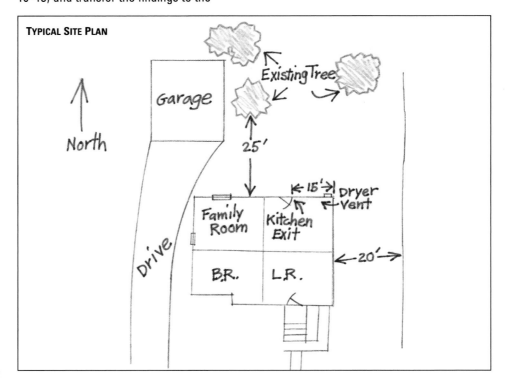

TYPICAL SITE PLAN

Don't forget the views

Keep three views in mind: the way the deck looks to passersby, what you see when you are sitting on the deck, and the view of the deck from inside the house.

■ **The view from the street:** Though a deck is primarily a horizontal surface, passersby and neighbors see the vertical elements—railings, steps, benches, overhead structures, planters, and skirting. If the deck has few vertical elements, budget for some furniture and flowerpots to dress it up.

■ **The view from the deck:** If the deck overlooks a beautiful view—be it a magnificent hillside or a lovely yard—orient the deck so that people can get a good look while they are sitting on benches or chairs. If you have small children, make sure you won't have to strain to see them while they play in the yard.

■ **The view from inside:** If you have a cherished view from your kitchen or living room, don't cover it up with a deck railing. If necessary drop the deck down two or three steps or build a deck low enough that it does not need a railing.

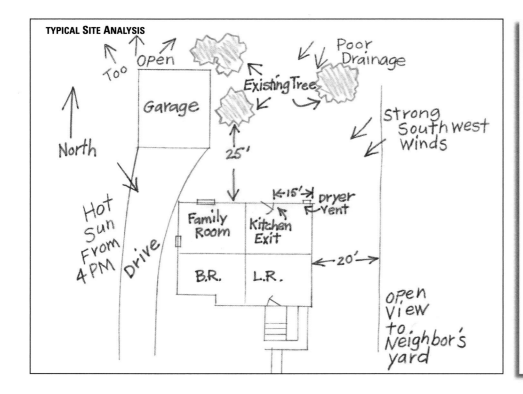

TYPICAL SITE ANALYSIS

Planning a new life for an old deck

If you already have a deck that you don't use, the planning steps might show how to make it into an enjoyable space you would use. Start by noting faults and assets, just as if you were planning a new deck.

If the deck is too large, subdivide it into smaller, more intimate areas with planters, container gardens, or movable seating. Perhaps you could add an outdoor kitchen, fire pit, or water feature (see pages 36–39). Maybe all you need is a little more room for a barbecue. Add a dining space and set up a portable or built-in grill where the furniture used to be.

If the deck is too small for all your guests and is cramping your party style, build an extension or put in a paved area by the deck (see page 8). If you don't have room to attach another deck to the old one, build a detached deck farther out in the yard and connect the two with a boardwalk or a third deck.

FROM BUBBLE PLANS TO MASTER PLAN

A bubble plan is simply a site plan with circles containing notes on it. It sounds simple, almost silly. But the bubble plan is the most useful planning tool you'll use.

Bubble diagrams let you play with your plans. They are designed to let your imagination run free so you can look at different ideas and situations to come up with the best deck plan. The site analysis you prepared (previous page) is a snapshot of your landscape as it exists now; the bubble plan helps you imagine how things could be.

Making a bubble plan

Tape a sheet of tracing paper over your site analysis and retrace the house and major features of the landscape. You should be able to read your site analysis notes through the top sheet, but if you can't, pull the site analysis to the side and use it as a guide.

Now look at the various areas in the yard and brainstorm how you could use them. Draw circles on the paper, identifying the purpose of each area—don't consider budget limitations or time constraints now.

Use abstract terms at this stage. For example, label an area close to the house as "entertainment," if you wish, but don't identify it specifically as "deck." You may discover other areas with the same purpose and find in later planning stages that a deck doesn't belong there at all. Similarly, "privacy" or "increase privacy" is a better label than "fence," "wall," or "trees." Indicate various needs in a general way and move them around to make the best use of your landscape.

If you want a place for entertaining large groups and a smaller space for family dining, move the bubbles around to see where they might fit. One solution might be to place them on different sides of the house. They might work with one area attached to the other. Or you might see a way to have one area completely removed from the house and the two connected by a path, or not connected at all. With the bubble plan, you can look at all the options.

When you make a bubble diagram, think about the purpose or function of an area first. Consider the kind of structure you need later. If you decide to finalize your design after you've drawn your first bubble plan, beware—there's a good chance you've forgotten something.

The final touches

Once you have found the best solution for your property, sketch in the structures that meet the purposes you have defined. Get as close to scale in this version as you can. It will be the launching pad for the plan views and elevations you'll need to take to your building department.

Put in the main structures first—the deck, landings, and pathways, and modify them if necessary. For example, if a rectangular deck doesn't look quite right or if a large oak interferes with one of its corners, don't reduce the size of the deck. Round the corner or cut it at 45 degrees. If the walk from the deck to the garden bed looks straight and boring, put curves in the path.

Trees and plants come next. Add planting areas with contoured bed lines, and use circles to designate new trees and shrubs. Then label the rooms in your house and make one last check to see that the uses of exterior space are compatible with the space inside. Finally, make notes of the tasks you need to accomplish: "remove this tree," "build fence here," "replant this garden," and so forth.

TYPICAL BUBBLE PLAN

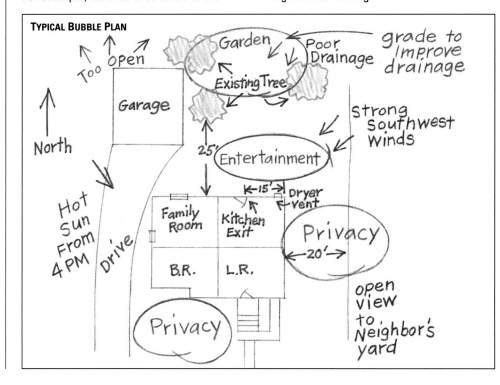

Dealing with inspectors

Building inspectors have an important job: They assure that structures built in their jurisdictions are strong and safe. To accomplish this goal, they have the authority to stop construction on any job they believe is being built incorrectly.

Work with an inspector in a respectful, businesslike manner. Present clean and complete drawings and materials lists. Find out how many inspections you will need and be ready for each. Do not cover up anything an inspector wants to look at, or you may have to dismantle your work. It's seldom a good idea to argue with an inspector. He or she knows more than you do, and getting on the bad side of an inspector can make a job miserable. Comply exactly with all of the inspector's directions.

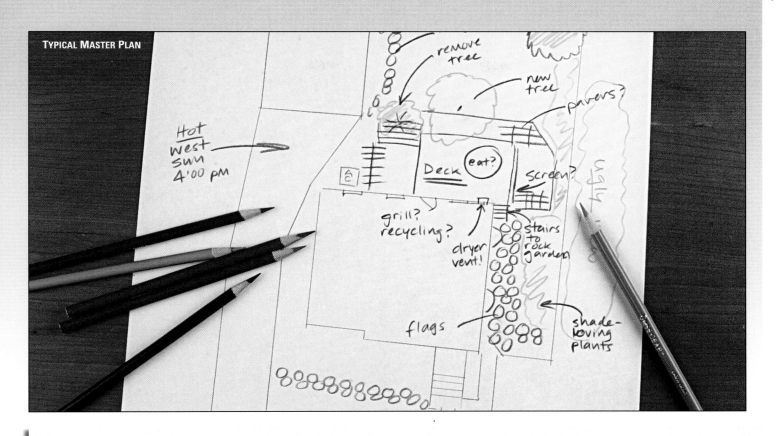

TYPICAL MASTER PLAN

REFRESHER COURSE
A quick look at deck planning

Putting your plans on paper is the final step of your planning activity. It allows you to sort out the considerations involved in locating and designing a deck that fits your site, reflects your personality, and will provide you with enjoyable space for years to come. Here's a quick glance at the things you should keep in mind when committing your design to paper.

Planning for purpose
List all the activities you foresee for your deck: lounging, barbecuing, entertaining, soaking in a spa, container gardening, storing gear, and more. In your design try to accommodate as many of these activities as possible.

Size and shape
Unless you expect to entertain large groups, there's little need for a huge deck. Just make sure you have ample space for all the activity areas you need.

A rectangular deck provides the most available space, and a simple shape may be the most attractive design. But don't be afraid to add an angle or two. An octagonal deck holds a round table nicely. Simple 45-degree angles add visual interest, often without sacrificing usable space.

Consider dividing the deck into two or more sections: one area for lounging and another for dining and cooking. Orient one section at a different angle, or use planters or steps to create a transition between the two areas.

A deck doesn't have to be right next to the house. A peninsula or an island deck offers a pleasant retreat from daily life.

Situations for comfort
As you plan your deck, note the sun and wind patterns in your yard. Situate the dining area in evening shade. Provide a lounging area with part shade and part sun. Put in plantings or a fence to minimize wind gusts.

Include amenities
Don't neglect the add-ons that make a deck more than just an outdoor floor. An overhead structure or trellis provides shade as well as a setting for climbing plants. A high railing with lattice panels provides privacy and screens undesirable views.

Built-in planters and benches unify different areas of a deck. You may prefer large flowerpots and attractive patio furniture, which can be moved to suit the occasion. If so, allow space for them in your plan.

Plan for lighting as well. Low-voltage lights are inexpensive and easy to install, and can be mounted around the deck. You may also need brighter standard-voltage lights and an electrical receptacle or two. Consult with an electrician about adding those features.

PLAN VIEWS AND ELEVATIONS

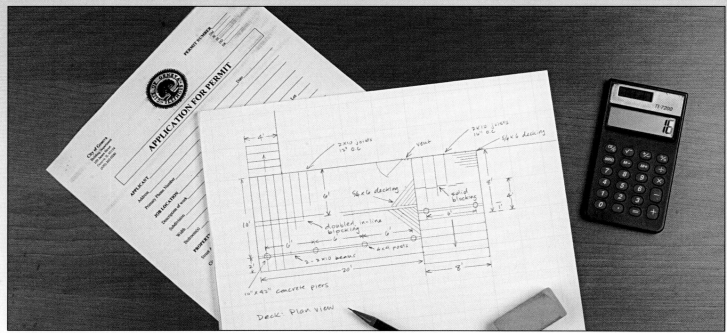

Draw a plan view from an overhead point of view. This important drawing must show all the joists, beams, posts, and stair framing. A plan view may also include a partial view of the decking, railing, and any other structures that are attached to the deck. Even though the drawing is to scale, be sure to include all dimensions, including overall length and width, how far apart the joists and beams are, and specific lengths of perimeter pieces. Show the locations and sizes of the house's windows and doors.

Include a materials list that states the number and size of all framing members as well as all hardware pieces.

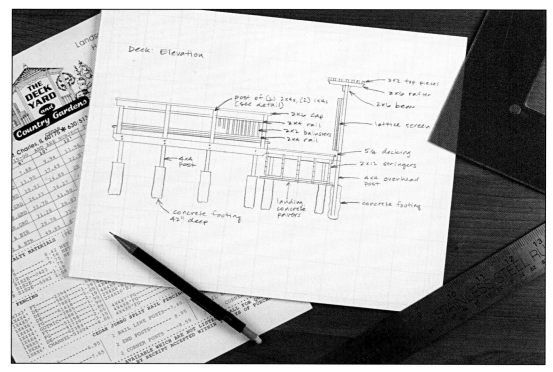

An elevation emphasizes vertical elements: footings, posts, railings, and any built-in planters, benches, or overhead structures. Produce one or two side views. Each elevation should show the size of the footings and the dimensions for the railing. Railing dimensions are particularly important. Indicate the height of the railing as well as how much space will be between balusters. Give the dimensions for all the railing pieces and describe how they will be attached.

Include information about fasteners. Indicate the size and number of screws or bolts used to attach the ledger, beams, and railing posts. If you will use special hardware, describe it in detail.

Drawing an elevation

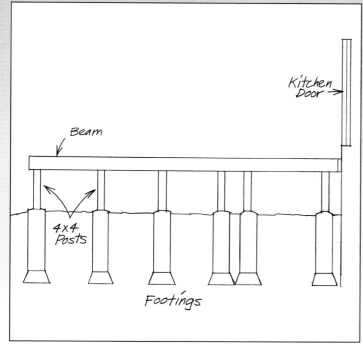

1 Start with a minimum indication of the deck location—here the back edge of the house. Use your ruler and graph paper to put in the footings, spaced to scale, then draw the posts and beams to the properly scaled dimensions.

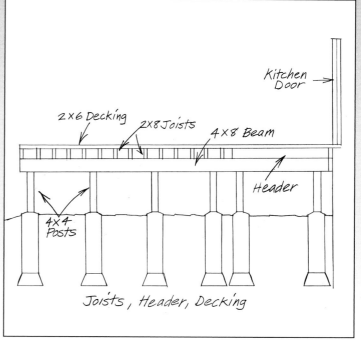

2 Add the joists next, again keeping them to scale. Where a framing member covers the view of the joists, as the header does here, use a cutaway view so you can see all the parts. Label the structural members with the proper size.

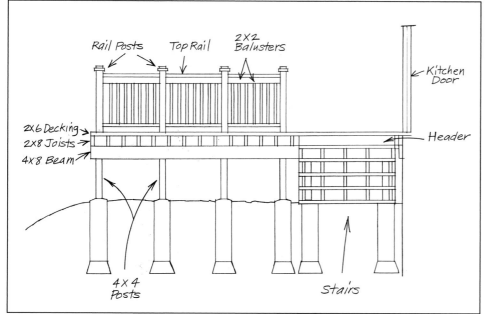

3 Draw in the railing elements and label their parts also. To the degree the graph paper will permit, render the balusters with the proper scaled spacing. Add the stairs last and show the details of the supports you will use.

Construction details

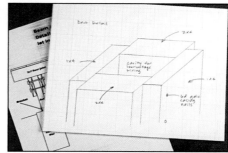

A separate detail drawing makes things clear. Use construction drawings to show framing for a change in deck levels, the method of attaching a ledger, or an unusual stairway. Show any element of the plan that isn't clear on the plan or elevation views. Your building department may want detail drawings for the railing or for any permanent benches, planters, or overhead structures.

TOOLS & MATERIALS

Compared with many home remodeling projects, deck building is easy and enjoyable. It is outdoor work, involves basic materials and carpentry skills, and won't disrupt everyday home life as other remodeling projects can. It's not a problem to leave the work half finished and pick up where you left off several days later.

No building job, however, including a deck, should be approached haphazardly. Making good decisions when you plan the project can save hassles later on, so be willing to spend as much time preparing as in actually building a deck.

Making plans

Walk around the site and make rough sketches first. Note the patterns of sun and shade, views worth preserving, and likely foot-traffic patterns. Gradually refine the drawings, and consult with your local building department to make sure that your plans comply with local codes (see pages 48–55).

Choosing tools and materials

Assemble the kit of carpentry hand tools shown at right. You may already have most of these tools. They are useful for many household projects and will be handy to have around the house long after the deck is finished, so invest in high-quality tools. Avoid bargain-bin, off-brand tools, which often break or bend easily, may not cut well, and may be less comfortable to use. Power tools that will make the job go more easily and quickly are shown on pages 58–59. In addition to saving effort, you can often make more precise cuts with a power saw.

This chapter also can help you decide which type of lumber to use for your deck and how to select the best boards. Synthetic decking, an increasingly popular option for deck builders, is explained on pages 66–67.

To make sure your deck will be safe, sturdy, and long-lasting, consult pages 68–69 for information about span lengths and other considerations.

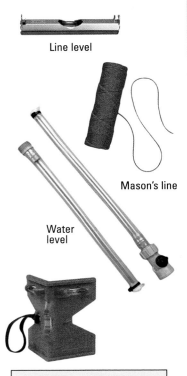

To check for level over long distances, use a carpenter's level atop a straight board, a line level, or a water level.

Line level

Mason's line

Water level

An inexpensive post level makes setting posts much easier. It allows hands-free work, and it indicates whether a post is plumb in both directions.

CHAPTER PREVIEW

For a successful project, choose the right tools and materials and draw detailed plans.

Power tools
page 58

Selecting lumber
page 60

Selecting the best boards
page 64

Synthetic decking
page 66

A 25- or 30-foot, 1-inch-wide tape measure is an all-purpose measuring tool.

Use a layout square to quickly mark for 90- and 45-degree cuts. It can also be used to mark other angles.

T-bevel

Hand sander

Carpenter's pencil

Pry bar

Cordless drill

Tool belt

Chalk line

Ratchet and socket

Carpenter's square

Squeeze clamp

Chisel

Bar clamp

Most homeowners prefer a 16-ounce hammer; a 20-ounce packs a wallop but requires a strong arm.

Sledge

Clamshell digger

Nail set

Handsaw

Computing the spans
page 68

Choosing fasteners
page 70

Building with quality and care
page 74

Footings
page 76

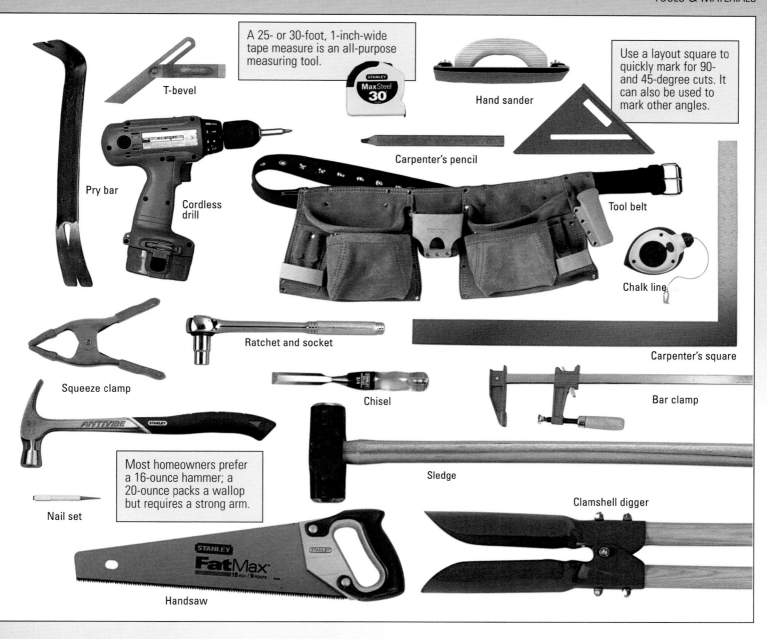

POWER TOOLS

If you already own some of the tools shown on these pages, test their quality before beginning a deck project. If you have difficulty cutting a straight line or boring a hole, try a new blade or bit. If the tool still is a struggle to use, buy a new one that will produce clean lines with ease.

The three most common power tools—circular saw, saber saw, and drill—are all you need for most deck work. Here's what to look for:

Power saws
A smooth-running **circular saw** equipped with a sharp blade will cut through lumber with ease and precision. Choose a saw that uses a 7¼-inch blade. The saw should be rated at 13 amps (1,560 watts) or higher and

be built with ball or needle bearings. Pick up the saw and handle it—it should feel comfortable in your grip. The knobs to adjust the cutting angle should be easy to use; make sure you can easily sight down the guide on the baseplate as you cut.

A 40-tooth **carbide-tipped circular saw blade** cuts rough lumber with ease and produces a fine, splinter-free edge.

A **jigsaw,** sometimes called a saber saw, is designed to cut curves. A cheap jigsaw will cut slowly and wobble, producing an uneven line. Choose a model with a large, solid baseplate that will stay firmly in place during cutting. The saw should draw at least 4.5 amps (540 watts). A sawdust blower is a useful feature: It clears sawdust off the guide line as you cut.

Purchase several **jigsaw blades** because they break easily. For most deck work, use medium- or heavy-duty blades, designed to cut through 2× material.

Power drills
To drill bolt holes and pilot holes for fasteners, you will need a **power drill**. A cheap drill will burn out under the load, so get a ⅜-inch, reversing and variable-speed drill that draws at least 3 amps (360 watts). It will drive screws too. A corded drill is handy, but for even greater versatility buy a cordless drill/driver. For deck work, a cordless drill/driver should be at least a 14.4-volt model. Buy the drill/driver in a kit with two rechargeable batteries so one can charge while you use the other.

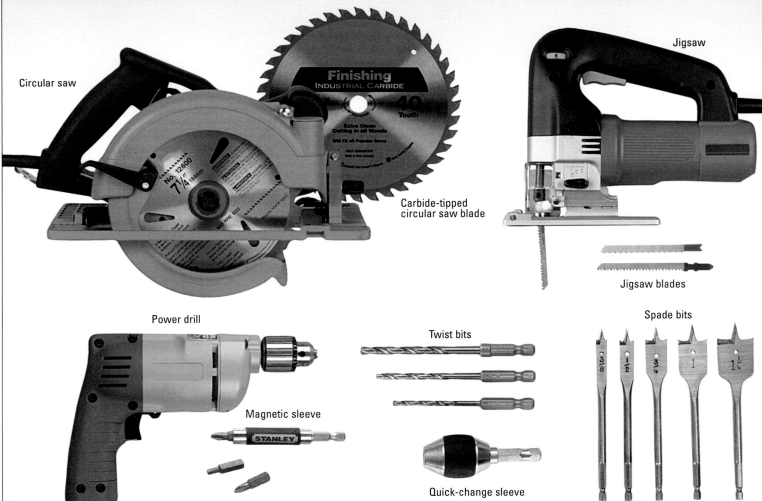

Circular saw

Finishing
INDUSTRIAL CARBIDE
40 Tooth

Carbide-tipped
circular saw blade

Jigsaw

Jigsaw blades

Power drill

Twist bits

Magnetic sleeve

STANLEY

Quick-change sleeve

Spade bits

Drill bits become dull quickly, especially if they hit a nail. Buy a complete set of **twist bits.** Titanium-coated bits last longer than cheaper bits. You may also need **spade bits** of several sizes. **Quick-change** and **magnetic sleeves** are timesavers.

Optional tools

Some tools may make the work go faster, and they help achieve a more professional look to the deck. For seldom-used tools, consider renting rather than buying; a rented tool may be of higher quality than one you buy.

A **power mitersaw,** commonly called a chop saw, makes precise cuts of any angle. To make 45-degree cuts through a 2×6 (or ¾×6 decking), you'll need a model with at least a 12-inch blade. A compound miter feature is not needed for deck work, but is useful for other work you may do with the saw.

A quick way to give railings and deck edges a custom look is to form them with a **router.** Use a self-guiding bit, which runs along the edge of the material and minimizes mistakes. A **roundover bit** produces a radius edge. Another woodworking tool, a biscuit joiner, is useful for some types of decking fasteners (page 73) and railing joints (page 74).

When you're attaching a ledger to a brick, block, or concrete surface, a **hammer drill** can reduce labor dramatically. With the hammer feature engaged, it pounds the surface with rapid blows while it drills.

A nail gun (page 73) drives a nail instantly with the pull of a trigger and can speed up a job. Different guns drive different sizes of nails. Most nail guns require a large air compressor. Some models are electrically driven or powered by a gas cartridge and a battery. If you want to use one for decking, experiment on scrap pieces of decking to make sure that the nails will not be driven too deeply.

Rent a **power auger** if you have several postholes to dig. See page 86 for instructions on choosing and using a power auger. A small concrete mixer (page 88) is better than hand mixing if you have many piers to pour.

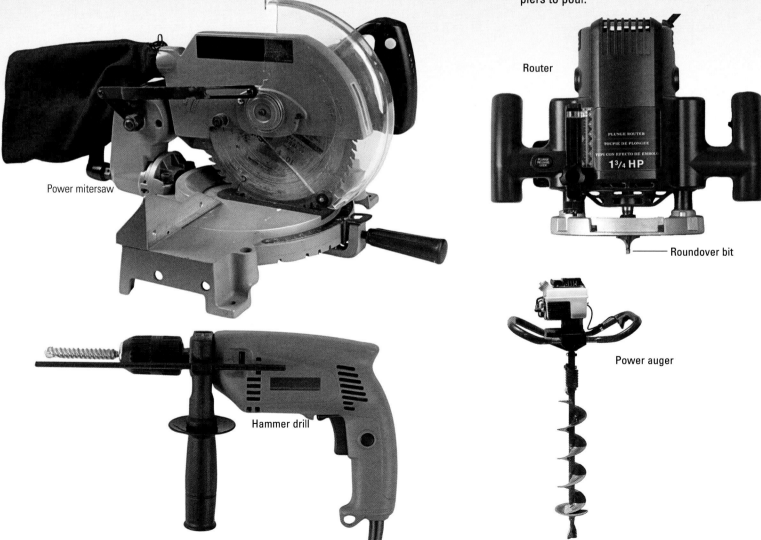

Power mitersaw

Router

Roundover bit

Hammer drill

Power auger

SELECTING LUMBER

Selecting lumber is a balancing act—among budget, beauty, and the function of the lumber (whether it will be used for framing or for decking and railings).

Types of lumber

Lumber used in deck construction generally falls into one of the following categories.

Pressure-treated lumber (PT), usually pine or fir, is infused with chemicals that make it extremely rot-resistant. The chemicals also give the wood a green or brown cast, which you can hide with stain or paint or let weather to a dark gray. Pressure-treated lumber is the least expensive, but you'll have to choose carefully to get stock that is straight and free of loose knots.

Naturally resistant species, such as cedar, redwood, and cypress, are resistant to rot and insects, a quality most characteristic of the heartwood, the dense centermost core of the tree. You can seal or stain these woods to retain their natural beauty, or let them weather to various shades of gray. Exotic species, such as ipe, cambara, and meranti, display similar color characteristics and are generally more durable, more difficult to work, and more expensive.

Where to use it

Framing: Unless your design requires the same wood throughout the entire structure (and your budget can withstand the sticker shock of natural heartwoods), pressure-treated lumber is a good choice for framing. Use lumber rated for ground contact for posts and framing members within 6 inches of the soil. Look for a grade stamp that says "ground contact" or indicates a treatment depth of 0.40 or greater. Some pressure-treated species are less porous than others, so they're incised before being treated. These incisions still show after treatment, so place this lumber where it will be less visible. Wood that has been kiln-dried after treatment (KDAT) is the highest quality.

For posts, 4×4s or 6×6s are standard. Cut cleats and stiffeners from 2×4s, joists and beams from 2×6s, 2×8s, 2×10s, or 2×12s. Pick PT lumber with care. Some boards will be smaller than standard nominal sizes. An untreated 2×10 will measure 9¼ inches, a PT 2×10 may only be 9⅛ inches wide.

Decking and railings: These are the most visible parts of your deck, so you'll want to use the best lumber you can afford. Redwood, cedar, and cypress, as well as the exotic species are good choices, but since most decking boards from domestic woods are sapwood and not rot resistant, you should treat them.

For the deck surface, you can use 2×4s, 2×6s, or ⁵⁄₄×6s. The ⁵⁄₄ decking (pronounced "five-quarter"), available in cedar and pressure-treated fir, is 1 inch thick and 5½ inches wide with rounded edges that make for a splinter-free surface.

Cedar 1× lumber usually has one rough side and one smooth side. Put the rough side down.

Grades and moisture content

Lumber is graded in an almost bewildering number of grades, which describe the prevalence of knots, its overall appearance, and its strength. For structural members choose a No. 2 grade or lumber graded as Standard. For decking and railings, Select grades are free of knots, but expensive. Choose the best your budget will allow.

A lumber grade stamp (page 62) will indicate the quality of the stock and will also note its moisture content. For framing, air dried lumber is adequate. Use S-dry or MC-15 lumber for decking and rails.

STANLEY PRO TIP

Pressure-treated precautions

Chromated copper arsenate (CCA) or ammoniacal copper arsenate (ACA) have been widely used for pressure-treating lumber. Research has shown arsenic compounds to be a potential health hazard, however, so production of such treated wood for residential use has been halted, effective in 2003. You may still find these products on the market, however, because the law allows suppliers to sell their existing stock. Lumber treated with other chemicals, such as ammoniacal copper quaternary (ACQ), is not considered hazardous.

No matter what kind of PT wood you purchase, wear protective clothing, a dust mask, and safety glasses while working with it. Sweep up thoroughly and dispose of scraps. Do not burn PT waste. Call your local environmental agency and ask about proper disposal methods. Keep children out of the work area.

Lumber sizes

Nominal Size	Actual Size
1×2	¾" × 1½"
1×3	¾" × 2½"
1×4	¾" × 3½"
1×6	¾" × 5½"
1×8	¾" × 7¼"
1×10	¾" × 9¼"
1×12	¾" × 11¼"
2×2	1½" × 1½"
2×4	1½" × 3½"
2×6	1½" × 5½"
2×8	1½" × 7¼"
2×10	1½" × 9¼"
2×12	1½" × 11¼"
4×4	3½" × 3½"

After it is cut, lumber is dried, planed, and smoothed, all of which reduces its thickness and width. The nominal size of a board refers to the size before drying and planing; actual size means the size you actually get, and it's less than its nominal size in thickness and width.

A very old, rough 2×4 may actually measure 2 inches by 4 inches. Today a nominal 2×4 is actually 1½ inches by 3½ inches.

Lumber from 2×6s on up can vary as much as ¼ inch in width—even if taken from the same stack at the lumberyard. Posts larger than 4×4 are prone to twists and cracks; consider sandwiching 2×s instead.

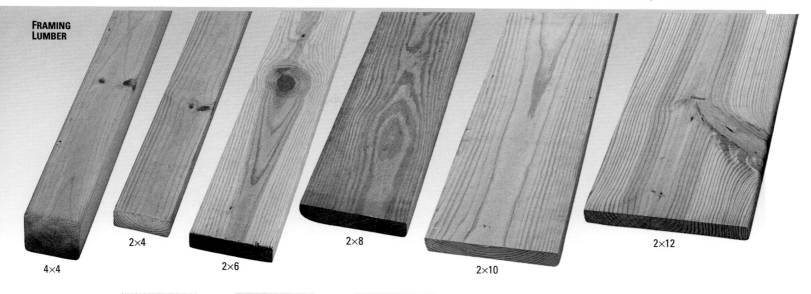

FRAMING LUMBER

4×4   2×4   2×6   2×8   2×10   2×12

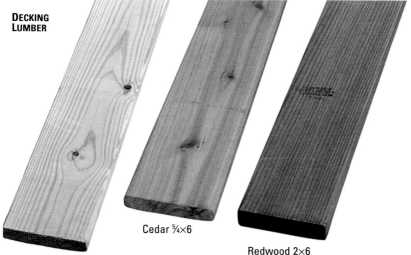

DECKING LUMBER

Pressure-treated ⁵⁄₄×6   Cedar ⁵⁄₄×6   Redwood 2×6

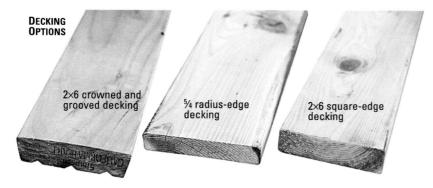

DECKING OPTIONS

2×6 crowned and grooved decking   ⁵⁄₄ radius-edge decking   2×6 square-edge decking

Decking comes in more than just square-edge configurations. Crowned and grooved decking lets water run off freely, and the grooves provide additional insurance from warping and splitting. Radius-edge decking offers a slightly different appearance and reduces splintering.

Exotic woods

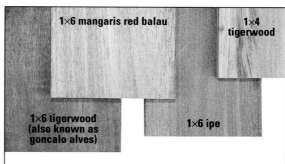

1×6 mangaris red balau   1×4 tigerwood

1×6 tigerwood (also known as goncalo alves)   1×6 ipe

Exotic hardwoods offer a more costly, but extremely durable alternative to domestic woods. Ipe, for example, can triple your material costs—and that's if you use it only on the deck surface and railings. On the other hand, ipe is twice as strong as PT Douglas fir.

As more retailers bring these woods to market, prices might come down a bit, but they will probably never be competitive with PT lumber. Sustainability is also an issue with these woods. Some of each species is cut from sustainable forests, but these products can be difficult to obtain. Check with the Certified Forest Products Council (www.certifiedwood.org) for information on sustainable wood products.

All of the exotic hardwoods are extremely dense and may prove difficult to work with. Predrilling is a must, as undrilled fasteners will split the boards. Fasteners made specifically for these woods are preferred to nails or screws. Ipe is so dense that it neither needs nor will accept stains or finishes. Other species can be finished with hardwood stains or oils.

SELECTING LUMBER *(continued)*

Sapwood and heartwood

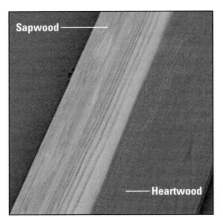

Redwood and cedar look better than PT lumber, but only the **heartwood** naturally resists rot. The light-colored **sapwood** may rot in a few years unless treated regularly with preservative.

Lumber grade stamps

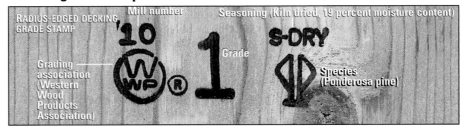

Grade stamps differ from species to species, and board markings differ from dimension lumber stamps. A PT stamp specifies the treatment chemical, treatment depth, and other data. Pay special attention to both the grade and the moisture content of untreated lumber.

Redwood grades

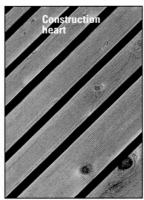

B-grade redwood has only tiny knots and is all heartwood—a desirable but expensive choice for decking.

Construction heart has knots but no sapwood. **Construction common** has large knots and is partly sapwood.

If you want to retain the brown color of these boards, plan to stain them every year or two; otherwise, allow them to weather (page 214).

How much lumber will you need?

For a small deck (10×12 feet, for example), determine how much lumber you'll need by counting all the pieces of each size—12-foot 2×4s, 8-foot 2×6s, and so on. Add 10 percent to framing quantities and 15 percent to decking to allow for waste.

Lumber lengths are in even 2-foot intervals. Most longer stock is slightly longer than stated—a 12-foot board may measure 144¼", for example. If you will cut several lengths from a board, remember to allow for the saw kerf when estimating.

For larger decks, you can calculate the total square footage of decking you need by multiplying the length of the deck surface times the width. Allow for overhangs. Then buy enough lineal feet of decking to make up the deck area plus the waste allowance. Make actual counts of posts, beams, joists, and other framing members.

Milled railings

The style of railing you employ in your deck design can enhance the appearance of your deck more than any other element. Square-cut posts and balusters are the most common, of course, and will complement almost any architectural style. You can dress them up with mortises, bevel cuts, and post caps. If you want something more stylish, look at the supply of milled stock carried by your home center.

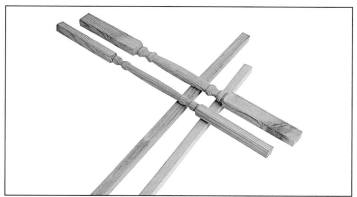

You might be surprised at the array of styles in different species. Turned balusters are available with numerous configurations and go well with Victorian or classic landscape designs. Milled stock increases your design options geometrically—you can keep the style consistent throughout, or mix various baluster styles with a consistent post design for more variety.

Storing lumber

Once you get your materials to the work site, protect them from direct sunlight and moisture, especially if you expect your deck building to spread out over several weekends. If your lumber is not kiln-dried, let it dry for several weeks. Stack the boards flat—keep them off the ground with concrete blocks or 4×4s and insert 2×2 spacers (called stickers) between them. The stickers will let air circulate evenly throughout the stack. Kiln-dried lumber is ready to use, but you'll need to protect it from the elements too.

Milled post caps and finials

Add style to your railings by adding milled post caps or finials. Finials come in a bountiful number of configurations and are proportioned to fit 4×4 or 6×6 posts. Some come complete with lag screws that only require predrilling the posts. Other styles need drilling for screws or dowels. To keep rainwater from rotting the top of the post, caulk the bottom edge with silicone before tightening the finial.

Post caps cover the tops of the posts completely and shed rain from the end grain. You'll find them fluted, corniced, and chamfered—in styles that will match any deck design.

SELECTING THE BEST BOARDS

Most lumber retailers have some warped and defective boards mingled in with the good ones. If you simply order a certain number of a particular size board and take what the lumberyard delivers, you're likely to get some substandard pieces. The best way to ensure you get strong and attractive lumber for your deck is to select them yourself; examine each board and choose only those that suit your needs.

Living with imperfection

It's rare to find a board that is completely free of defects. So think about how each board will be used and make sure it is free from *important* defects. For instance, framing lumber that will be hidden needs to be straight and free of major cracks, but it need not be pretty. Decking and fascia boards need have only one good-looking side. You can accept some boards that are bowed or even a little twiste, because you

can straighten them when you install them. Boards used for the railing will be seen from both sides, so they need to be straight and attractive on both sides.

Defects to look for

■ A **bow** is a bend along the wide face of the board. A related defect, a **crook,** is a bend along the narrow face, visible as you sight down one edge. The high side of a crook is called the **crown**. Bows are not usually a problem as long as fastening makes them straight. A slight crook—no more than ¾ inch in an 8-foot board—is not a problem for any board except the top cap of a railing.

■ A slight corkscrew shape in a board is known as a **twist**. If the twist is noticeable, reject the board.

■ A **check** is a crack that appears on the surface only and is usually only a cosmetic problem. However, if the crack runs more

than halfway through the thickness of a board, reject the board.

■ A short crack running through the thickness of the board at its end is a **split.** If the cracked portion plus an inch or so can be cut off, then accept the board.

■ A **knot** is primarily a cosmetic problem; if it is tight it usually does not affect the strength of the board. If a knot is larger than 1 inch in diameter or feels loose, it may come out.

■ A **wane** is a rounded-off corner along the edge of a board, where bark used to be. It is usually only a cosmetic problem, though it slightly reduces a board's nailing surface.

■ A curve across the width of a board is a **cup.** Unless it is severe, cupping is not a problem for framing lumber. In a decking board, slight cupping can be taken out by screwing down each side of the board.

IMPERFECTIONS TO WATCH FOR

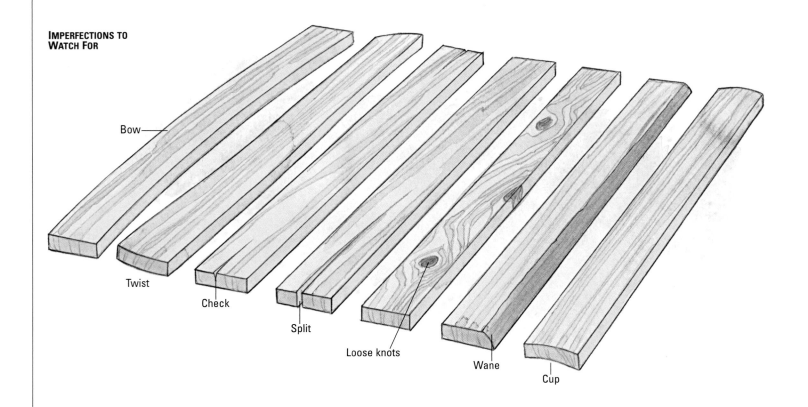

Bow

Twist

Check

Split

Loose knots

Wane

Cup

Vertical and flat grain

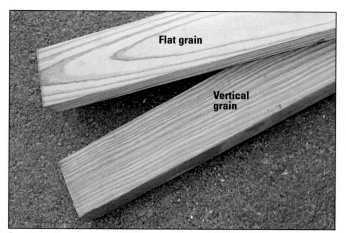

Boards with narrow parallel lines, called **vertical grain**, are stronger and less likely to warp than boards with widely spaced curved lines, called **flat grain**. Many boards have both vertical and flat grain. When possible, choose boards with more vertical grain than flat grain.

Examining a board

It takes about 10 seconds to examine a board. Check for twist and crook by picking up one end and sighting down its length. Then examine both sides and the edges for defects such as loose knots, cracks, and wane. When using lumber for framing, place the board so that the **crown** (a slight upward crook) is up.

Sealing cut edges

Cedar and redwood benefit from rot-preventing treatment. In addition, pressure-treating often does not reach the center of a thick board; this means that when the board is cut, untreated wood is exposed. To keep a board from rotting, give the cut edge a quick soak in sealer or apply sealer with a paintbrush. It's usually easier to apply sealer before installing the board.

STANLEY PRO TIP

Check for moisture

A board that is wet—either with sap or with pressure treatment—will warp when it dries out unless it is tightly stacked or firmly nailed in place. It will certainly shrink in width and perhaps in length as well.

Consult a board's label to find out its moisture content. Kiln-dried stock is the driest. A board with a moisture content above 15 percent will probably warp unless it is fastened securely.

The label describes a board's moisture content when it left the mill. If a board has been in a lumberyard for months, it may have dried out or become wet. To check a board for moisture, hit it with a hammer. If you see a small spray of liquid or if the indentation feels moist, then the board holds significant moisture.

Wet decking can be installed, but be aware that it will shrink in width. When builders install wet decking, they often fit the boards snugly against each other. When the boards dry out, 1/8-inch gaps will develop between them.

Once removed from the stack, wet lumber can dry quickly, especially if the weather is dry. If left out in the sun, a loose board may warp in an hour. Keep boards tightly stacked until you use them and then fasten them securely with nails or screws.

SYNTHETIC DECKING

Technology has created a host of synthetic materials that bring a number of advantages to do-it-yourself deck building. Wood composites, vinyl, and fiberglass-reinforced decking are becoming more widely used because they avoid or minimize many of wood's drawbacks: splitting, splintering, warping, and deteriorating with age. The synthetics are waterproof and maintenance-free. Their principal drawback is that they are not strong enough to be used as structural members, and most systems call for joists spaced 16 inches on center.

Composites
Molded from a compressed and heated mixture of wood fibers and plastic resins, wood composites are the closest of the synthetics to real wood. The manufacturing process results in a surface that mimics the grain of real wood, and the boards can be cut with a circular saw equipped with a large-toothed blade. Installation of some composites is also wood-like—with screws predrilled into the decking. Others are girder-shape and employ blind screws and a tongue-and-groove system for fastening.

Most composites are environmentally friendly, and many products are made from recycled materials. Some manufacturers even go as far as to introduce chips of aromatic cedar into the decking so it smells like real wood.

If the sun will beat on the deck, choose a brand that has proved colorfast. Many types fade dramatically over the years. Some but not all can be stained when they fade.

Vinyls
Made from recycled plastics or from the same polyvinyl chloride (PVC) as drainpipes, vinyl decking is lightweight, strong, and weatherproof. For wood lovers, however, its appearance may leave something to be desired. Currently this kind of decking comes in only three colors: white, tan, and gray. The plastic surface is etched to provide some slip resistance.

On the other hand, vinyl decking can be ordered to size in kits that come complete with fastening hardware, making installation easy. Blind screws covered with sliding covers or T-clips are the recommended fastening technique. PVC's primary drawback is that it is more prone than

other synthetics to expansion and contraction in temperature extremes.

Fiberglass-reinforced decking
This is decking that is virtually indestructible and could well last you a lifetime. It's stronger than wood, fade resistant, and unaffected by harsh sunlight or extreme cold. Like other products, you can order your deck to size (in even multiples of the stock lengths and widths of the material), but if necessary, you can also cut it with a circular saw fitted with a masonry blade. Retaining clips hold the decking in place; individual pieces snap on the clips.

General considerations
Synthetic decking comes in a variety of forms and thicknesses. Most common are $\frac{5}{4}$ decking and 1½-inch extruded girders. Manufacturers have designed their products to comply with most building codes, but some localities may not allow synthetic materials. Always check with your local building code officials before placing an order for synthetic decking.

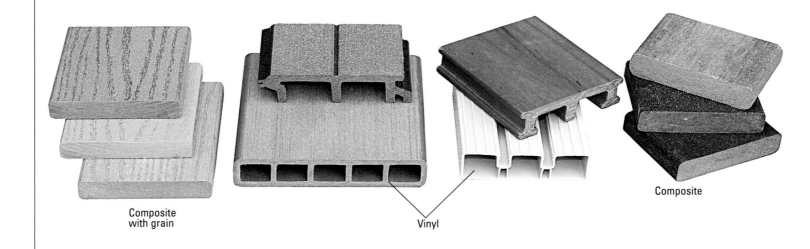

Composite with grain

Vinyl

Composite

Synthetic decking gives the color and often the texture of wood decking, as shown in these examples. The synthetics don't have knots and the edges won't splinter like wood, which makes them more comfortable for bare feet. Synthetic decking remains waterproof without periodic refinishing, but the color may fade in harsh sunlight. Some materials can be stained to bring back their color.

Composite railing components

Wood/plastic composite framing members, such as 4×4s, 2×4s, and 2×2s, can be used for building railings but are not structurally suitable for deck framing.

Railings made of synthetic material can be plain or fancy. They are sturdy and require little maintenance. Some railing components fasten together with screws using wood-style joints; others are assembled with special brackets and hardware.

COMPUTING THE SPANS

Five basic components make up any deck: decking, joists (and when attached to a house, a ledger), beams, posts, and footings. To ensure that a deck is safe and strong, local building departments have strict code requirements for these components.

Lumber type
The strength of a board depends on two factors: its species and its quality. Among lumber commonly available in pressure-treated form for deck framing, Douglas fir and Southern yellow pine are strongest, but Southern pine has more of a tendency to warp. Hem-fir is a designation that includes hemlock, fir, and other species that grow in the same stands. Some hem-fir is strong and stable, some is weak and likely to warp and crack. Consult with a lumber dealer and the building department before using hem-fir.

Lumber quality also has a bearing on a board's strength. Boards graded No. 2 and better are the best choice for deck building. Construction grade, common, and No. 3 stock have defects that make them unsuitable for a deck. Select grade or No. 1 boards are top-quality, but are usually not worth the extra cost for use in deck building.

Footings
In areas with freezing winters, most codes require concrete footings that extend below the frost line. In warmer areas a shallow footing is allowed, but codes will specify a minimum amount of mass in the footings. If an area has marshy or sandy soil, massive footings may be required.

Posts
For most decks, 4×4 lumber is strong enough for structural posts. If a deck is raised more than 6 feet above the ground, codes may require 6×6 posts.

Beams
The farther a beam must span—that is, the farther apart the posts are—the more massive a beam must be. The chart below lists approximate recommended spans. Beams made of two or more pieces are usually at least as strong as solid beams of the same size. For instance, a beam made of two 2×8s is probably stronger than a solid piece of 4×8. They are also less likely to crack.

Joists
The required width of a joist depends on its span—how far it must travel between beams or between a beam and a ledger. It also depends on the joist spacing; for instance, joists that are placed 24 inches apart must be wider than joists placed 16 inches apart. See the chart below and study your local code.

Decking
Decking boards span from joist to joist. If you use ⁵⁄₄ decking, joists must be no farther apart than 16 inches. Decking made of 2×4s or 2×6s can span up to 24 inches. If you will run decking at an angle, you may need to put the joists closer together; know your local codes.

Stick to standard lengths
Lumber comes in even lengths. Your computations, plans, and construction will be easier if you plan your deck with this in mind. You'll do a lot less cutting if you build a 12×16-foot deck rather than one that's 11 feet 7 inches × 15 feet 10 inches. There will be less waste too.

Recommended beam spans

Beam spans	Beam	Joists span up to	Beam span
Distance between	4×6	6'	6'
posts, using No.2 and	4×8	6'	8'
better Southern pine	4×8	8'	7'
or Douglas fir	4×8	11'	6'
	4×10	6'	10'
	4×10	8'	9'
	4×10	10'	8'
	4×10	12'	7'

Recommended joist spans

Beam spans	Joist	If joists are spaced	Span
Distance a joist spans	2×6	16"	9½'
between a beam and	2×6	24"	8'
a ledger or between	2×8	16"	13'
beams, using No. 2	2×8	24"	10½'
and better Southern	2×10	16"	16½'
pine or Douglas fir	2×10	24"	13½'

Local codes

Your local building department has regulations designed to ensure a strong and durable deck. While a few requirements may seem dated or unusual, most are based on the following common concerns:

■ **Span** requirements listed at left ensure your deck won't sag or collapse during a party or under snow load. Codes specify maximum spans according to the type of wood used.

■ A deck more than 2 feet or two steps above ground must have a **railing.** Codes dictate how high the railing must be, as well as how far apart the balusters can be. Small children must not be able to climb it.

Some codes require handrails, not just cap rails, for stairs.

■ If you attach the deck to the house with a **ledger,** code states how many fasteners of what type must be used. Metal flashing of a specific type may be required.

■ Many codes demand that posts be held in place by a specific type of **post anchor.**

■ In cold areas many codes require **footings** that extend below the frost line so that the deck does not get raised up in the winter by frost heave. Other departments may allow a floating deck with shallower footings that rise and fall during freeze-and-thaw cycles.

DECK TERMS

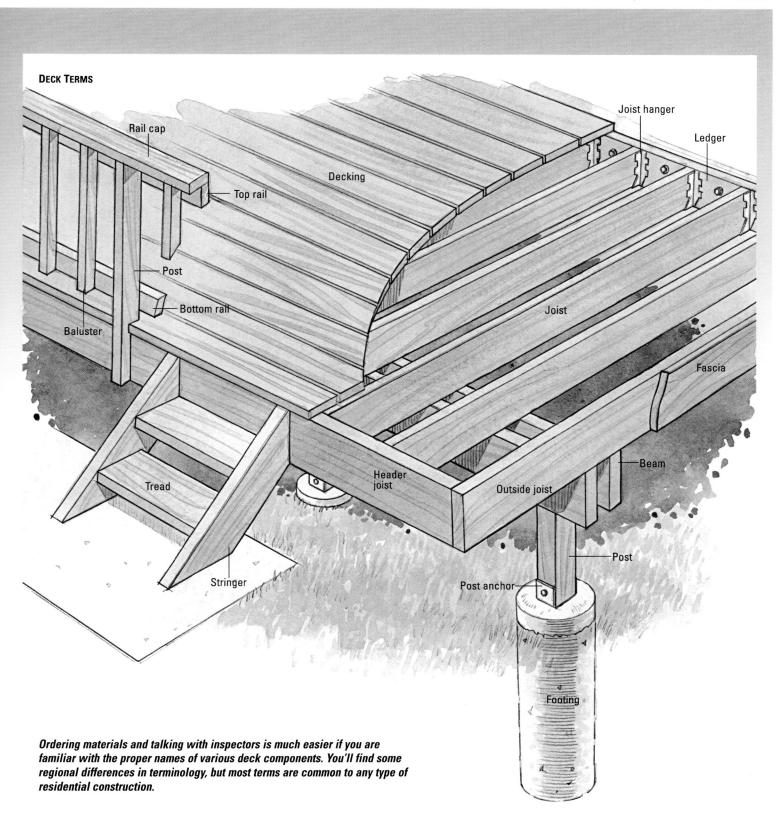

Rail cap

Joist hanger

Ledger

Decking

Top rail

Post

Joist

Bottom rail

Baluster

Fascia

Tread

Header joist

Outside joist

Beam

Stringer

Post

Post anchor

Footing

Ordering materials and talking with inspectors is much easier if you are familiar with the proper names of various deck components. You'll find some regional differences in terminology, but most terms are common to any type of residential construction.

CHOOSING FASTENERS

Screws, nails, and anchoring hardware have to stand up to many years of moisture. Standard galvanized fasteners have a single protective coating, which may flake off and rust. Double-dipped galvanized fasteners are better protected, but you'll get the best life from coated fasteners made for decks. Stainless steel is costly, but the best.

Nails

Nails are sized by their length, designated by a penny, or d, size. Gauge, or diameter, increases as the penny size increases; a 16d nail is both longer and fatter than an 8d.

Common nails, used for general framing, have large heads and thick shanks. They hold well but are hard to drive and may split the wood.

Box nails, thinner than common nails of the same size, reduce splitting in ¾-inch or thinner stock.

Ringshank and spiral nails grip the wood fibers and don't easily work their way out. They are very difficult to remove.

Finishing nails have slender shanks and small, barrel-shape heads. Use them for trim work and countersink the heads.

Casing nails are heftier versions of finishing nails and provide more holding power.

Screws

Screws come in an astonishing array of styles. A good all-around choice is #10 decking screws—generally in 2½- to 3½-inch lengths. Decking screws are coated for corrosion resistance, are sharp, tapered, and self-sinking. With a cordless drill/driver you can drive them about as fast as nails.

Be sure to match your screwdriver bit to the screw head (or vice versa). Decking screws generally are machined with a phillips, square, or a combination head. Square heads drive more securely.

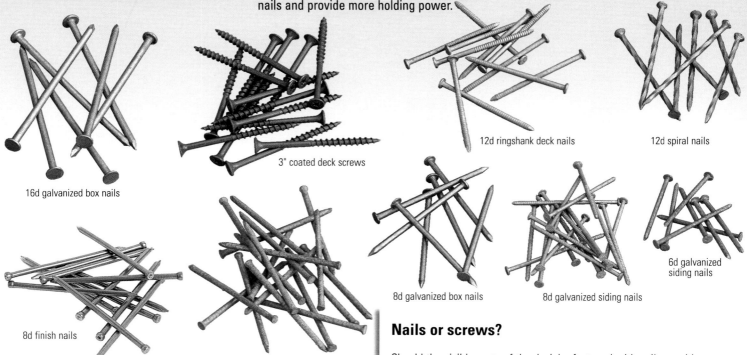

16d galvanized box nails

3" coated deck screws

12d ringshank deck nails

12d spiral nails

8d galvanized box nails

8d galvanized siding nails

6d galvanized siding nails

8d finish nails

10d galvanized casing nails

10d galvanized box nails

³⁄₁₆"×3¼" masonry screws

Nails or screws?

Should the visible parts of the deck be fastened with nails or with screws? Both fasteners have pros and cons.

Screws are nearly as quick to drive as nails and have greater holding power. As long as you drive them accurately, without stripping the head, screws are easier to remove than nails. However, many people don't like the way screw heads look because a small amount of water will puddle inside them. Water will not puddle on a nailhead unless you drive it too deep. To an experienced builder, driving nails is a bit faster than driving screws.

On the negative side, if you miss a nailhead with the hammer, or if you drive the nail too far, you will mar the wood. And it is difficult to remove a nailed board without damaging the board.

You can build the framing with either screws or nails.

Framing hardware

Framing connectors strengthen the joints between framing members. Not too long ago, framing members were joined with nails or screws, but most current building codes now require framing hardware.

Attach joists to the side of a ledger or beam using **joist hangers**. At the corner either cut a joist hanger in half using tin snips or use an **angle bracket.** Angled joist hangers accommodate joists that attach at a 45-degree angle.

Where a beam sits on top of a post, a **post cap** provides a reliable joint. If joists sit on top of a beam, many local codes allow you simply to angle-drive screws to secure the joists to the beam. Other local building departments require special **seismic (or hurricane) ties,** which add lateral strength.

A **post anchor** secures a post to a concrete pier and supports it so the bottom can dry between rainfalls. Get the style that you can adjust so you can fine-tune the posts and keep them on the same line.

Heavy-duty screws and bolts

To fasten a large piece like a post, use either a **lag screw** or a **carriage bolt.** Bolts are stronger and can be tightened in future years if the lumber shrinks. Always use washers under the head of a lag screw or the nut on a carriage bolt so that the fastener does not sink into the wood.

Attach a ledger to brick, block, or concrete with **lag screws** and **masonry anchors.** Hold a ledger temporarily with **masonry screws,** which are not quite as strong but are easier to drive and don't require anchors.

Seismic tie

Joist hanger

Angled joist hanger

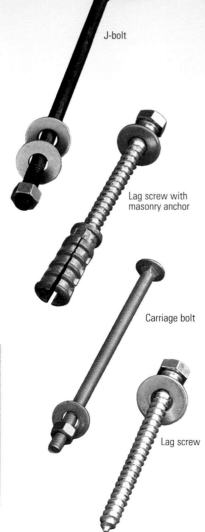

J-bolt

Lag screw with masonry anchor

Carriage bolt

Lag screw

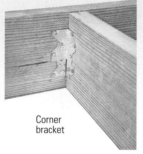

Corner bracket

Joist connector

Post-to-beam bracket

Adjustable post anchor

Nonadjustable post anchor

CHOOSING FASTENERS *(continued)*

What size fastener?

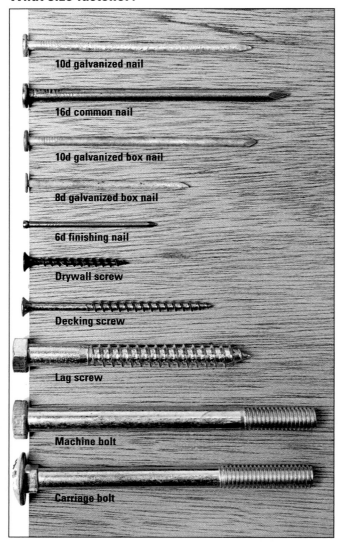

10d galvanized nail

16d common nail

10d galvanized box nail

8d galvanized box nail

6d finishing nail

Drywall screw

Decking screw

Lag screw

Machine bolt

Carriage bolt

Decking: Fasten ⁵⁄₄ decking with 2½-inch coated screws or 12d ringshank or spiral nails.

Railings: Attach 1× trim, rails, and cap rails with 10d, 8d, and 6d galvanized, finishing, or casing nails.

Framing: Use 10d or 16d common, spiral, or ringshank nails or decking screws in 2× stock, 8d or 10d box or ringshank nails or shorter deck screws in thinner stock. Attach framing hardware with the fasteners supplied by the manufacturer, 16d nails, or 3-inch deck screws. Check with your building inspector—some codes prohibit attaching framing connectors with screws.

Invisible decking fasteners

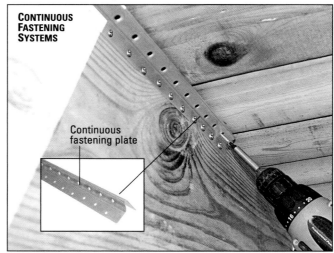

CONTINUOUS FASTENING SYSTEMS

Continuous fastening plate

You can avoid visible nails and screws completely with invisible deck fastening systems. Invisible fasteners come in many forms. They are more expensive and more time-consuming to install, but they leave a

A close look at masonry fasteners

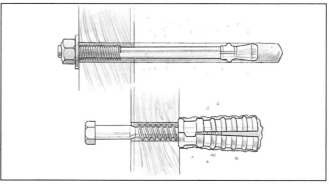

An anchor bolt comes preassembled so its sleeve expands against the sides of a predrilled hole as you tighten the bolt. Drill a hole of the same diameter and at least ½ inch longer. Blow out the dust and drive the bolt with the nut just at the top of the threads. Make sure the bolt doesn't turn when tightening.

Plastic or soft-metal expansion shields are designed to spread their sides as you tighten the fastener. Drill a hole of the same diameter and length of the shield, and tighten the screw.

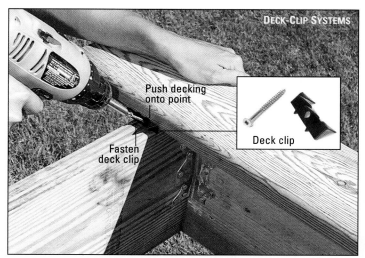

DECK-CLIP SYSTEMS

Push decking onto point

Fasten deck clip

Deck clip

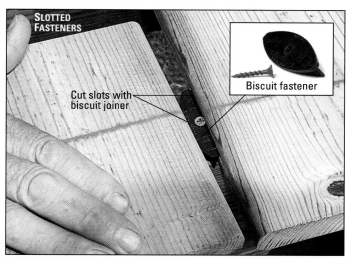

SLOTTED FASTENERS

Biscuit fastener

Cut slots with biscuit joiner

clean, uncluttered deck surface. They are especially useful in contemporary designs or with complicated decking patterns because they don't distract from the pattern of the decking itself.

Deck clips are the easiest to install—you can work from the top of the deck. Continuous fasteners require driving screws from underneath and are better suited to raised decks.

Power fasteners

CORDLESS SCREW GUN

To fasten decking faster and more neatly, consider renting or purchasing a screw gun that uses bandolier-style deck screws. The strip-mounted screws do cost more than standard screws.

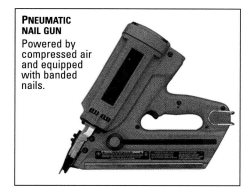

PNEUMATIC NAIL GUN

Powered by compressed air and equipped with banded nails.

POWDER-ACTUATED FASTENER

Powered by an explosive gunpowder charge. Especially useful for attaching framing to concrete, such as when fastening decking sleepers to a slab.

Power fasteners—nail guns, screw guns, and powder-actuated fasteners—speed up carpentry projects. Some are powered by compressed air, others use a power cell or chemical or explosive charges. Power fasteners are expensive, but you can rent the tool you need at most rental stores. Many can be set to countersink the fasteners or leave them flush with the surface.

Advantages of power fasteners over a hammer and nails.
■ The gun can be operated with one hand, leaving the other hand free to steady the work and keep it aligned.
■ A single blow drives the nail from the gun, eliminating the repeated hammer blows that can jolt a piece out of alignment.

■ The risk of bending a nail or missing the nailhead and denting the deck is eliminated.
■ Nails used in nail guns are thin and have blunt tips that seldom split the work piece.
■ You can nail in places or positions that would be difficult to reach with a hammer.

BUILDING WITH QUALITY AND CARE

Compliance with building codes ensures that your deck will be solid and long-lasting. However, you may want to go beyond basics and add features to enhance the strength and beauty of your deck. Here are some suggestions.

Better-than-average materials
Though it will increase the cost, consider buying top-quality lumber for the visible parts of the deck. Redwood costs a lot more than pressure-treated, but it has a classic look that nothing else can match.

No matter which lumber you choose, carefully select boards for the most visible parts of the deck, such as the cap of the railing. Select or No. 1 grade lumber or lumber with a low moisture content will look good years later; No. 2 lumber may not.

Wherever fasteners will be visible, think carefully about how they will look. Stainless-steel screws or nails may seem like an extravagance, but they're worth it if you really like the way they look.

Planning visible joints
Wood joints on outdoor structures tend to separate over the years. Plan a deck with as few joints as possible and take a little extra time to make all the joints stronger.

Avoid fancy joinery unless you are an experienced carpenter using stable lumber. Setting boards into notches, for instance, may look good when first installed, but once the wood shrinks, the result will look sloppy. Avoid miter joints whenever possible; butt joints are easier to construct and less prone to separating.

Sometimes you can avoid butt joints in the decking if you buy extra-long boards; 18- or 20-foot-long boards may cost more and be hard to find (and handle), but they may be worth it if they eliminate joints.

Whenever there is the slightest chance that a nail or screw may split the board, drill a pilot hole before driving the fastener.

For the tightest joints, rent or buy a power mitersaw (page 59), which makes more accurate cuts than a circular saw.

If butt joints are necessary in the decking, attach a 2×4 cleat on the side of the joist to provide twice the nailing surface. Drill pilot holes before driving screws or nails through the decking boards. Consider installing a divider strip (page 144).

The outside corner of a railing top cap is a notorious trouble spot. Wood biscuits reinforce this joint invisibly. While a biscuit joiner is expensive (you'll likely want to rent it), it is far easier, more forgiving, and stronger than dowels or other fasteners.

STANLEY PRO TIP: **2×4 decking with fewer fasteners**

Decking made of 2×4s rather than the standard 2×6 (or 5/4×6) makes a closer decking pattern that many people find worth the extra cost and effort. If you use stable lumber with a low moisture content, you need only one nail or deck screw per joint to hold the decking firmly. If using nails, be sure to buy galvanized spiral or ringshank nails. Screws should be galvanized or corrosion-resistant.

Excavate the area and take steps to block weeds before building a deck, even if codes do not require these steps. This will help prevent mosquitoes from breeding in vegetation and keep unwanted shade-loving plants from growing up through the decking.

Cantilever the joists a few feet past the beam to hide some of the framing. If the underside is still visible, consider installing a skirt (pages 178–179). Add an access door so you can store items under the deck.

This four-part rail post takes some time to build, but it has a more interesting appearance and is less likely to develop problems over the years than a single piece. Thick, wide boards are more likely to split than smaller boards. Even 4×4 posts often develop cracks.

Anchor stairway posts so they won't wobble from side to side. Most posts gain lateral strength by being attached to outside joists. However, the posts at the bottom of a stair rail are not connected to the deck and will be stronger if attached to a post anchor or sunk into a concrete footing (page 77). Position the post back far enough so it has maximum contact with the stringer.

FOOTINGS

Decks and overheads require load-bearing posts to support the framing, and each post needs to be set in a footing. Typically a footing is a round hole dug into the ground, extending below the frost line and filled with concrete. Different building codes, climates, and soil conditions may allow for alternative footings, for example, piers set in concrete or tamped earth (see options below). Ultimately the type and dimensions of the footing you'll need will depend on the height of the deck, the types of materials you plan to use, how deep the ground freezes, and the load-bearing capacity of the soil.

Loading a deck
Footings must support two kinds of loads inherent in any structure—dead loads and live loads. The dead load of a deck is the weight of all its permanent elements—posts, beams, framing, decking, planters, stairs, and railings—before transient items (snow, furniture, and people) are put on it. Most building codes will require the construction of a deck to support a dead load of 10 pounds per square foot and a live load of 40 pounds per square foot. This means that footings, along with the other support elements, must be constructed to support a total weight of 50 pounds per square foot. All of the elements work together—the ledger carries a portion of the weight, which it transfers to the foundation of the house; beams carry the intermediate loads; and footings support the loads that are transferred to the perimeter.

Soils
Soil consistencies vary (page 10) and thus their ability to support a load. Loose soils have minimum load-bearing capacity and may require more or larger footings than heavy clay or compacted soils. Local codes take local soil conditions into account, so it's important to contact the building department before you start planning your deck. You may find that local codes specify different spacings or construction methods than the ones shown in standard span tables.

Climate
In cold climates, the freezing and thawing of the soil causes it to expand and contract—sometimes dramatically. If the posts are improperly set, any movement of the soil will be transferred to the posts and the deck structure above them, shifting or cracking portions of the deck and causing severe structural damage. Regions have a different maximum level (called the frost line) at which the ground freezes during the winter. Local codes specify the depth of this line and how far below it you must dig to set your footings. In warm climates you may be able to get by with a minimum footing—a concrete pad about 6 to 12 inches deep and 1 to 2 feet square. Even in some winter climates, codes will allow you to set posts in a tamped-earth footing.

Slopes
Posts set in sloping terrain call for special attention. Not only do you have to meet specifications of local codes for depth and construction, but also most codes require at least 7 feet of soil from the bottom of the footing horizontally to the surface.

Drainage
Most localities require 3 to 6 inches of gravel in the bottom of the footing hole to allow water to drain away from the bottom of the post. Even if it's not required, it's a good idea.

FOOTING OPTIONS

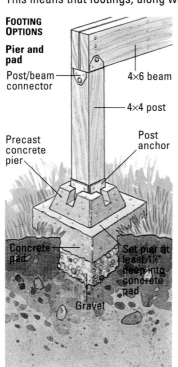

Pier and pad

Post/beam connector

4×6 beam

4×4 post

Precast concrete pier

Post anchor

Concrete pad

Set pier at least 1½" deep into concrete pad

Gravel

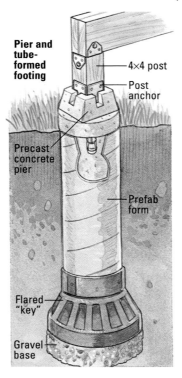

Pier and tube-formed footing

4×4 post

Post anchor

Precast concrete pier

Prefab form

Flared "key"

Gravel base

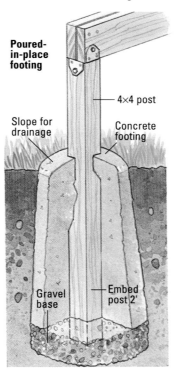

Poured-in-place footing

Slope for drainage

4×4 post

Concrete footing

Gravel base

Embed post 2'

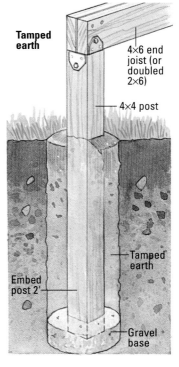

Tamped earth

4×6 end joist (or doubled 2×6)

4×4 post

Tamped earth

Embed post 2'

Gravel base

Footing materials

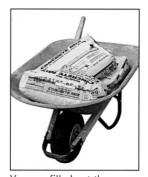

Precast concrete piers are available at your home center and may be used with or without footings, depending on local codes. They may be used without hardware, as shown here, to simplify construction of ground-level decks.

When using a precast pier to support a post, install a post anchor in the center or purchase piers with the hardware already mounted.

Home centers and material retailers carry prefab tubes that form the concrete in a footing. The tubes are made from a composite material that is strong but allows easy cutting to the proper depth.

You can fill about three footings with four 90-pound bags of premix concrete. For larger projects mix your own with a power mixer or call in the ready-mix truck. Carry the concrete to the holes in a wheelbarrow.

Before you dig footing holes, see if your home center has plastic forms that attach to the tube. They add strength and stability to the footing but require a wider hole than you would normally dig.

Post anchor in poured-in-place
Post anchor
Concrete forms
Concrete footing

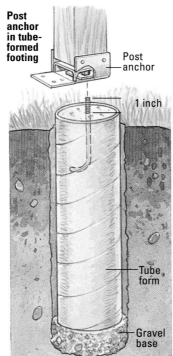

Post anchor in tube-formed footing
Post anchor
1 inch
Tube form
Gravel base

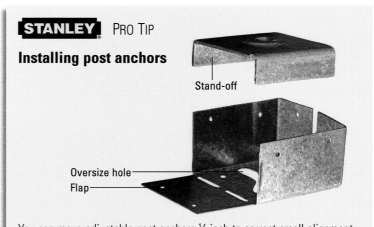

STANLEY PRO TIP

Installing post anchors

Stand-off

Oversize hole
Flap

You can move adjustable post anchors ½ inch to correct small alignment errors. Buy anchors with a stand-off to hold the post away from moisture.
Install the anchor with one flap down and finger-tighten the hold-down nut. Install the posts and drive nails or screws to secure the posts. Use string lines to check that the posts are lined up correctly. When you are sure it's right, tighten the nuts, using an open-end or adjustable wrench. Bend up the flap and attach it to the post.

A QUICK GUIDE TO DECK BUILDING

Whether you're building a deck from a kit or published plan or following your own design—simple or elaborate—remember that all decks go together in pretty much the same way. To keep the project moving smoothly, do all the steps in order.

There also are critical steps that precede construction. If you haven't done so already, you should make a construction schedule that lists and organizes all the tasks you have to complete. Make sure you include everything. At a minimum your list should look something like this:

■ Research and decide on materials
■ Conduct site analysis and determine deck location
■ Draw plans and elevations
■ Estimate material quantities and costs; develop budget
■ Apply for building permit and schedule inspections as required
■ Modify plan if necessary to meet code; resubmit permit application
■ Order materials
■ Grade site and install drainage lines
■ Organize materials and set up on-site workstation
■ Strip sod and prepare site
■ Attach ledger
■ Set batterboards and lay out site
■ Locate, dig, and pour footings
■ Set anchors and posts
■ Install beams and joists
■ Lay decking
■ Build railings and stairs
■ Apply deck finish
■ Throw deck party

Once you've made your list, jot down the names of prospective helpers and add expected completion dates. Note any plans you have for contingencies, such as weather delays. And familiarize yourself with how a deck is constructed, shown in the illustration on page 69.

When you get started, complete each task before beginning the next one. When you finish each day's work put everything away, even if your neighborhood is safe and the forecast promises sunny, bright weather for the next two months. Keeping the project site orderly lets you get right to work the next time without having to hunt for materials or tools.

Build your deck as carefully as you planned it. Any extra care you invest will make it look like it was built by a pro.

CHAPTER PREVIEW

Installing a ledger
page 80

Laying out the site
page 82

Digging footings
page 86

Pouring footings
page 88

Removing the sod before you lay out the site with batterboards will make the layout go more smoothly. Drive temporary stakes at the approximate corners of the footprint of the deck and tie mason's lines between them. Mark the ground with upside-down paint. Remove the sod. Then lay out the site, dig the holes, and set the posts. Rake in gravel and cover it with landscape fabric.

Installing post anchors
page 90

Setting and cutting posts
page 92

Installing beams
page 94

Hanging joists
page 96

Installing decking
page 98

Designing stairs
page 100

Building railings
page 104

INSTALLING A LEDGER

A ledger is a joist attached to the framing of the house. It carries the weight of the deck and transfers it to the foundation of the house. If you are installing an attached deck, your layout and installation will begin with a ledger. If you are building a freestanding deck, it will be supported on all sides by posts and footings, and you should skip to the next step.

Because the ledger functions as the first step in laying out an attached deck, you must position it precisely—level and firmly attached to the framing of the house. This means that the lag screws that fasten a ledger to a frame structure need to go through the sheathing and penetrate the band joist or studs. On brick, block, or concrete, use heavy-duty masonry anchors drilled into the masonry.

Cut your ledger from the same size lumber as your joists—3 inches shorter than the width of the deck so you can attach the end joists to the ends of the ledger. In most cases you will have to remove siding to install the ledger. (See also pages 132–133.)

PRESTART CHECKLIST

☐ **TIME**
About six hours to remove siding, position ledger, and fasten it

☐ **TOOLS**
Tape measure, hammer, chalk line, speed square, circular saw, 4-foot level, cordless drill, tin snips for metal siding, chisel, caulk gun, socket wrench and sockets

☐ **SKILLS**
Lifting, cutting, drilling, driving fasteners

☐ **PREP**
Locate internal framing members in house—band joist, studs

☐ **MATERIALS**
2× lumber, felt paper, fasteners, flashing, caulk

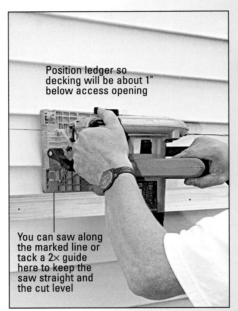

Position ledger so decking will be about 1" below access opening

You can saw along the marked line or tack a 2× guide here to keep the saw straight and the cut level

1 Mark the ledger outline by holding the cut ledger in place or by using a straightedge. Extend the marks 1½ inches on both ends for the end joists. Set your saw to cut the siding, not the sheathing, and cut to the corners. Chisel out wood corners; cut metal corners with snips.

Metal flashing keeps water off the ledger

2 Replace damaged waterproofing on the sheathing with 30-pound felt paper. Cut metal Z-flashing or roll flashing to the length of the cutout and slide it at least 1 inch under the siding above the cutout. Pressure will keep it there. Overlap flashing joints by 3 inches and notch it for the doorway.

FASTEN A LEDGER
Optional ledger attachment

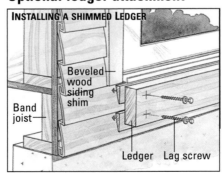

INSTALLING A SHIMMED LEDGER

Beveled wood siding shim

Band joist

Ledger   Lag screw

Some localities allow ledgers to be installed on the surface of the siding. This installation requires shims to keep the surface of the ledger vertical. Cut shims from siding stock and tack them upside down on your ledger location. Drill pilot holes and fasten the ledger to the rim joist with lag screws.

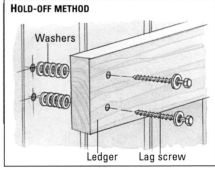

HOLD-OFF METHOD

Washers

Ledger   Lag screw

If your local code requires that the ledger be held away from the siding so it can dry out quickly, attach the ledger temporarily and drill all the pilot holes. Remove the ledger, push the lag screws through the holes, and slip on four or five washers behind the ledger. Drive the screws into the pilot holes.

Level ledger

2×4 braces
hold ledger
in place

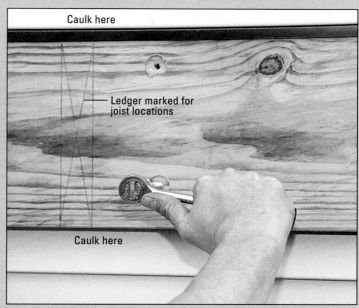

Caulk here

Ledger marked for
joist locations

Caulk here

3 Mark the ledger (and the header joist) for joist locations. If you're working alone, prop 2×4 braces at either end of the cutout and hoist the ledger in place, resting it on the braces. Center the ledger in the cutout, leaving 1½ inches on either side for the end joists. Adjust the brace on one end to position the ledger exactly at the correct height and tack this end to the sheathing with a 10d nail or deck screw. Level the board and tack the other end.

4 Counterbore lag-screw locations that fall on joist markings, then drill pilot holes for the lag screws through the ledger and about ½ inch into the band joist or studs (on a deck above the band joist). Drive washered lag screws into the framing with a socket wrench, stopping just when the screw won't turn without excessive force. Caulk counterbored holes, the joint above the flashing, and the bottom of the ledger. Don't caulk the ends yet.

WHAT IF...
The ledger anchors to brick, block, or concrete?

Pilot hole

Locator hole

Anchor

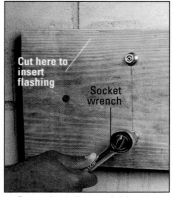

Cut here to insert flashing

Socket wrench

1 Drill the ledger for lag screw pilot holes. Then use masonry screws or braces to hold it firmly in place while you drill locator holes with a small masonry bit.

2 Remove the ledger. Drill holes using a masonry bit the correct size for the masonry anchors. Drill at least ¼ inch deeper than the length of the anchors and blow out any dust.

3 Tap masonry anchors into the holes until they are flush or slightly recessed.

4 Brace the ledger and drive the screws into the anchors. Tack a guide to the ledger. With a masonry blade, cut a kerf ⅜ inch deep for the flashing. Install and caulk the flashing.

Laying Out The Site

Laying out a site so the posts are in line and the corners are perfectly square relies on the simplest of homemade tools—batterboards. You'll need two batterboards for each corner (unless you can't drive batterboards close to the house). Make them from 2-foot pointed 1×2 or 2×4 legs and an 18- to 36-inch 1×4 crosspiece.

Start your layout by driving batterboards perpendicular to each other and about 3 feet beyond the outside corners of the site where you have removed the sod. String mason's line tightly between them and fine-tune the batterboards so the crosspieces are at the same height. Drive in the legs so the crosspieces are level (check them with a torpedo level).

Then follow the steps illustrated on this page to lay out an attached deck, beginning by plumbing the ledger location to establish the center line for the outside posts. If you're laying out a freestanding deck, you won't have a ledger as a guide but the rest of the steps will be the same. See pages 108–111 for more information on laying out a freestanding deck.

Prestart Checklist

☐ **Time**
About six hours for a 12×16-foot deck, excluding sod removal and preparation

☐ **Tools**
Tape measure, cordless drill, small sledge hammer, plumb bob, mason's line, line level, wooden stakes

☐ **Skills**
Measuring, leveling, driving stakes, making simple calculations

☐ **Prep**
Remove sod

☐ **Materials**
Scrap 2×4s and 1×4s, deck screws, masking tape, landscape spikes

Centerline of side posts

1 Using your dimensioned plan, mark the ledger to establish the centerline of the side posts. This line is often 1½ inches in from the edge of the ledger, but different construction methods, such as cantilevering or the use of beams, will place the posts on a different line.

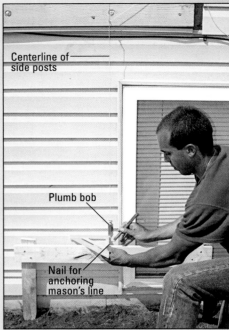

Centerline of side posts

Plumb bob

Nail for anchoring mason's line

2 Tack a nail on the ledger at your post centerline and drop a plumb bob from it. Drive a batterboard close to the house with its crosspiece level, centered on the plumb bob, and level with the batterboards on the outside corner. String a line to the outer batterboard and level it with a line level.

Working close to grade

4-foot level, set plumb

Centerline of side posts

Batterboard

If your ledger is only a few feet off the ground, using a plumb bob to establish the post centerline may prove cumbersome. Instead mark the ledger as shown above and use a 4-foot level (holding it plumb) to transfer the line to the batterboard.

What if...
You can't drive batterboards close to the house?

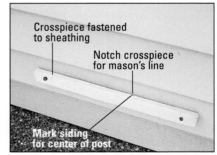

Crosspiece fastened to sheathing

Notch crosspiece for mason's line

Mark siding for center of post

If you can't drive batterboards close to the house, attach a crosspiece to the siding. Notch the back edge of the crosspiece so you can wrap the mason's line around it and fasten it securely with screws that penetrate the sheathing. On masonry use self-tapping masonry screws. Caulk the holes when you remove the piece.

Mark location of plumb bob line and tie mason's line

Screw for attaching mason's line

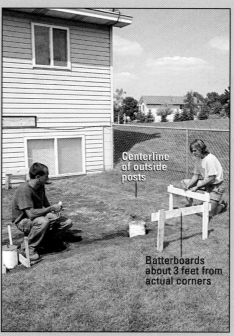

Centerline of outside posts

Batterboards about 3 feet from actual corners

Drop plumb bob from camera tripod if working alone

3 Let the plumb bob come to rest and pencil-mark its location on the crosspiece. Drive a small screw near the mark and wrap the mason's line around the crosspiece, lining it up with the mark on the last wrap. Repeat the layout of the post centerline on the other side of the site.

4 Establish the centerline for the outside corner posts and mark the crosspieces. Pull all the mason's lines tight, and reset the batterboards, if necessary, so the lines touch at their intersections. Square the corners using a 3-4-5 triangle.

5 Drop a plumb bob with its line just touching the intersection of the mason's lines. Let the plumb bob come to rest and have a helper mark its location on the ground with a landscape spike. Remove the plumb bob and drive the spike into the ground. Mark the spikes with painted Xs.

Square the corners

4'
3'
5'
Tape

To square the corners with a 3-4-5 triangle, measure out 3 feet on one line, and mark the measurement precisely with a piece of tape. Measure out 4 feet on the other line and mark it. With the aid of a helper, hold the edges of a tape measure on the marked pieces of tape. If the distance between them is 5 feet, your corner is square. If it's not, move the line on the crosspiece and remeasure. On large sites use even multiples of 3, 4, and 5 feet. The larger the numbers, the more accurate your layout will be.

Mark all the crosspieces

Mark final line position

Once you have squared the corners, mark the crosspiece where the mason's line crosses it. This will give you a reference point against which you can reset the line if necessary, for example, when rechecking the layout after you've completed it.

Accurate plumbing
Although adjustable post anchors will let you fine-tune your layout, you want it as accurate as possible from the start. Use a plumb bob, not a chalk line, to plumb the post locations.

Locating line footings

1×4 spacing template marked for post spacing and laid on mason's line

Mason's line establishes center of line posts

To space the line posts (those between the corner posts), stretch mason's line between the corner spikes. Then mark your post-spacing interval on a 1×4. Center the first mark on the corner spike and drive another spike at the next mark. Repeat for each post.

Footings at 45 degrees

To mark 45-degree footings, lay out the rectangular footprint of the deck. On each line, measure equal distances from the intersection. Drive stakes outside the lines and tie mason's line to the stakes so it intersects the marks. Drop a plumb bob at these intersections and drive in spikes.

Laying out a small job

To lay out a small project, such as a concrete landing pad for stairs, you can use the corners of a 4×8 sheet of plywood instead of batterboards. Make sure the plywood is square to the rest of the site, then drive landscape spikes at the corners.

Laying out with boards

If the deck is small you can lay it out with straight 2×6s instead of batterboards and mason's lines. Position the boards with their inside edges where the lines would be. Use a 3–4–5 triangle (page 83) to square the boards to each other and to the house. Measure along the boards and mark the post locations on the ground. You'll need to reassemble this layout jig when you insert the J-bolts into the concrete footings.

Stake to firmly hold frame

Square boards with 3-4-5 triangle

Laying out an octagon

Plywood locator template

45°

45°

45°

1½"

2×6 layout frame

To build an elaborate deck with an octagonal base, use this method to locate the footings—it is accurate for sites up to about 20 feet in diameter. First compute the length you want each side (or face) to be. Then divide that dimension by .4166 to get the diameter of the structure. Using this formula a structure with 60-inch sides will have a diameter of about 12 feet (60/.4166=144.02 inches or 12 feet). Set 2×6s (they won't move around as much as 2×4s) on the ground and stake the corners as shown. Fasten the corners of the frame with one deck screw. Square the corners with a 3-4-5 triangle (page 83). Mark the side length on four boards, leaving a few inches at each end, and screw them diagonally across the corners. Cut a plywood locator template like the one shown, and use it to place landscape spikes. When you have the spikes in place, remove the frame and paint the spikes with an X.

STANLEY Pro Tip: **Build the frame first**

If your deck is a square or rectangle and the yard is level, build the deck frame first, then use it to lay out the footings.

Assemble the outside joists (pages 120–121) and lay them on the ground where the deck will be built. Check the corners for square and drive stakes to hold the boards firmly in place, marking the footing locations. String mason's lines and measure from the house to mark the post locations.

Outside joist

Stake to secure frame

Set string to align piers

Header joist

Digging Footings

If building codes allow shallow footings and your deck requires only a few of them, you're in luck. You can probably dig the footings with a clamshell digger. In soft soil it's easy and inexpensive.

If you have a lot of deep footings to dig, however, rent a power auger. Rent a one-person machine (page 112) if you have a way to get it home. Otherwise go for a two-person auger. In either case make sure the auger has a bit the right diameter for your footings. It should come with extensions so you can start close to the ground and dig to the proper depth.

Working a power auger can be a lot like working out at a gym. You and your assistant should plant your feet firmly and keep a tight grip on the machine. And when you lift the bit out of the hole, bend your legs and lift with them, not your back.

Don't try to dig through rocks. Remove the auger and try to pry the rock with a pry bar. If you hit bedrock, your code may allow you to pour concrete directly on top.

Prestart Checklist

☐ **Time**
Figure about one hour for each 42-inch footing with a flared bottom

☐ **Tools**
Clamshell digger or power auger, round-nose shovel, small sledge, handsaw, pry bar, 2-foot level

☐ **Skills**
Digging or using a power auger, leveling

☐ **Prep**
Remove sod, lay out site

☐ **Materials**
Footing tube forms, mason's line, 2× lumber and stakes, gravel

1 If you haven't done so already, mark the center of the footing by spray-painting an X on the landscape spike you have driven in your layout. Use upside-down paint (available at your home center). Untie the mason's lines to get them out of your way, and remove the spike.

Tape on handles marks approximate depth of hole

2 To start the hole, spread your feet about a foot on either side of the X and with the handles of the clamshell digger parallel to each other, drive the blades into the soil. Put your shoulders into the work; your arms will tire quickly. Let the weight of the digger do as much of the work as possible.

Codes for slopes

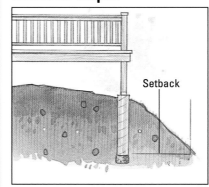

Setback

When setting footings on a slope, check your local codes for the amount of setback required. Most codes specify that the bottom of the footing needs to be at least 7 feet horizontally from the surface so the weight of the deck won't push the footing out of the slope.

Using a power auger

Start the hole with the extension that will put the handles about waist high. As the bit spins, rock the tool slightly from side to side to give it a fresh bite in the soil. Add extensions as necessary, and flare the bottom of the hole by rocking the auger more. Pull out loose soil at the bottom with a clamshell digger.

3 Pull the handles apart to capture soil between the blades, then lift the digger straight up. Move the digger to the side and push the handles together to release the soil. Knock clumps from the blades with a 2×2. At the proper depth, work the digger at an angle to flare the bottom of the hole.

4 Clean out any loose soil from the bottom of the hole and pour in a layer of gravel. Tamp the gravel with a tamping bar or a 2×4 to the depth required by codes. The gravel allows water to drain away from the bottom of the footing and helps reduce frost heave.

5 Mark your tube form so it will be long enough to reach the point where the flare begins in the bottom of the hole—plus about 2 inches so you can attach it to braces. Cut the form with a handsaw, keeping the saw perpendicular to the form.

Installing the tube form

Attach one end of brace first, then level the brace and attach the other end

1 Before setting the tube in place, fasten it to 2× braces with short screws. Set the tube in the hole and drive stakes at both ends of the braces. Fasten one end of each brace to a stake and set a 2-foot level on the form. Raise or lower the brace to level the tube, then screw the braces to the stakes. (See page 112 for another method.)

2 Backfill around the outside of the tube, tamping the soil lightly with a 2×2 as you go. If the hole you've dug is more than 3 inches wide on all sides of the tube, tamping the soil may fill the flared bottom of the hole. In this case pour the footing first, then backfill.

POURING FOOTINGS

Whether you're pouring a lot of footings or just a few, it's better to have someone help you. Even power mixing is strenuous, and pushing concrete around with a mixer or wheelbarrow can quickly tire you.

If your deck is small, with footings at only its four corners, preparing premixed bags of concrete in a wheelbarrow is quick and cost-effective. Pouring more than four to six footings is best done with a power mixer or ready-mix from a concrete truck.

Rent a small mixer with wheels, if available. Move the mixer to each hole, prepare the concrete, and pour. Don't try moving the mixer with concrete in it. If a portable mixer is not available, rent a stationary model and move the concrete to the holes in a wheelbarrow. Laying a ramp of 2×12s will make this task easier and will minimize damage to your lawn.

No matter how you prepare the concrete, measure the dry ingredients first (in shovelfuls), mix them in the power mixer or wheelbarrow, then add the water.

PRESTART CHECKLIST

☐ **TIME**
About an hour per footing to mix, pour, and place J-bolt

☐ **TOOLS**
Power mixer, wheelbarrow, round-nose shovel, mason's hoe, speed square

☐ **SKILLS**
Mixing, pouring, screeding

☐ **PREP**
Dig holes and install tube forms

☐ **MATERIALS**
Concrete (premixed bags or loose materials), 2×4 screed, J-bolts

Guide the concrete with a shovel

1 Bring a mixer or wheelbarrow to the hole and mix the concrete. If working alone, shovel the concrete into the hole. With a helper, position the mixer or the wheelbarrow so the concrete will pour from it when tipped. Guide the concrete with a shovel.

2 When the footing is half full (and again when full) consolidate the concrete in the tube by working a 2× up and down in the mix. This will remove air from the mix and bring water to the top, aiding in the proper curing of the mix.

Mixing concrete in a wheelbarrow

1 If you're mixing concrete in a wheelbarrow, get a large one—a lot of concrete will spill from a small wheelbarrow as you mix it. Pour the contents off a complete premixed bag into the wheelbarrow (never a partial bag) or measure in the dry ingredients with a shovel. Mix the dry mix together with a hoe, then mound it into the center of the wheelbarrow and make a depression in it.

2 Add about one-half of the total water into the depression and work the dry mix into the water with a hoe. Then work the mix back and forth the entire length of the wheelbarrow with the hoe, scraping up dry material from the bottom. Add water as necessary, working it into the mix before adding more. When the concrete clings to a trowel turned on edge, it's ready.

Seesaw the screed across the surface

3 Overpour the concrete into the tube and screed off the excess with a short length of 2×4. Seesaw the 2×4 as you pull it across the top of the tube to level the mix. Simply pulling the 2×4 straight across will drag mix out of the form.

4 Let the concrete set up just until it begins to firm, and insert a J-bolt into the center of the form. Set the bolt as precisely as possible, checking with a tape measure on opposite sides of the form. If the bolt ends up slightly off center, you can correct this with an adjustable post anchor.

5 Push or pull the J-bolt to leave 1 inch of thread above the surface of the concrete. Make sure the bolt is vertical by checking it with a speed square. Repack loose concrete with a pointed trowel, adding a little more if necessary. Let the concrete cure before installing post anchors.

Power mixing

If using premix, empty complete bags into the mixer. Using partial bags can result in an improper mix. If using dry mix, measure the right proportions of cement, sand, and aggregate into the mixer in shovelfuls. Turn the mixer on to mix the dry materials thoroughly. Then add about one-half the prescribed water, and mix thoroughly. Continue mixing, adding water a little at a time, until the mix just clings to the side of a shovel turned on edge.

Bedding precast piers

Recess supports post anchor
Cross grooves support joists

Precast concrete piers are engineered to accommodate joists for ground-level decks without footings or posts and anchors set in footings. If you bed a pier in a concrete footing, however, you need to soak it in water. A dry pier set in a wet footing will draw moisture out of the concrete, weakening it. Soak the pier in a tub of water for several minutes, then center it on the footing before the concrete sets up.

INSTALLING POST ANCHORS

Installing post anchors utilizes many of the same methods you employed when you initially laid out the site—measuring, squaring, lining things up. This time, however, everything needs to line up as precisely as possible—and that's where adjustable post anchors come in. Unlike fixed anchors, adjustable models allow you to correct as much as a ½-inch discrepancy in any direction if you have made an error when placing footings or J-bolts.

You'll find adjustable post anchors at your home center in a number of configurations and with a varying number of pieces, but all of them do the same job. A bottom plate is made with an opening that allows lateral movement in all directions, a clamping plate holds the bottom plate in place under the pressure of a nut and washer, and a pedestal raises the post off the surface of the footing to allow water to drain away.

Before you get out the measuring tape to square things up, install all the anchors loosely on the footings, then line them up using the techniques shown here.

PRESTART CHECKLIST

☐ TIME
About five minutes to initially fasten each anchor. Allow three hours to place the anchors for a 12×16-foot deck.

☐ TOOLS
Socket wrench and socket, tape measure; hammer drill and speed square for drilling epoxied holes

☐ SKILLS
Tightening nuts, drilling with hammer drill, measuring

☐ PREP
Install footings

☐ MATERIALS
Post anchors, mason's line, threaded rods or all-thread for epoxied studs

Placing anchors

1 Set the base of the anchor, the pressure plate, and the washer over the threads of the J-bolt. Start the nut on the threads and tighten it finger-tight. You should be able to move the anchor with moderate pressure. Install all the anchors before moving on to the next step.

2 Start with the footings opposite and parallel to the house. Set a long straight 2×4 across the front edges of the anchors. Measuring from the house to the front edge of the 2×4, line up the anchors so all of them are an equal distance from the house. Tighten each nut about one-half turn more.

WHAT IF...
You want to install threaded studs?

Keep drill perpendicular

1 Threaded studs are an alternative to J-bolts and you can install them after the footings have cured. Using a hammer drill, drill a hole ⅛ to ³⁄₁₆ inch larger than the stud diameter and to a depth that will leave 1 inch of threads exposed.

3 On the batterboard crosspiece next to the house, mark to the outside of the centerline at one-half the thickness of a post. This mark represents the outside edge of the post. Mark the corner crosspiece at the same point, and restring the lines. Drop a plumb bob from the line at the outside corner, and adjust the anchor so its edge lines up with the point of the plumb bob. Measure the diagonals, and adjust the anchors until the diagonals are equal.

4 Tighten each anchor nut firmly with a ratchet handle and socket. When the nut feels secure, tighten it one-quarter turn more so the anchor can't move. Don't strip the J-bolt threads. Measure the diagonals again to make sure the anchors are still in line.

2 Mark the top of the stud with a 1-inch piece of tape (which will also keep the threads clean). Then blow the dust out of the hole with a shop vacuum. Using a quick-set epoxy syringe, inject epoxy into the hole and push the threaded stud into the hole immediately. If a small amount of epoxy doesn't issue from the hole, pull out the stud and inject more epoxy.

3 Plumb the exposed end of the stud with a speed square and let the epoxy cure for the length of time specified by the manufacturer. When the epoxy has cured, measure the height of the threads. If more than 1 inch protrudes from the hole, thread on the nut until its top face is an inch above the concrete. Cut the stud with a hacksaw and remove the nut.

SETTING AND CUTTING POSTS

Setting the posts for your deck requires careful work, but it can also be exciting because the posts are the first visible sign that your deck is going up. Even though you still have a lot of work to do after you set the posts, getting them up can make you feel like you're halfway there.

Setting posts will go more than twice as fast if you have someone help you. Two helpers are even better; you won't have to move back and forth from one post to another to adjust them.

Posts must be plumb, so they have to start out with square ends. Check the bottom of each post with a speed square and cut it if necessary. Dip cut ends in a preservative before setting them in the anchors and let the preservative soak in overnight.

To make the job go quickly, do everything in stages—square all the posts, set them in the anchors with a temporary brace, then plumb, align, and brace all of them, letting their height run wild, then mark and cut them to a consistent height.

PRESTART CHECKLIST

☐ **TIME**
About 20 to 30 minutes to plumb and cut each post

☐ **TOOLS**
Speed square, framing hammer, post level, mason's line, wrench, tape measure, water level, reciprocating saw

☐ **SKILLS**
Measuring, plumbing, driving fasteners, cutting

☐ **PREP**
Set footings and anchors

☐ **MATERIALS**
Lumber, fasteners, masking tape

Setting the posts

1 The day before you set the posts, make sure their ends are square. Mark the cut lines with a speed square and make the cuts with a mitersaw or circular saw. Dip the cut ends in preservative and let them sit overnight.

2 Set each post in its anchor. While someone holds it plumb, drive one nail through the anchor hole and about halfway into the post. This will keep the bottom in place but allow you to move it when you plumb it. Tack 1×4 bracing to the post (see next photo) and stake in position.

Adjust the bottom of the post

Adjustable post anchors are made to be moved—right up to the last minute. To make an adjustment insert an open-end wrench in the slot and loosen the nut just slightly. Tap the post into place with a hammer and a piece of 2×4 scrap, and retighten the nut.

Cutting the posts

1 Use a water level to establish the height of each post. Fasten one end of the water level so the water line is even with the bottom of the ledger (or level with whatever edge your plan prescribes). Hold the water level on each post and mark the post at the water line. Transfer the mark around the posts as shown on the next page.

3 When you've set and temporarily braced all the posts, restring the mason's lines on the marks that represent the outside edge of the posts (page 91, Step 3). Clamp a second 1×4 brace to the post and stake it. Plumb each post with a post level, keeping its outside face against the mason's line.

4 Recheck the post alignment by sighting down the mason's line. Replumb any post that looks out of line and adjust the bottom of the post if necessary. If you have a post that's plumb but slightly bowed (no more than ⅛ inch), you can force it into place when you install the beams or joists.

5 Drive the remaining fasteners into the post anchor. Some anchors are made to accept nails or screws only. Others are fabricated to accept a lag screw also. Predrill for the lag screw before driving it.

2 You can mark the cut line for the posts by using the depth of the joist and/or beam, depending on your construction plan. Starting at the line that is level with the bottom of the ledger, measure down the depth of the joist and mark this point.

3 Transfer the cut line to all the faces of the posts, using a speed square and a carpenter's pencil. Make this line dark enough so you can see it when the sawdust flies. You will need to be able to see the line to keep the blade from wandering.

4 Holding the weight of a circular saw at right angles to the post can prove cumbersome (and even dangerous), especially when standing on a ladder for a raised deck. A reciprocating saw will prove more accurate. Keep the shoe of the saw on the surface of the post and make sure the blade cuts straight along the line.

INSTALLING BEAMS

A beam runs across the posts, parallel to the ledger, and supports the joists.

First consider your construction options: The beam can be a single piece of lumber, a built-up piece with or without spacers, or two pieces of lumber fastened to the sides of the posts.

Local codes may help you narrow your options. Some localities consider a beam with spacers stronger than a single board, and others don't. After code compliance your chief concern is how much the beam will show (and therefore how you want it to look) and the amount of space your plan allows for it.

A cantilevered front edge on the deck helps hide the beam unless you're building a raised deck. Then you can hide it with skirting. A low deck might not leave you much vertical space for a beam so you would have to use smaller stock and install an additional post. Instead of digging more holes, you could build a beam that doubles as the header joist, then hang the deck joists between the ledger and the beam (see "What if. . ." on page 119).

PRESTART CHECKLIST

☐ **TIME**
About three hours for a 16-foot beam constructed from two 2×10s

☐ **TOOLS**
Tape measure, circular saw, framing hammer, caulk gun, cordless drill

☐ **SKILLS**
Measuring, cutting, driving fasteners, drilling, caulking

☐ **PREP**
Set and cut posts

☐ **MATERIALS**
2× lumber or beam stock, deck screws, beam framing hardware, bracing lumber, caulk

1 Sight down each member of your beam and make sure you have the crowns side by side. Cut them to length and clamp them with all edges flush. Place the assembly on a firm work surface and drive three fasteners every 12 inches.

2 Install post/beam connectors to each of the posts, orienting them in the same direction. Move the completed beam assembly to the deck site and lower the beam onto the connectors. Center the beam on the deck site.

Construction options

A single-piece 4× beam reduces construction time, but long pieces of 4× lumber may be hard to find and expensive.

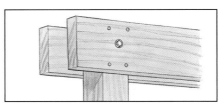

Caulk this joint

Fill this space with ½" spacer

Build your own beam from 2× stock. This construction is strong, less expensive, and comes together quickly.

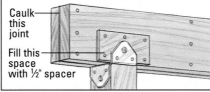

Two lengths of 2× stock fastened to the sides of posts won't be as strong, but may be required by the details of your design.

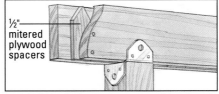

½" mitered plywood spacers

Add ½-inch plywood spacers with mitered tops to a built-up beam to bring its width consistent with dimensioned lumber and hardware. Miters allow water to drain.

3 Stake a 1×4 brace into the ground and with a helper holding a 2-foot level, plumb the face of the beam and keep it in place by driving a toenailed screw through the brace and into the beam.

4 Install another staked brace on the opposite side and add braces to secure the beam plumb along its length.

5 With the beam braced, secure it to the post/beam connectors with screws or nails. Screws will be less apt to push the beam out of alignment, but may not be permitted by some local codes. Remove the braces when you hang the joists.

Seams in the beams

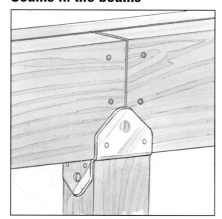

Leaving a splice in a beam unsupported will weaken the structure and could cause it to fail. Wherever you have to splice a beam, make sure it's offset from a splice in the other 2× member by at least 8 feet and center the splice in a post/beam connector.

Bracing the posts

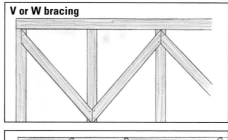

V or W bracing

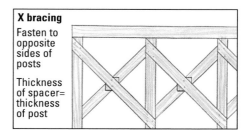

X bracing

Fasten to opposite sides of posts

Thickness of spacer= thickness of post

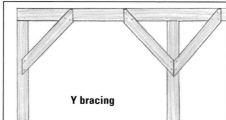

Y bracing

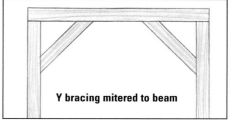

Y bracing mitered to beam

Decks more than 5 feet above grade, located in hurricane-prone or high-wind regions, or set with footings in loose soil may require bracing. Local codes may limit you to a certain configuration, but try to bring as many aesthetic qualities to your brace design as code restrictions allow.

HANGING JOISTS

The simplest and most reliable way to hang joists is to attach the rim joists and header to the ledger and beam, then install the inner joists. Building the outer frame first makes production easy—you can gang-cut all the joists at the same time, mark and install all the hanging hardware, then hang and fasten the joists. Install the joists with the crown edge up (page 64).

Unless you plan to cover the header and rim joists with cedar or a similar fascia, select the straightest, most knot-free, and least blemished boards for them. Square the ends before measuring. Predrill all the holes for fasteners so you don't split the ends, and take care to avoid dinging the wood when nailing or leaving protruding screw heads. If a screw won't seat properly the first time, draw it back about 1½ inches and drive it again.

If you haven't marked the ledger and header for the joist locations, do it after you square the frame. Remember that the internal space between the rim joist and the first inside joist is 13¾ inches; spacing between the rest is 14½ inches.

PRESTART CHECKLIST

☐ **TIME**
About two hours for a 12×16-foot deck no more than 5 or 6 feet above grade

☐ **TOOLS**
Tape measure, cordless drill, hammer, circular saw, speed square, framing square

☐ **SKILLS**
Measuring, cutting, fastening, squaring

☐ **PREP**
Install posts and beams

☐ **MATERIALS**
2× joists and blocking, fasteners, framing hardware

Installing joists

1 Measure and cut the rim joists to length. Set one edge of a rim joist on the beam with the top edge of the other end flush with the ledger. Fasten the boards with two 3-inch deck screws. Fasten the other rim joist the same way. (Install angle brackets after you square the frame.)

2 Set a square inside the corner at the ledger and adjust the rim joists until they square. If everything is just right, the outer face of the rim joist should be flush with the end of the beam. Tack the rim joists to the top of the beam with a toenailed screw.

Installing blocking

Blocking stiffens the frame and helps keep joists from twisting

1 Tack a 1×4 on top of each joist to keep their centers spaced at 16 inches (or on the centers required by your plan). Find the midpoint of the deck (half the distance from the house to the beam) and snap a chalk line across the top of the joists.

2 Measure each bay (the space between the joists) and cut 2× blocking to this length. Don't cut all the blocks the same size—the thickness of the joists may vary. Install the blocking on alternate sides of your chalk line, face nailing or screwing them. Then fasten the joists to the beam with seismic ties.

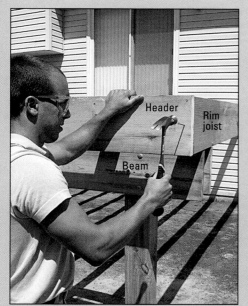

3 With a helper holding the header, fasten it to the ends of the rim joist—corners flush. Square the corners with a framing square and check with a 3-4-5 triangle. Remove the toenailed fasteners at the beam and adjust. Redrive the toenailed fasteners and set angle brackets in the corners.

4 Stabilize the frame on the beam with seismic ties and mark the joist locations on the ledger and header. Cut the joists to length and tack temporary flanges to the ends to hold the joists flush at the top. Set the joist on the marks, then slide a joist hanger tight to the bottom and fasten it.

5 Continue fastening temporary flanges to each joist and with the aid of a helper lower them in place. Fit the hanger to the bottom and screw or nail the hanger on the marks. Wherever the header is bowed slightly have a helper push it toward the joist while you drive the hanger fasteners.

Trimming wild joists

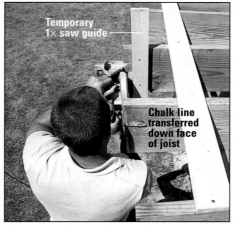

You could install the joists first and fasten the header to them after they're in place. Attach the joists to the ledger using joist hangers, then tack a 1×4 brace across the top of the joists to stabilize them and keep their spacing correct.

Measure out from the ledger along each rim joist the distance specified in your plan. Mark both rim joists at this point. Stretch a chalk line across the joists at these marks and snap it. Transfer the marks down the face of the joists

with a speed square. Tack a temporary 1× guide to each joist so the saw blade will cut just on the waste side of the cutting line. Trim the ends of the joists with a circular saw and face-nail the header to them. Then install joist hangers.

INSTALLING DECKING

Decking is a visible element of your project, so install it with care. Naturally resistant woods and KDAT treated lumber will not shrink much after installation, so spacing between them can be about ⅛ inch. Make a spacing jig to speed the job. PT lumber will shrink after you install it, so lay PT boards without any spacing.

You can fasten your first board for parallel decking either at the house or at the edge of the deck, and work toward the opposite side. Decking boards are not all exactly the same width, so you may need to rip the last few boards to make them fit. The width variation may be visible, so it's generally best to install the starter board at the edge of the deck. That way the ripped boards will be next to the house where they will be less visible. Most other decking patterns begin in the center of a module, and you will need to reduce their width as you approach the edge.

To make the decking more attractive, stagger the joints so they do not fall in a straight line. Center the end of the board on a joist and add a cleat to the joist so you won't have to drive a nail or screw right at the end of the board.

PRESTART CHECKLIST

☐ **TIME**
Five to seven hours to install decking on a 12×16-foot deck

☐ **TOOLS**
Tape measure, chalk line, cordless drill, circular saw, spacing jig, pry bar, wide putty knife, speed square, mitersaw, jigsaw

☐ **SKILLS**
Measuring, cutting, driving fasteners

☐ **PREP**
Install framing

☐ **MATERIALS**
Decking, fasteners, 1×4 and 8d nails for spacing jig

1 Measure from the house to the inside edge of the starter board and mark both rim joists at this distance. Snap a chalk line at the marks. The position of the first board will vary, depending on whether you will overhang the decking or install fascia. Make allowances for these details.

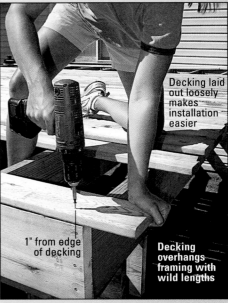

Decking laid out loosely makes installation easier

1" from edge of decking

Decking overhangs framing with wild lengths

2 To save time, lay out the decking boards loosely on the deck so they're within reach. Plan staggered joints ahead, pre-arranging the boards and installing cleats where necessary. Align the starter board with the chalk line and face-nail or screw two fasteners centered on the joists.

Make a spacing jig

To space decking evenly, make this jig from a 1×4 and 10d nails. Space the nails at the joist spacing (16 inches, for example) and drive them about an inch through the 1×4. Blunt the tips of the nails so they won't snag or damage the decking. Set the jig with the tips of the nails on either side of the joists.

Joints over joists

Strengthen each joint by fastening 2×4 cleats on both sides of the joist under the joint. Predrill the decking to minimize splitting, and drive the screws on a slight angle toward the joist.

 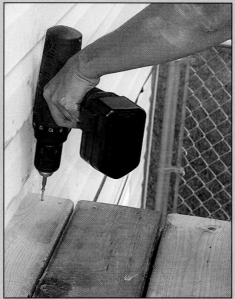 

3 Insert the spacing jig against the starter board and pull the next decking board against it. Fasten this board, moving the spacing jig down its length as you go. Make sure joints are cleated and centered on the joists. Continue installing the decking until you are three boards from the end.

4 Dry-lay three boards, maintaining spacing. If the last board fits without trimming, install the remaining decking. If not, lay two boards and trim the last one. Or rip the three boards to equal widths. Trim the last board to length for the overhang; you can't trim it in place.

5 Mark the overhang on the first board and snap a chalk line from this mark to the edge of the last board. Trim off the wild ends of the decking with a circular saw. You can tack down a long straight 2×4 to guide your saw. Bevel the edges with a palm sander, and seal the cut ends.

WHAT IF...
A deck board is bowed?

To pull a bowed edge toward you, hammer the blade of a pry bar solidly into the joist and pull the decking into place. Hold its position with one hand and drive the fasteners with the other.

To push a bowed edge away from an adjacent board, insert a wide putty knife between the boards, followed by a pry bar. Pull the pry bar back and hold the board in position. Then drive in the fasteners.

Notching a deck board

1 Set the decking board against the post or other obstacle, and mark the edges of the post on the decking. Mark the depth of the notch and square the lines with a speed square.

2 Cut the notch with a jigsaw and test-fit the cut. Fasten cleats on the posts to provide a nailing surface for the inside edge of the board. Fasten the board to the joist and the cleat.

DESIGNING STAIRS

The ascent should be gradual for outdoor stairs—short risers and deep treads are the rule.

At first glance, designing stairs for your deck may seem mysterious, but a simple rule makes it easy: twice the riser height (the height of each step to the top of the tread) plus its run (the front-to-back depth of the tread) should equal between 24 and 27 inches (see "Figuring rise and run," opposite page).

Start by measuring the total rise and run for your stairs. You can plan a specific location for the stairway landing pad and cut stringers (the diagonal supports) to meet it. Or you can decide how many steps and what rise and run you want and position the pad according to the stair calculations. Even better is to start with a prospective pad location and estimate whether the resulting rise and run will be comfortable and aesthetically pleasing.

Stringers are the key stair components. Choose straight, clear 2×12s, preferably boards with vertical grain. Don't settle for second-best boards for stringers; buy the best lumber you can find. See pages 147–153 and 172–173 for other tips.

PRESTART CHECKLIST

☐ **TIME**
About seven hours to measure and cut the stringers and install the treads, not including installation of concrete pad

☐ **TOOLS**
Tape measure, framing square, stair gauges, circular saw, jigsaw or handsaw, cordless drill, socket wrench

☐ **SKILLS**
Using simple mathematical formulas, measuring, cutting, fastening

☐ **PREP**
Install decking and landing pad

☐ **MATERIALS**
2×12s, fasteners

Marking the stringers

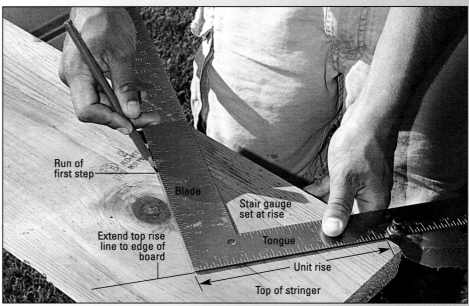

Run of first step — Blade — Stair gauge set at rise — Extend top rise line to edge of board — Tongue — Unit rise — Top of stringer

1 Calculate the rise and run for each step and place stair gauges (see page 148) at these measurements on your framing square. Set the gauge for the rise on the tongue of the square and for the run on the blade. Starting at what will be the top of the stringer, set the framing square on the stringer so the tongue (the short side) intersects the corner. Mark the rise and run lines. Extend the line for the rise to the opposite edge of the stringer (you will cut at this line later).

MEASURING THE TOTAL RISE AND RUN
The height and length of the stairs

To measure the total rise of your stairs, hook the tape over the decking and measure to the ground or post footing. On level ground, that's the total rise of your stairs.

On sloped ground mark the prospective end of the stairs with a stake and extend a 2×4 to the stake. Prop the 2×4 on scrap until it's level, then measure the space between the bottom of the board and the ground (assuming the pad will be level with the grade). Add this measurement to the first one. This is the total rise.

To measure the total run of the stairs, extend a level 2×4 (or keep the one from the previous measurement) and measure from the edge of the deck to the stake. This is the total run of the stairs. Compute the rise and run for each step from these measurements, and adjust them so they give the look you want and meet the guidelines for comfort.

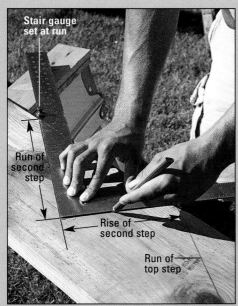

2 Slide the framing square along the edge of the stringer until the rise marker lines up with the end of the previous run line. Mark the rise and run lines for the second and each subsequent step, keeping the stair gauges against the edge of the board.

3 When you have marked the rise and run for the bottom step, extend the last rise line to the edge of the board. Then set the framing square on the opposite edge of the stringer so the run length lines up with the extended line.

4 Move the framing square up the board by the thickness of the tread, and mark a line parallel to the bottom run line. You will actually cut on this second line because the stringer needs to be shortened by the thickness of the tread. Otherwise the bottom step will be too high.

Figuring rise and run

For easier climbs, deeper stair treads should have a shorter rise. The standard formula is: Twice the riser height plus the run should equal between 24 and 27 inches. (If rise is 7 inches and run is 11 inches, for example, 2 times 7 equals 14; adding 11 equals 25.)

To calculate rise and run, measure the total rise of the stairway (see box, opposite) and divide by the amount of rise you want for each step. Round to the nearest whole number; this is the number of rises. Then divide the total rise by the number of rises to find the exact rise for each step.

If you want each rise to be about 7 inches, for example, and the total rise is 58 inches, divide 58 by 7. The result is 8.28; round that down to 8 rises. Divide 58 by 8 rises to find

the unit rise, 7.25 (7¼) inches. To find the total run, or length, of the stairway, multiply the run you want, say 11 inches, by the number of rises minus one (remember, the last rise is up to the deck surface). In this case 7×11 = 77. So the stairway will end 77 inches away from the deck.

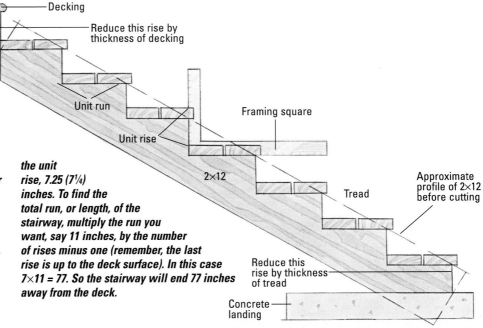

Cutting the stringers

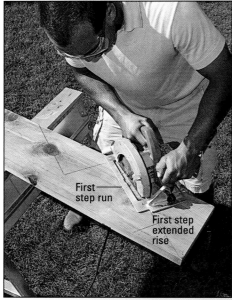

1 Go back to the top of the stringer and cut the run for the first step using a circular saw and a sharp blade. Then reposition your saw and cut the first step rise and the extended rise from one edge of the board to the other.

2 Cut the next rise with a circular saw, stopping the blade just before it touches the line for the run. Cutting into the corners will weaken the stringer. Cut the run with the circular saw, stopping it also before it reaches the corner.

3 Finish the cuts with a jigsaw fitted with a standard blade (the teeth cut on the upstroke, making the saw easier to control). Slip the blade into the cut before you turn the power on. Cut the outside edge of the kerf and hold the waste with your free hand.

What If...
You want closed stringers?

1 If your design requires only two closed stringers, mark them as you would an open stringer (page 100) but cut only the top extended rise and the bottom edge and rise. If your design calls for more than two stringers, those in the middle will be open stringers. Mark and cut one stringer and use it as a template to mark the others. Do not cut the outside stringers.

2 Mark the tread locations as a guide for positioning the stair brackets. Then cut the bottom edge and rise and the extended rise at the top of the stringer.

Assembling stairs

1 Lay out and pour a landing pad, if required (see pages 150–151). Let the concrete cure. Mark the location of the stringers on the rim joist or header and fasten the stringers with angle brackets. Square the stringers to the deck frame and fasten them at the bottom with brackets. Then fasten a stair bracket at each tread on the closed stringers, keeping the top of the flange lined up with the tread line.

4 Cut the remaining steps in a similar fashion, starting each cut with a circular saw and finishing them with a jigsaw as you go. If your design does not include a toe-kick (pages 152–153), the stringer is finished.

5 If your design includes a toe-kick, mark the dimensions of the board (usually a 2×4) and cut the notch with a jigsaw.

6 Test-fit the stringer in the location of the stairs and use it as a template to mark the second board (and third, if required by the design). Clamp the boards securely and outline the second stringer with a carpenter's pencil.

2 Continue fastening stair brackets at each tread location on the open stringers, keeping the top of the flange lined up with the surface of the cutout. To help keep them flush, set a 2×4 scrap on the cutout, push the bracket under it flush, hold the bracket securely, and drive the fastener. Installing treads will go faster with one person under the stairs and the other holding the treads in place.

3 Measure the opening between the stringers and cut the first tread to length. Slip the tread in place and drive the fastener through the bracket into the underside of the tread.
  If you're working with open stringers throughout the design, measure and cut your tread stock so it overhangs the stringers by 1½ inches. Fasten the treads to the brackets.

4 When you get to the bottom of the stairs and there's no more room to work, fasten the treads with lag screws and a socket wrench.

BUILDING RAILINGS

You can construct your railings with a number of different methods, but the most common (and generally the easiest) is to attach the posts to the rim joists and headers and install railing sections between them. Most railing designs go up rails first, then balusters or infill, then the cap rail.

When installing the posts, overhanging decking can get in the way. You can either notch the post or notch the decking so the bottom of the post rests flat against the joist. Notched decking is the method illustrated on these pages—it minimizes the possibility of weakening the posts.

Creating level lines is especially important in railing construction. That's because railing components are viewed against the background of the house. Exercise care when establishing level lines. For example, use a water level to mark the placement of the bottom of the posts. Using a line level or setting a carpenter's level on a long board will likely prove inaccurate over long spans. A ½-degree error at one end can mean a discrepancy of several inches at the other. See pages 154–157 for other tips.

PRESTART CHECKLIST

☐ **TIME**
About 16 hours to cut and install railings for a 12×16-foot deck

☐ **TOOLS**
Circular saw, mitersaw, post level, 4-foot level, 2-foot level, cordless drill, spade bits, twist drill, socket wrench, spacing jig, hammer, square

☐ **SKILLS**
Measuring, cutting, fastening, leveling

☐ **PREP**
Install decking

☐ **MATERIALS**
Lumber, fasteners, lag screws and washers

Use post level to plumb the posts

Notched decking keeps post flat against joist

Fasten posts with counterbored land staggered lag screws

Center rail joints on post

1 Calculate the post length—start with its height above the deck and subtract the thickness of the cap rail. Add the length of the joist, less a 1-inch reveal. Cut all your posts to this length. Mark the reveal at one end of the joist and at the other end with a water level. Snap a line and install the posts at the proper spacing.

2 Hold an uncut piece of rail stock in place to mark its length (spacing between each pair of posts may be fractionally different). Cut each rail to fit. Screw the top and bottom rails to the posts in predrilled holes. Don't overdrive the screws.

DESIGN OPTION
Different post styles

Install a double corner, spacing the posts at least a post-width from each side of the corner. Join the rails in the corner with butt joints or miter cuts.

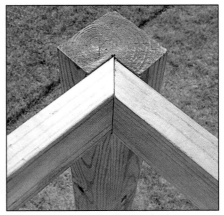

Notched line posts require notched corner posts. Mark the profile of the notch and cut the shoulder with a circular saw, stopping just short of the base of the notch (page 199). Chisel out the waste.

Spacing
jig

Handle simplifies
placement of jig

Scarf joint improves
appearance and drainage

3 Clamp a stop block to your mitersaw table at the baluster length and cut all the balusters. Bevel the bottoms and tops or make other decorative cuts. Calculate baluster spacing and cut scrap wood to that width to use as a spacing jig. Set the jig in place, then a baluster, and fasten the baluster to the top and bottom rail. When you get within the last three or four balusters, check the remaining space and adjust the spacing slightly if necessary.

4 Miter the end of the cap rail (commonly a 2×6) and hold it in place to measure its length. The cap rail has to run to a corner or if jointed, the joint must be centered on a post. Mark the square end of the cap rail and cut it, making a scarf joint over a post. Always cut the miter first, then the end. Drive two fasteners on both sides of a joint and one every 12 inches between posts. Smooth the cap rail (both the top and the edges) with a pad sander.

CUT ALL YOUR POSTS
Making production cuts

To gang-cut posts or any stock, square the ends of the boards and line them up against a straightedge or straight 2×4. Clamp them together with bar clamps. Use a square to mark the cutouts and cut them with a circular saw. Chisel out the waste.

THE CAP RAIL
Mitering the cap rail

Mitered cap rails dress up the appearance of your railing, but they are notorious for coming apart. First make sure the edges fit together precisely. Recut them if they don't fit correctly. Apply a thin bead of construction adhesive to the faces of the miter and push them together, clamping them with a corner clamp if you have one. Drive finish nails into the top rail and posts and also into the corners.

DESIGN OPTION
Custom railing inserts

A custom-made railing insert will make your railing design unique. Cut balusters to form a sunburst pattern or notch and rout 2×2s to form a lattice. Let your imagination go free and measure the pieces of your design carefully. Remember that custom inserts have to comply with code requirements for minimum spacing.

FREESTANDING BASIC DECK
PLANTERS & BENCHES

The upper rectangular platform of this deck overlaps the lower one by 2 feet. Planters and benches help define two distinct areas. Because it sits low to the ground, no railing is required.

Footings and beams
The soil near the foundation of a new home—soil that was backfilled after the concrete basement was poured—is unstable. Local codes usually require that concrete footings within 3 feet of the foundation must be 8 feet deep. To avoid the time, effort, and expense of such deep footings, this plan makes use of heavy-duty beams that rest on footings placed farther away from the house. The beams,

made of three 2×10s, run perpendicular to the house and are strong enough to cantilever 3 feet past the footings. The middle beam supports both deck levels.

Framing
The decking is pressure-treated ⁵⁄₄×6 laid at a 45-degree angle to the house. For proper support the joists must be spaced no more than 12 inches apart. If thicker 2× decking is used, or if the ⁵⁄₄ decking is run perpendicular to the joists then the joists could be placed 16 inches apart (see the span chart on page 68).

Framing for the upper level rests on top of the lower-level framing and overlaps by 2 feet.

Using pressure-treated wood
Inexpensive pressure-treated lumber is used for the visible parts—the decking, benches, and planter—and the structural members. Many decks made of pressure-treated lumber lose their looks: The wood warps, splits, and turns an ugly gray. But with a little extra care a treated-wood deck can look great for many years.

Choose boards that are straight, dry, and free of large knots (pages 64–65). Pressure-treated wood may twist and warp as it dries, so stack it tightly until you install it and fasten it securely. After a month or so, check to see whether any fasteners are working loose. If so, remove them and install longer fasteners.

This basic deck makes use of low-cost materials and basic construction techniques.

CHAPTER PREVIEW

Laying out the deck
page 108

Forming footings
page 112

Installing posts
page 116

Framing
page 118

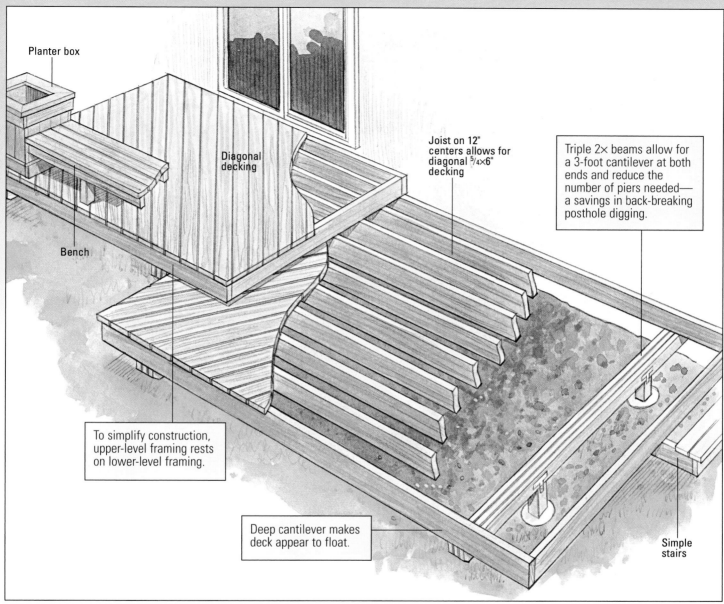

Planter box

Diagonal
decking

Bench

Joist on 12"
centers allows for
diagonal $^5/_4\times6"$
decking

Triple 2× beams allow for
a 3-foot cantilever at both
ends and reduce the
number of piers needed—
a savings in back-breaking
posthole digging.

To simplify construction,
upper-level framing rests
on lower-level framing.

Deep cantilever makes
deck appear to float.

Simple
stairs

*A two-level deck eases the
transition from doorstep to yard
while adding enough visual
interest to make even a small
deck a stylish addition to a home.
This deck is built with pressure-
treated lumber exclusively.*

Angled decking
page 124

Simple stairs
page 127

**Bench with
planters**
page 128

LAYING OUT THE DECK

The simple design of this deck includes fail-safe features—for instance, the beams may be off by an inch or so without weakening the structure. Don't take the project lightly, however. Produce an accurate scale drawing and get it approved by your building department (pages 48–55). Keep in mind that the decking will overhang the joists by 1½ inches or so on all sides. If the yard is heavily sloped, see pages 136–137 for tips.

Planning the footings and beams
Because they extend 3 feet beyond the footings, massive beams made of three 2×10s are required. Large beams call for larger-than-average supports—4×6 posts and 12-inch-diameter footings.

PRESTART CHECKLIST

☐ **TIME**
Four to five hours to build batterboards, figure the layout, stretch lines, and determine footing locations

☐ **TOOLS**
Drill, sledgehammer, tape measure, mason's line, carpenter's square, shovel

☐ **SKILLS**
Measuring and checking for square, fastening with screws, pounding stakes

☐ **PREP**
Get drawings approved and double-check them for accuracy, study the way the deck will be assembled

☐ **MATERIALS**
1×4 or 1×2 for stakes, 1⅝-inch screws, masking tape

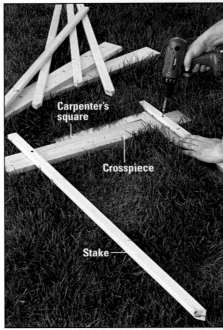

1 Construct batterboards using 1×2s or 2×4s and a 1×4 crosspiece. Stakes can be from 16 to 36 inches long. If the ground is hard, make them shorter; if soft, make them longer. Cut the crosspieces about 30 inches long. Assemble the pieces with a single screw at each joint.

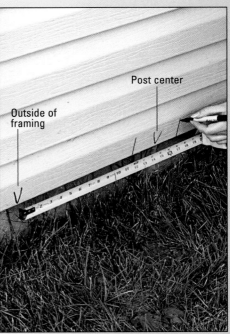

2 Mark the house wall for the positions of the posts. First mark the outside of the framing (the decking will overhang it by 1½ inches). Then measure over and mark where the post will be located. Make sure you identify the center of the post.

LOCATING PIERS

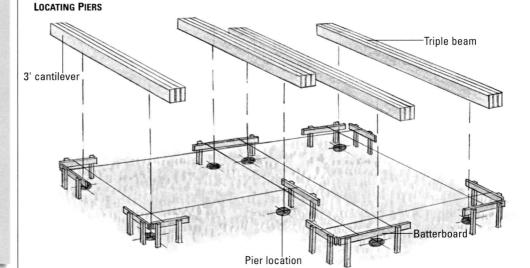

Batterboards support strings that help pinpoint the center of each post and pier. In this case the piers are positioned 3 feet from the house to avoid the backfill next to the foundation of this new house.

3 Near the house drive a batterboard into the ground, more or less centered over the post location. Pound the stakes until the crosspiece is 6 inches or so above the ground and stable. For soft, wet soil, use long stakes; shorter stakes are fine for hard ground.

4 Measure out from the house for the position of a post and drive in another batterboard. Position all batterboards about 2 feet beyond the post locations. To keep your estimated post locations roughly perpendicular to the house, hold a carpenter's square against the house and run a tape measure along its side, as shown.

Alternate framing

To make a two-level deck, you can build two decks as shown in this chapter. Another way is to let the beam of one section serve as the rim joist or header for the other.

Set the posts (pages 112–117), but build your beam from two 2× boards fastened to opposite sides of the posts (page 94). This gives you essentially two headers at the same level. (You could consider them rim joists, too, if you want to change the decking orientation.) Build frames on both headers and hang joists in the section that will be the lower deck. Don't hang joists in the other section; instead build a frame on top of it and hang the joists in this raised platform. Repeat for multiple levels.

This method requires you to lay out the sections with separate sets of batterboards.

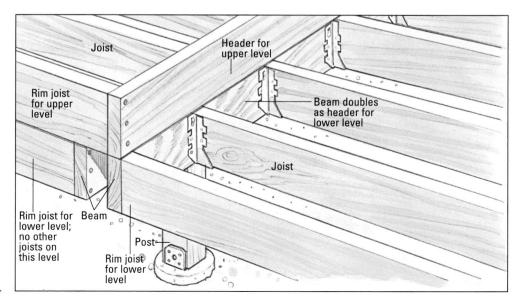

Laying out the deck (continued)

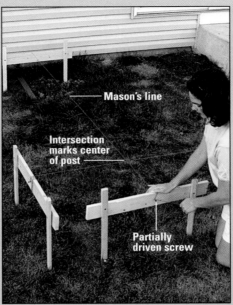

Mason's line

Intersection marks center of post

Partially driven screw

5 Estimate the location of the other postholes. Place additional batterboards 2 to 3 feet beyond the post locations. You can approximate the footing locations by driving temporary stakes into the ground.

6 Drive a screw partway into the middle of each batterboard's crosspiece. Stretch mason's line to form a grid. Use the screws to anchor the string. The mason's lines should intersect at roughly the same height. Drive one of the batterboards deeper into the ground, if necessary, to align the lines.

7 Adjust the line that runs parallel to the house until it is equally distant from the house along its entire length and lined up with the center of the footings. Anchor this line firmly to its batterboards so you won't bump it out of position.

MULTIPLES OF 3, 4, AND 5
Laying out a large deck

Laying out a large deck calls for the same techniques as laying out a small one, but is slightly complicated by the length of the sides and by the necessity of keeping the line posts (those set between the corner posts) lined up.

Set your batterboards firmly in the ground and tie the mason's lines tightly onto the crosspieces so they don't sag or move around in the wind.

When you square the corners with a 3-4-5 triangle, use larger multiples of 3, 4, and 5, such as 6, 8, and 10 or 9, 12, and 15. When the sides of the deck are long, the larger numbers will keep your measurements accurate. Measure the diagonals of the site as a final check, and adjust the lines if necessary.

After you mark the location of the corner posts, lay out and mark the line posts. Use a template (page 84) to keep them spaced properly, driving stakes or landscape spikes to mark them.

Mark line with tape.

10'

6'

8'

Mark exact string location.

8 Check the mason's lines for square. Measure 6 feet along one line and mark the spot with a piece of tape. Measure 8 feet along the perpendicular string line and mark it the same way. (Make sure you know which side of the tape indicates the exact spot.) Measure the distance between the two marks; if it is exactly 10 feet then the lines are square to each other. If not, adjust one line. With this method you can substitute 6, 8, and 10 with any multiples of 3, 4, and 5; for example 9, 12, and 15; or 12, 16, and 20. The larger the numbers, the greater the accuracy.

9 Once you have found the correct position for the line, mark its position on a batterboard with a pencil. You can remove the screw and drive it under the line or leave the screw in place. Just make sure you wrap the line tightly on the mark and tie it to the screw.

STANLEY PRO TIP

Keep it stable

Layout problems often arise not because of inaccurate measurements but because things get bumped. So drive batterboards into the soil until they're firm. Clearly mark the correct spot for the line on each crosspiece. Keep neighborhood kids away from batterboards and mason's lines. When walking around the job site, step carefully around or over the lines. Most important, check and double-check measurements to keep things square. Check measurements:
- When you start to dig the holes
- When you insert the tube forms
- When you insert the J-bolts

REFRESHER COURSE
Locating posts precisely

To mark the center of a posthole, hold a plumb bob (a chalk line will work in a pinch) with its string barely touching each layout line. Drive a stake or landscape spike into the ground to mark the spot.

If the design calls for three or more posts supporting the same beam, the middle posts do not require intersecting string lines. Just measure along the line or use a spacing jig (page 84) to mark the center of the footing.

FORMING FOOTINGS

Check with a building inspector for advice on how to excavate your site and prevent the growth of weeds. In some locations there is no need to excavate—building the deck will kill all foliage under it. More likely, however, you must remove the sod, lay down landscape fabric, and cover it with gravel to keep things from growing. You can remove the sod before or after you have laid out the footing locations.

Local codes will specify posthole depth and width, as well as how the concrete should be formed and how the post will attach to the concrete. These steps show the most common method, using a tube form and a post anchor that attaches to a J-bolt.

Digging in

Digging is back-straining work, especially if you are not used to doing it. Don't rush it. When possible work with your back straight rather than bent. Consider renting a power auger (below right) and hiring some help. Or call fencing or landscaping contractors and ask how much they would charge to dig the holes.

PRESTART CHECKLIST

☐ **TIME**
To dig a posthole, from 15 minutes to two hours, depending on soil conditions

☐ **TOOLS**
Posthole digger or power auger, spade, level, layout square, trowel

☐ **SKILLS**
Using a spade or a posthole digger

☐ **PREP**
Have utility companies mark locations of water, gas, electric, and phone lines. Double-check that the locations for the postholes are correct.

☐ **MATERIALS**
Sand or flour for marking the ground, plastic sheeting, gravel, concrete, tube forms, J-bolts

1 Remove the mason's lines, but keep the batterboards in place. Take care not to disturb the batterboards as you work. Mark the perimeter of the deck with sand or upside-down spray paint. Dig away the sod from the deck area.

2 It may be possible to slice lines in the sod with a straight shovel or spade and roll up the sod for use elsewhere. Leave the stakes that mark the post locations in place, or pull them up and replace them as soon as you have rolled up the sod around them.

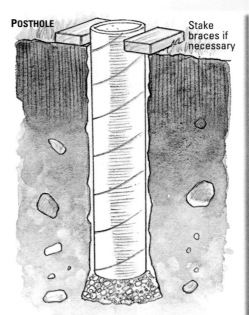

If your ground is level, here's a method for bracing the tube forms that's easier than the one shown on page 87.

Rent a power auger

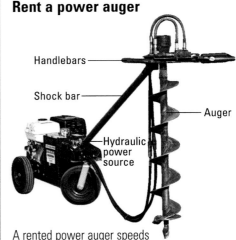

A rented power auger speeds up the digging and makes holes that are more precise than those dug by hand. A handheld auger (page 86) may be difficult to use, especially if the soil is rocky or full of roots. This type has a bar that helps absorb the shock when the tool bucks as it hits a root or rock.

3 At each posthole mark a large X with flour, sand, or spray paint. Remove the stake and dig a hole wide enough to accommodate the tube form that you will use. Shovel a few inches of gravel into the hole and tamp it down.

4 Set a tube form into the hole and mark it about 2 inches above grade. Cut the form with a handsaw or a knife. Check that the top of the form is close to level; recut the form if necessary. Anchor the form with screws driven into 2×s and add braces, if necessary, to keep the top of the form level.

5 Don't fill the tubes with concrete until the inspector has signed off on the holes. Fill any spaces around the form with well-packed soil. Mix the concrete and pour it into the form. Poke a pole or a piece of 1×2 into the concrete several times to remove any air bubbles.

WHAT IF...
You need lots of concrete?

If you have a lot of concrete to pour, using dry-mix bags will be time-consuming and expensive. Explore some other options:

■ Most ready-mix concrete companies deliver only large loads, but some have special trucks made for small jobs. The company can help you figure out how much concrete you need. Plan how to move the concrete from the truck to the holes—having a couple of helpers and wheelbarrows is a good idea since the drivers will not wait around for a long time.

■ Consider renting a gas- or electric-powered concrete mixer. Pour bags of dry-mix into the mixer and add water, or have cement, sand, and gravel delivered to your yard and mix your own. A common ratio is one part cement, one part sand, and two parts gravel.

REFRESHER COURSE
Mixing concrete

A 60-pound bag of dry-mix will fill an 8-inch tube form about 20 inches deep; a 10-inch form, 13 inches; or a 12-inch form, 9 inches. If you need more than 40 bags, consider having concrete delivered (see box at left).

To mix concrete, pour a bag of dry-mix into a wheelbarrow or tub and dig out a small depression in the middle. Pour or spray water into the hole, taking care not to add too much. Mix with a shovel or a hoe. Scrape the tub or wheelbarrow as you mix so there is no dry powder left at the bottom.

A good mix is just loose enough to be pourable but not too runny. It should hold its shape and cling for at least 1 second to a shovel turned on edge.

Forming footings *(continued)*

6 Drag a short board across the top of the form in a seesaw motion. This removes excess concrete and partially smooths the concrete surface.

7 Reattach the mason's lines and check that they are square. Directly below intersecting lines insert a J-bolt into the concrete. Wiggle it downward until about an inch sticks up. Drop a plumb bob from the intersection to help center the J-bolt.

Bolt should protrude 1"

8 Use a layout square to check that the bolt is pointing straight up. Smooth the concrete with a small trowel and check the bolt again.

J-bolt

STANLEY PRO TIP: **Set some piers**

In areas where the ground does not freeze in winter, deep footings may not be required. Some local codes will require only shallow footings, others, only piers with no footings at all. If the ground is subject only to minor frost heave or none, the whole deck will float as a unit. Because it's not attached to a house, it won't be damaged.

If the ground is stable and you don't mind using more concrete, you can skip the tube form and pour a shallow footing directly into a hole in the ground. However, you'll need to form the top of the footing so that you have concrete a couple of inches above ground level.

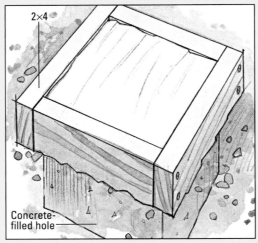

2×4

Concrete-filled hole

A 2×4 frame set atop a wide, shallow hole is a simple way to form a footing. Check that the frame is level.

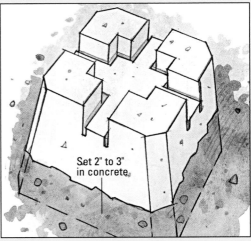

Set 2" to 3" in concrete

A precast pier can be set into a bed of concrete while it is still wet. Local codes may allow setting a series of precast piers directly on firm soil.

9 Once the concrete has set, smooth the landscaped area and tamp it firm by walking on it. Fill any indentations that would create puddles. Make sure that the footings stick up at least 2 inches above the ground. Spread heavy-duty plastic sheeting or landscape fabric over the deck area to prevent the growth of weeds. Use gravel or stones—not soil—to hold the sheeting in place. If you need two or more sheets, overlap them at least 1 foot.

10 Pour 1 or 2 inches of gravel on top of the sheeting and rake it smooth. The gravel will poke small holes in the plastic, which will allow water to seep through. However, avoid large holes or tears that may permit weeds to grow.

Groundcover options

For long-lasting insurance against weed growth, lay down black plastic sheeting that's 6 mils thick. Landscaping fabric protects against weeds but does not last as long as plastic. Purchase landscape staples to hold the sheeting in position.

You'll be walking on top of the gravel while you build the framing, so choose gravel that is free of sharp edges, which could tear the plastic. Pea gravel or lava stone are two good choices.

Landscape fabric

Heavy-gauge plastic

Pea gravel

Lava stone

River rock

WHAT IF...
Drainage is a concern?

If rain and melting snow threaten to cascade off the edges of the deck and erode planting areas, dig a trench—6 inches deep or so—around the deck and fill it with gravel. This catches runoff from the deck and lets it seep into the ground. If drainage problems threaten your foundation or crawlspace, you may need to dig a long drainage trench that slopes away from the deck. Lay perforated drainpipe in the trench and have the pipe end in a dry well—a gravel-filled hole in the ground that is at least 1 foot in diameter and 2 feet deep.

INSTALLING POSTS

Allow a day or two for the concrete to set and start to cure; it will take a week or so to achieve full strength.

A post level is an indispensible tool for installing posts. It tells you at once whether the post is plumb in both directions and leaves both hands free to work.

High-quality pressure-treated posts are fully saturated with a chemical that will keep them from rotting for decades. For extra protection soak the cut ends in a bucket of sealer before installing them (page 65).

Use a level and a long board to estimate the height of each post. Set posts about a foot longer than you will need them; you will cut them to exact height later.

These steps show how to cut posts that will have beams placed on top of them. For a sandwiched beam, see pages 163–164.

PRESTART CHECKLIST

☐ **TIME**
About 30 minutes to install a post anchor, temporarily brace a post, measure and cut a post to height

☐ **TOOLS**
Post level, hammer, drill, tape measure, circular saw, layout square, wrench

☐ **SKILLS**
Driving screws, checking for level and plumb, cutting with a circular saw

☐ **PREP**
Pour footings with J-bolts. Use string lines to mark the footings for posts that are correctly aligned (pages 108–111).

☐ **MATERIALS**
Posts (usually 4×4s), adjustable post anchors, 1×4s or 1×2s for braces and stakes, 2-inch screws

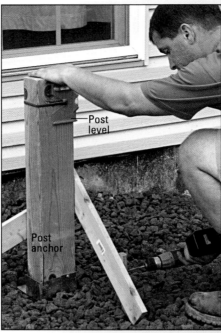

1 Install a post anchor and finger-tighten the hold-down nut so that the anchor is fairly stable but movable. Insert a post, fasten it to the anchor with one screw, and attach a post level. Stake and brace the post—position the post so it is plumb and screw the braces to the post.

2 Use a level to mark the first post for the height of the decking. Make sure that the decking will be at least 1 inch below the threshold of the doorway.

WHAT IF...
You have to add a bolt after the concrete has set?

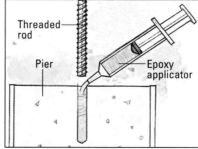

If a J-bolt is seriously misaligned, cut it off and buy threaded rods and epoxy made for retrofitting concrete anchors. Drill a hole in the footing using a masonry bit slightly larger in diameter than the rod. Vacuum out all the dust. Inject epoxy into the hole and insert the threaded rod. The epoxy will set firm in about a day.

STANLEY PRO TIP

Clamp the braces

Plumbing a post and bracing it, even with a post level, can often require more hands than you have available. To make this job easier, and more accurate, attach your 1×4 or 2×4 brace to a ground stake with one screw. Hold the brace against the post and plumb it with a post level or carpenter's level. When the post is plumb, clamp the brace onto it. Drive two screws through the brace into the post and add another screw to the ground stake.

Top of decking
Top of joist
Top of beam
Mark post at bottom of beam, and cut to that height

Cutline for post

3 Measure down from the top of the decking. Strike marks to indicate the thickness of the decking, the width of the joists, and the width of the beam. Cut the post at this height with a reciprocating saw.

4 You can use a line level or a water level to mark all of the posts for cutting level to the first post. Over short spacing you can use a straight board and a carpenter's level, as shown. Set one end of the board on the first post. If you are holding the board against more than one post, it might help to have someone hold the other end of the board. Mark all the posts and double-check that the marks are all level with each other; then cut the posts.

REFRESHER COURSE
Options for setting posts

Some deck designs call for posts that are set in holes filled with concrete or tamped dirt. The concrete method is challenging because all the posts must be perfectly aligned when the concrete is poured.

A 42-inch-deep hole is typical for both methods. Tamp the bottom of the hole and throw in a few inches of gravel. Tamp the gravel. Insert the post.

If you will be filling around the post with concrete, brace the post plumb in both directions. Drive several 16d nails into the post to help anchor it in the concrete.

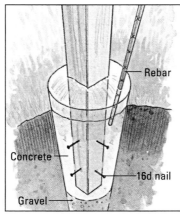

Rebar
Concrete
16d nail
Gravel

As you fill around a post with concrete, poke down with a piece of metal reinforcing rod or a 1×2 to eliminate air pockets. Mound the concrete around the post above the hole to drain water.

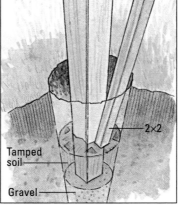

2×2
Tamped soil
Gravel

When setting a post in soil, tamp down every few inches of soil. Check frequently that the post remains plumb in both directions as you tamp and fill.

STANLEY PRO TIP

J-bolt too long?

If a J-bolt is too long for the post anchor (a common problem), add a few washers before screwing down the nut. Or trim the bolt with a hacksaw. Before you saw it, spin on a nut to below the cut line. After cutting, remove the nut to clean and realign the threads.

FRAMING

The beam for this deck is made of three 2×10s. (For other methods of beam construction see pages 94 and 139.)

Many older decks were built using massive timbers—4×6s or 4×8s—for beams. Some builders still do it that way; using a one-piece beam can save time. But large timbers are heavy and hard to handle. They often warp beyond remedy, and they almost surely will crack over the years. Fastening multiple pieces of 2× lumber together actually creates a beam that is stronger than a single piece of 4× or 6× lumber.

If a deck design is complicated, it often makes sense to build a beam that is about 1 foot too long and cut it to length after the framing is in place (page 142). The beams for this deck can be cut to exact length before they are installed.

PRESTART CHECKLIST

☐ **TIME**
About 2 hours to build a 14-foot-long beam made of three 2×10s with plywood spacers

☐ **TOOLS**
Tape measure, circular saw, drill, long bit, hammer, clamps, adjustable or socket wrench

☐ **SKILLS**
Measuring and cutting a board, fastening with screws and bolts

☐ **PREP**
Set up two or three stable sawhorses and lay the beam pieces on them

☐ **MATERIALS**
Lumber for the beam pieces (2×10s in this case), pressure-treated plywood, 1¼-inch deck screws, 3-inch deck screws, ⅜ × 6-inch carriage bolts with nuts and washers

A. Making a beam

1 Stack the three 2× beam members on top of each other with their crowns (page 65) facing the same direction. Square the ends and cut them to length. If you choose to do so, cut a decorative angle at one or both ends.

2 Cut pointed spacers from a sheet of ½-inch pressure-treated plywood (the points prevent rainwater from sitting on the plywood and soaking in). Fasten the spacers, points up, to two beam lengths with 1¼-inch screws. Attach the spacers at 16-inch intervals.

OVERVIEW OF BEAM LOCATION

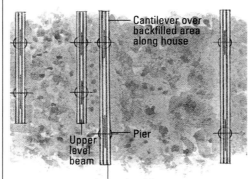

Be sure to assemble the beam so the 2×s have the crown sides up. Miter-cut ends of plywood spacers and point them upward.

Sandwiching the post

Sandwiching posts between two 2×s is a common way to build a beam. Begin by cutting your posts about 1 foot longer than needed. Set them in place with temporary support. Position the members and fasten them with carriage bolts.

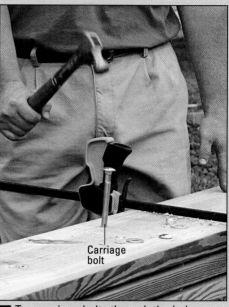

Set ends flush

Bolt hole

Carriage bolt

3 Stack two beam pieces with the spacers sandwiched between. Align the ends and clamp them together. Drive 16d galvanized box nails or 3-inch screws every 16 inches, alternating the distance from the edge of the beam. Add the third beam piece and repeat the process.

4 Starting about 2 inches from the edges of the beam and at 16-inch intervals, counterbore two holes on the inside (or least visible side) of the beam for carriage bolt nuts. Drill through the beam with a long bit the same diameter as the bolts.

5 Tap carriage bolts through the holes. On the flip side, add a washer and nut and tighten the nut with a socket wrench.

WHAT IF...
The deck is close to the ground?

Low decks might not provide enough vertical space for joists attached to the top of a beam. The solution is a flush beam, which is essentially a header that has been doubled for strength. Cut two headers (the boards that will be perpendicular to the joists) and mark lines on them indicating where the joists will go (Step 3, page 121). Fasten them to the posts so they are level. Double up the headers to make them flush beams. Drive a pair of nails or screws every 16 inches to bind the pieces together firmly. The second piece is 1½ inches longer than the header on each end to accommodate rim joists on both sides of the frame.

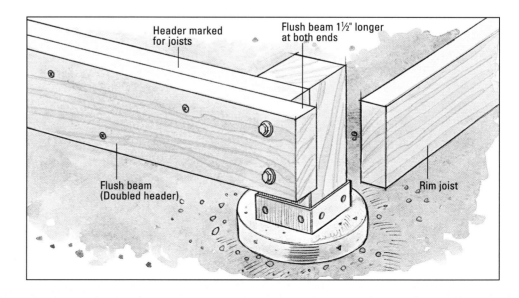

Header marked for joists

Flush beam 1½" longer at both ends

Flush beam (Doubled header)

Rim joist

B. Beams, headers, and outside joists

Mark beam by
amount of
overhang

T-bracket

1 Mark the beam where it will overhang the posts on both ends. In this case the beam is marked 3 feet from each end. Then have someone help you place the beam on top of the posts. For the longer beams you may need two helpers. Make sure that the beams are flush to the posts on both sides.

2 Check the beam for level. If it isn't, trim one of the posts. If trimming will lower the deck too much, cut and install a new post; do not shim the beam to level it. Attach the beam to the post with a post/beam connector or with T-brackets and joist-hanger screws on both sides.

FRAMING OVERVIEW

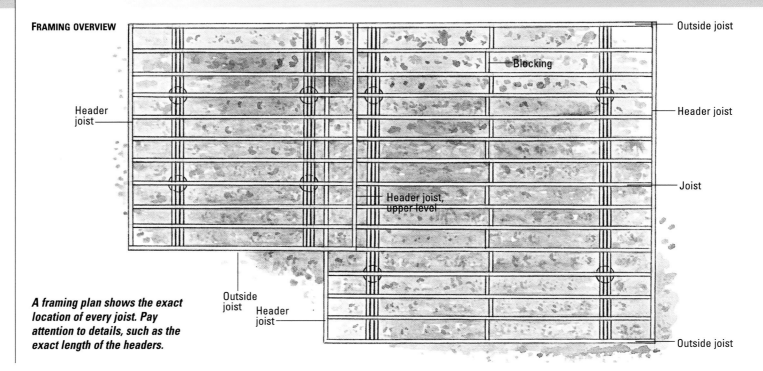

Outside joist

Blocking

Header joist

Header joist

Joist

Header joist, upper level

A framing plan shows the exact location of every joist. Pay attention to details, such as the exact length of the headers.

Outside joist

Header joist

Outside joist

Joist goes on this side of the line

3 Cut the two header joists to length. Use the straightest boards possible. Lay them on a flat surface, side by side, with crowns facing in opposite directions and the ends perfectly aligned. Mark the headers with the joist locations indicated on the framing plan, 12 inches apart in this example. Every 12 inches make a V-shape mark. Draw square lines through the marks as shown. Draw an X on the joist side of the line.

Header joist

Outside joist

4 Cut the outside joists to length—usually the width of the framing minus 3 inches for the thickness of the two headers. On a flat surface assemble the outside joists and the headers. Make sure the headers face each other correctly with their crowns up and the Xs on the same sides of the layout lines. Use a framing square to check that the frame is square. Drill pilot holes and drive nails or screws to attach the boards at the corners.

5 Check again for square, using a 3-4-5 triangle. Attach a temporary brace at each corner to keep the frame stable when you lift it up. For the brace use a 1×4 or larger, and attach it with two screws at each joint.

6 With a helper or two, lift the frame and set it on top of the beams. Measure the frame at all four points to make sure it overhangs the beams by equal amounts on all sides. Check again for square with a 3-4-5 triangle. Attach the frame to the beam with a seismic tie (page 71) or similar hardware at each joint.

C. Inside joists

Pattern joist

Temporary cleat

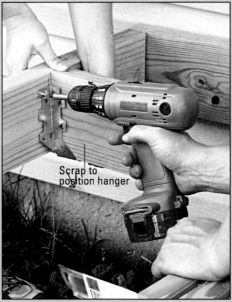

Scrap to position hanger

1 In this design the inside joists are the same length as the outside joists. Gang-cut the inside joists using production methods. Set up a cutting platform so you can move boards on and off easily and work comfortably. Make sure the boards will be properly supported while you cut. Check the ends; if one is not square or has a split, cut off 1 or 2 inches. Use one joist as a pattern, attaching a temporary cleat to one end to keep it flush with the others. Measure and mark for the cut; draw an X to indicate which side of the line will be cut. Cut with a power mitersaw or a circular saw.

2 Install the joist hangers on the outside joists. Line up one side of the hanger on the vertical mark on the header so that the hanger overlaps the X. Fasten one side in place, then have a helper hold a scrap of joist so you can position and fasten the other side of the hanger.

WHAT IF…
The deck wraps around a corner?

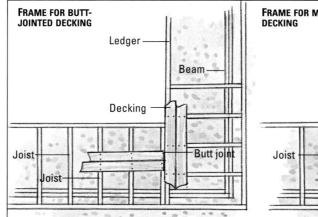

FRAME FOR BUTT-JOINTED DECKING

Ledger

Beam

Decking

Joist

Joist

Butt joint

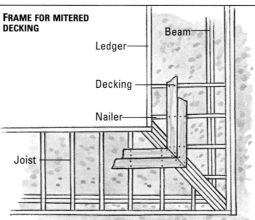

FRAME FOR MITERED DECKING

Beam

Ledger

Decking

Nailer

Joist

If a deck will turn a corner around a house, special framing is needed. The decking pattern determines the framing configuration. If the deck boards will meet in a butt joint (left), the framing is simple.

If the decking will meet at a mitered corner (right), support the miter joint with two joists installed at a 45-degree angle; attach a 2×4 nailer to each side, for added nailing surface.

Attaching framing hardware— nails or screws?

Some building inspectors insist on nails designed exclusively for joist hangers—and they want one placed in every hole in the hanger. Others want screws made for hangers and assert that too many fasteners can split the joist. Check your local requirements. In any case use only fasteners that are specially hardened and strong enough for use with joists.

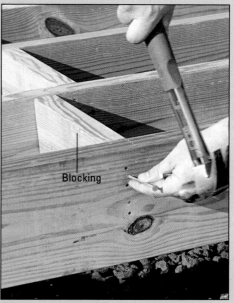

3 To attach the remaining joists, screw a temporary block to the top of the joist and use it to hang the end of the joist at the marks on the header. Slide a joist hanger tight to the bottom of the joist. Drive joist hanger nails or screws into each hole.

4 Check that the outside joists are straight with a line strung as shown. Measure several points along the line to make sure that it is an equal distance from the end joists. Use a 3-4-5 triangle to confirm that the frame is square.

5 Blocking keeps joists from warping and stiffens the framing. Snap a chalk line down the center of the joists. Measure the space between each joist as you go, and cut blocking from the same stock as the joists. Install them in a staggered pattern that allows you to face-nail each one.

STANLEY PRO TIP: **Attaching joists to the beam**

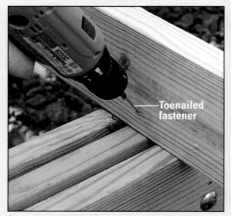

For extra stability, fasten the joists to the beam. Local codes may recommend simply toenailing or screwing as shown above: Drill a pilot hole, then drive a 16d nail or 3-inch screw at a fairly steep angle through the joist and into the beam.

Some localities may require framing hardware, such as hurricane or seismic ties. Slip one into place and drive four nails or screws to fasten it.

WHAT IF...
Joist hangers aren't required?

Local codes may allow you to back-nail (or back-screw) instead of attaching with joist hangers. Have a helper hold the joist in position while you drive 16d galvanized nails or 3-inch deck screws through the header and into the joist.

ANGLED DECKING

Installing decking at a 45-degree angle is not difficult. Practice cutting some scrap decking to make sure you can consistently cut a precise 45-degree angle. Measure carefully to see that the first boards are installed correctly. The rest of the deck will go on quickly.

Cutting the angles

A radial-arm saw or a 12-inch power mitersaw is ideal for cutting 2×6 or 5/4 decking. With a 10-inch power mitersaw you may have to finish each cut with a handsaw—a time-consuming extra step. With practice you can make accurate 45-degree cuts with a circular saw, using a layout square or a jig as a guide (page 225). Some circular saws manage this more easily than others; often the blade guard gets in the way at the beginning of the cut.

PRESTART CHECKLIST

☐ **TIME**
Most of a day to cut and install angled decking on a 300-square-foot deck

☐ **TOOLS**
Power mitersaw or radial-arm saw, circular saw, tape measure, chalk line, flat pry bar, chisel, hammer, drill, handsaw, layout square

☐ **SKILLS**
Making accurate 45-degree cuts, driving screws or nails, cutting with a circular saw

☐ **PREP**
Check that the framing is securely fastened at all points

☐ **MATERIALS**
Decking, screws or nails

¼" plywood strip

1 To help maintain a straight line near the house, temporarily attach a strip of ¼-inch plywood against the siding, on top of the ledger. Fasten the screws above the decking thickness so you can remove it after you install the decking.

2 Choose two straight boards and cut one end of each at a 45-degree angle. A 10-inch power mitersaw will not cut all the way across the board. Complete the cut with a handsaw. If you are experienced using a power mitersaw, lift up on the forward edge of the board to finish the cut.

STANLEY PRO TIP: **Buy the right lengths**

If possible buy decking boards long enough so you will not need to make any butt joints. Make a scale drawing that shows every piece of decking, and measure to find out how many boards of each size you will need (see page 62). The shortest boards you can buy usually are 8 feet long. If you need two 4-foot pieces, buy an 8-footer; if you need two 6-foot pieces, buy a 12-footer.

Spacer strip

Measurements should be equal

Automatic-feed screwdriver

Spacer

3 Set the two boards on the joists with the mitered ends pressed against the spacer strip. Measure from the corner to the edge of the decking in both directions. When the two measurements are equal, the decking is at a 45-degree angle to the house.

Check the first board for straightness and fasten it to the joists with nails or screws. You may drive all the fasteners as you go, or drive only a few at this point and snap chalk lines to line up all the other fasteners.

4 Attach decking by driving two fasteners wherever a board intersects a joist. Insert a spacing jig between the boards (see page 98 and below). An automatic-feed screwdriver makes the job go quickly. Set the nail or screw heads slightly below the face of the decking.

REFRESHER COURSE
Bending a warped board

Chisel

1 If a decking board is bowed, you will need to bend it into place. Insert spacers and fasten one end of the board. Then move along the board, straightening it as you go. Where a board needs persuading, drive a fastener partway into the board, push it into position, and finish driving the fastener.

2 If pushing does not do the trick, dig the point of a chisel or pry bar into the joist, right up against the decking board, and pry the board into position. If a board is so badly bowed that neither of these techniques works, replace it with another one.

Easy spacers for tight places

Traditionally decking boards are spaced using 16d nails. To keep the spacing consistent, make a spacing jig as shown on page 98. For tight places or short boards, drill a pilot hole through scrap blocks and drive nails through the blocks.

Angled decking *(continued)*

5 To mark the decking for a 1½-inch overhang, hold a piece of 2× lumber (which is actually 1½ inches thick) under the decking as a gauge to mark both ends of the cut.

6 Give your chalk line box a good shake to make sure the line is well-loaded with chalk. Hook the line onto a nail or screw driven partway into the side of one of the marked boards. Be sure to pull straight up when you snap the chalk line.

7 With clamps or deck screws, temporarily attach a straight board to the decking to serve as a guide for cutting along the chalk line. Cut the line with a circular saw.

STANLEY PRO TIP: **Doing it right**

Decking can be tedious work, but maintain your focus to achieve a deck surface with consistent joints and straight boards. Follow these tips:

■ Sort the boards and lay them loosely on the deck before you cut and install them. Choose the best-looking side to face up, and return bad boards to the lumberyard.

■ Drill a pilot hole if driving a fastener less than 3 inches from the end of a board. Otherwise the board may split.

■ Keep in mind that when you trim the edges, your circular saw cannot reach all the way to the house. Cut the board or two that will be nearest the house before you install them (page 144).

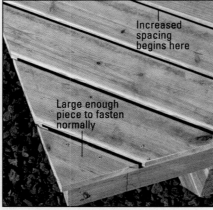

■ Once you're within 3 feet of a corner, measure to see how wide the last piece will be. If it looks like you'll end up with a tiny corner piece, try avoiding it by increasing the spacing between the last four or five boards.

WHAT IF...
You're stuck with a small piece?

If the last piece is large enough (as shown at left), install it as you did the other boards by drilling pilot holes and driving fasteners down through the face of the board. If the piece is small, cut and attach it after making the chalk line cuts. Drill horizontal pilot holes and attach the piece with screws or nails driven into the adjoining deck board (above). There will be no space between these two boards.

SIMPLE STAIRS

For complete instructions on planning and building stairs, see pages 100–103 and 147–149. If the deck is less than 2 feet above grade and you need only a set of standard steps, you can simplify the process. A standard step has a rise (vertical distance) of 6 to 8 inches and a run (horizontal distance) of 10 to 12 inches.

You may end the stairs on a landing made of either concrete (pages 150–151) or patio pavers (pages 172–173). Or you can suspend the steps (as shown here) above the ground until the landing is installed.

Home centers sell precut stringers. This is the simplest solution if you need only a few steps. These usually have 7-inch rises and 11-inch runs. Cut the top of a precut stringer to fit against the deck joist (page 102). You may need to cut the bottom so that the last step is shorter than the others.

The method shown on this page works if you have one or two steps. You can adapt the dimensions to suit your site. If possible make all the steps (including the bottom step) the same height.

PRESTART CHECKLIST

☐ **TIME**
Once the landing is installed, a couple of hours to construct and attach a simple step or two

☐ **TOOLS**
Tape measure, circular saw, drill, hammer, carpenter's level, layout square

☐ **SKILLS**
Figuring rise and run for a couple of steps, measuring and cutting boards, fastening with nails or screws

☐ **PREP**
Determine stair location and dimensions

☐ **MATERIALS**
Lumber for framing and treads, hurricane ties, stake

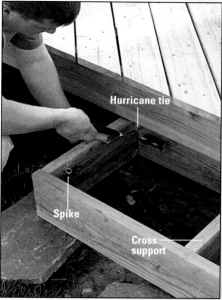

1 Build a simple box frame for the step from 2×6 or 2×8 pressure-treated lumber. If the treads are ⁵⁄₄ decking, add a cross support every 16 inches; if they're 2×s, add a support every 24 inches. Attach the box to the outside joist with hurricane ties and add a spike to avoid twisting.

2 Cut the treads to length and fasten them in place using 2-inch fasteners for ⁵⁄₄-inch decking (shown above) or 3-inch fasteners for 2× treads.

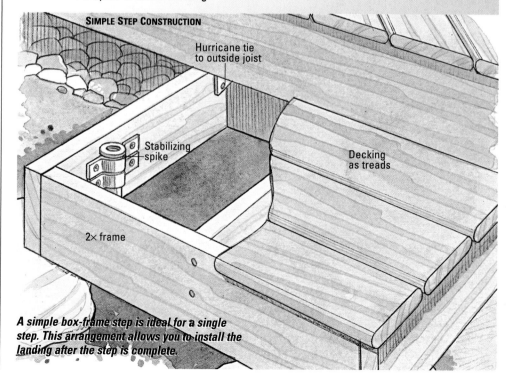

SIMPLE STEP CONSTRUCTION

A simple box-frame step is ideal for a single step. This arrangement allows you to install the landing after the step is complete.

BENCH WITH PLANTERS

Some deck planters are wood containers that actually hold soil. Others serve as decorative containers into which you can place potted plants. The type shown here combines the features of both: an attractive planter box that holds a large plastic tub with holes in the bottom for drainage.

Tubs are available at garden or home centers. Another option is to order a galvanized liner from a sheet-metal shop; the liner can be custom-made to fit any size planter.

Whichever type of planter you choose to make, be sure that water can drain freely out of the bottom and plan where that water will go. Drained water trapped in a cavity below the planter could cause decking to rot. Most decorative plants need less than 1 foot of soil depth. Rather than loading a tall planter with unnecessary soil, build a shelf inside.

A bench is even easier to build than a planter. A platform that is 16 inches wide and 17 inches high will be comfortable for most people.

PRESTART CHECKLIST

☐ **TIME**
Several hours to build two planters and a bench

☐ **TOOLS**
Tape measure, level, drill, hammer, circular saw, layout square, framing square, squeeze or pipe clamps

☐ **SKILLS**
Measuring and cutting boards, fastening with nails or screws

☐ **PREP**
Purchase a liner and design a planter to fit around it

☐ **MATERIALS**
Lumber for the planter and the bench, screws or nails, L-shape strap ties with screws, 6-inch carriage bolts

1 Cut pieces of ⁵⁄₄ decking for the sides of the planter. To build each side, clamp the pieces and attach a 2×6 brace, which also acts as a cleat to hold the bottom pieces (Step 2). Cut the brace 2 inches shorter than the width of the side and attach it with screws.

Leave equal spaces of at least 1" on each side

Cleat

Shelf for container

2 Hold three of the sides together with clamps and drive nails or screws to fasten them together. Attach the fourth side in the same way. Cut pieces of decking for the shelf. Check the structure for square, then attach the shelf pieces to the cleat. Add the top and bottom trim pieces.

PLANTER CONSTRUCTION

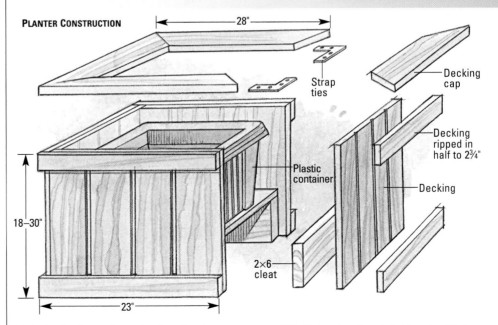

28"

Strap ties

Decking cap

Plastic container

Decking ripped in half to 2¾"

Decking

2×6 cleat

18–30"

23"

This simple planter is made primarily of pressure-treated ⁵⁄₄×6 decking. Vary height and width to suit your deck. The cleat can be set to suit the height of the plant container you'll use. Trim pieces can be butt-jointed or mitered.

3 To make the cap, cut decking boards with 45-degree miters and assemble them with L-shape strap ties. The frame should overhang the top trim by 1½ inches on all sides. Set the liner in the box and then fasten the cap using 2-inch deck screws sunk into the top trim piece.

Position L-shape strap ties inside the perimeter of planter

Framing square

4 Toe-fasten the planters in position with 3-inch fasteners. For each bench measure between two planters and construct a 2×4 frame with crosspieces every 2 feet or so. Set the finished frame between the planters and fasten it into the planters with four 3-inch fasteners.

Planter

Crosspiece

Bench frame

5 If a seat is longer than 8 feet, add 4×4 supports every 6 feet or so. Cut seat slats from decking lumber and fasten them to the frame with screws or nails driven into the seat joists. Space the seat slats as you would for decking and allow them to overhang the frame by 1 or 2 inches.

6" carriage bolts

4×4 post

BENCH CONSTRUCTION

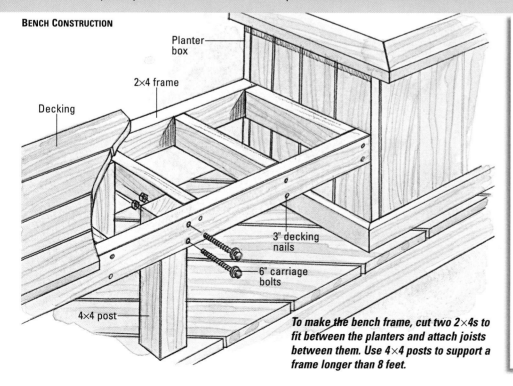

Planter box

2×4 frame

Decking

3" decking nails

6" carriage bolts

4×4 post

To make the bench frame, cut two 2×4s to fit between the planters and attach joists between them. Use 4×4 posts to support a frame longer than 8 feet.

REFRESHER COURSE
Toe-fastening posts

To attach the posts and the planters to the deck, drive toenails or angled screws. Drill a pilot hole 2 inches above the deck at about a 60-degree angle. Install a 3-inch deck screw or 16d nail.

DECK ON A SLOPED SITE
STAIRS & RAILING

A deck attached to the house is quick to build and makes efficient use of materials. The angled corner of this design adds an attractive, space-saving feature that requires only about an extra half-day's labor.

Framing the deck
A ledger board provides a secure way to attach a deck to a house. It also functions as an ideal starting place for laying out the site. After the ledger is installed, all layout measurements start from it.

Once the ledger is set, reference down from it to the ground and lay out the post locations. Where the deck has an angled corner, two posts must be placed at a corresponding angle. Fortunately these two footings can be off by an inch or two without weakening the deck structure.

The beam in this design rests on top of the posts. You may prefer (or your building inspector may require) a sandwich-type beam; see page 162. This deck uses the simplest type of beam—two 2×10s fastened together.

Building stairs
If the deck is only 1 or 2 feet above fairly level ground, you can build simple stairs using precut stringers available at home centers. If the deck is higher or the ground slopes, careful planning is required to make sure that all the steps (including the bottom one) are the same height. This chapter presents complete instructions on how to build the stairs.

Working on a slope
A site that slopes away from the house presents challenges for a deck builder. Extra care must be taken to ensure that posts are plumb and the deck is level.

If a slope is severe, special measures may be needed to keep the footings from slowly sliding down the hill. In extreme circumstances the footings may have to be connected to the house's foundation; hire a professional for this type of work.

For safety and convenience work with at least one helper whenever possible.

Working from a ledger attached to the house, here's how to cope with a sloped site.

CHAPTER PREVIEW

Anchoring the ledger
page 132

Laying out a sloped site
page 136

Framing
page 138

Laying the decking
page 144

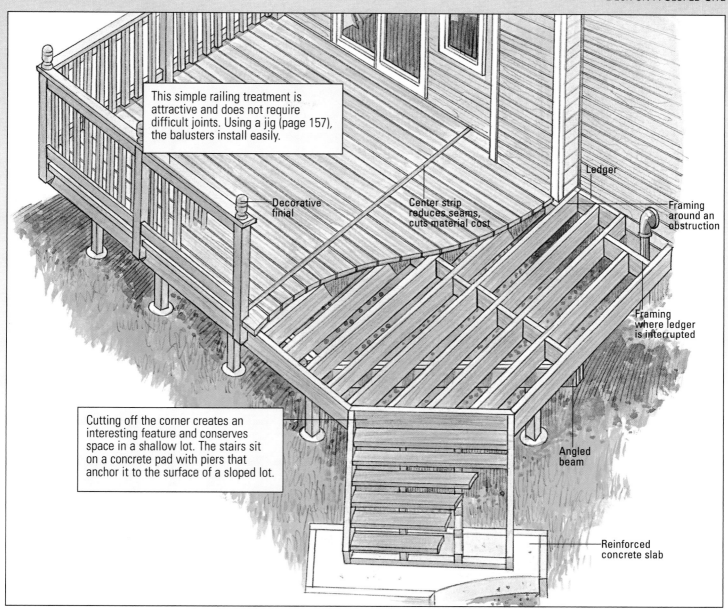

This simple railing treatment is attractive and does not require difficult joints. Using a jig (page 157), the balusters install easily.

Decorative finial

Center strip reduces seams, cuts material cost

Ledger

Framing around an obstruction

Framing where ledger is interrupted

Angled beam

Cutting off the corner creates an interesting feature and conserves space in a shallow lot. The stairs sit on a concrete pad with piers that anchor it to the surface of a sloped lot.

Reinforced concrete slab

A deck installed on a sloped site calls for special layout techniques and often is more challenging to frame. A ledger provides a level starting point; its height and length are helpful reference points while you're laying out the posts, beams, and framing.

Laying out stairways
page 147

Forming a concrete pad
page 150

Building the stairs
page 152

Adding the railing
page 154

ANCHORING THE LEDGER

Most decks are attached to the house with a ledger because it easily adds strength to the structure. In some areas with unstable soil, however, a deck must be unattached to prevent damage to the house and deck if it shifts. (See "Freestanding Basic Deck" beginning on page 106.)

Make it level and strong

The ledger will act as the reference point for laying out the entire deck, so take time to position it precisely and level. If the siding or door is not level, you may be tempted to install the ledger out of level for appearance's sake. Resist the temptation: An angled ledger greatly complicates the rest of the construction process.

Attach the ledger with lag screws driven into framing members—not just into the sheathing. Most homes will have an exterior joist (sometimes called a band joist) just below the door sill. That's where the ledger goes. Drill test holes to make sure the screws will have a hefty 2× board to grab.

PRESTART CHECKLIST

☐ **TIME**
Four to five hours to cut and install a 16-foot ledger board on a frame house; longer to attach to masonry

☐ **TOOLS**
Layout square, tape measure, level, circular saw, hammer, drill, socket wrench

☐ **SKILLS**
Measuring and cutting boards, testing for level, driving lag screws

☐ **PREP**
Draw the exact location of the ledger on the house

☐ **MATERIALS**
Ledger board(s), lag screws with washers, shims if necessary

Thickness of decking plus 1"

Level line

1 To mark the top of the ledger, measure down from the bottom of the door sill the thickness of the decking plus 1 inch. This small step-down will keep most rain and melted snow out of the house.

2 Using a carpenter's level or a water level and a straightedge, draw a level line on the house siding to indicate where the top of the ledger should be positioned.

REMOVE SIDING
Unlock the siding

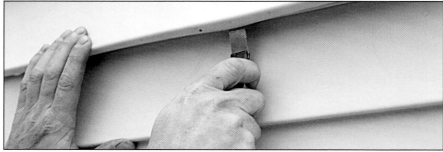

If you're cutting a ledger recess into vinyl siding, you may be able to save some time by unlocking the siding with a zip tool (available from your home center or siding distributor).

If the width of the ledger is the same as a full siding panel (or close to it), unlock the panel, install the ledger, and reinstall siding pieces cut to fit around it.

If the ledger is a different size and you cut the siding, you may be left with corners that you have to remove.

To unlock the siding push the zip tool up between the locking flanges of the siding and slide it along the length of the panel. The tool will push the edges of the flanges apart, allowing you to remove the siding.

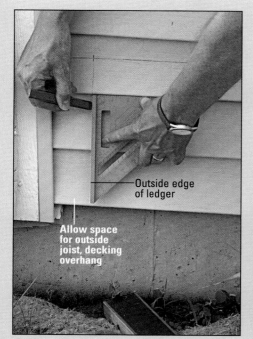

Outside edge
of ledger

**Allow space
for outside
joist, decking
overhang**

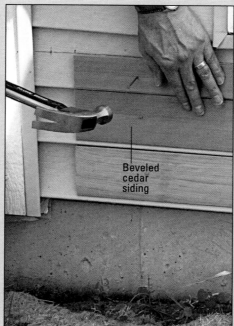

Beveled
cedar
siding

Mark for cutout

3 Mark the outside edges of the ledger on the siding. You may be able to remove siding. If you are cutting the siding, extend this mark 1½ inches (the thickness of the rim joists) past the actual length of the ledger on each side. This will allow you to fasten the rim joists to the ends of the ledger.

4 If you have beveled siding you can cut out a recess for the ledger (below) or if your codes allow it, install beveled cedar siding as a flat backing. Rip-cut the cedar so its thickness matches the thickness of the siding. Attach each piece with a nail every few feet.

5 If there is an existing concrete stairway, your inspector may want you to remove it. If you do not remove it, you'll need to cut the ledger to fit around it. Hold the ledger in place and mark for a cutout so that the ledger will rest on top of the concrete.

Setting a ledger into siding

In many areas it is common to cut and remove a section of siding and then set the ledger inside the cutout. The potential problem with this method is that it exposes the house sheathing, which is not pressure-treated and can rot if it gets wet, even it it's covered with builder's felt. If your inspector requires this method, follow these steps:

■ Cut vinyl or wood siding using a circular saw with the blade set to cut just through the siding and no deeper. (For aluminum siding turn the saw blade backward.)

■ Finish the cuts at the corners using a knife, a chisel, or tin snips.

■ Staple on a layer of 30-pound felt to protect the sheathing.

■ Cut drip-cap metal flashing to fit and slide it up under the siding. The flashing must cover the top edge of the ledger.

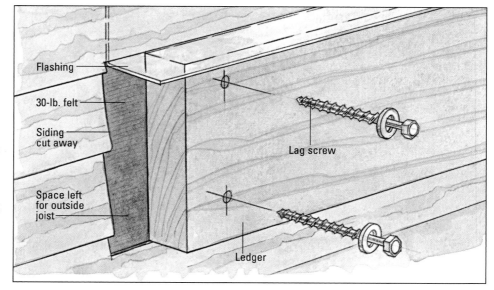

Flashing

30-lb. felt

Siding
cut away

Space left
for outside
joist

Lag screw

Ledger

Anchoring the ledger (continued)

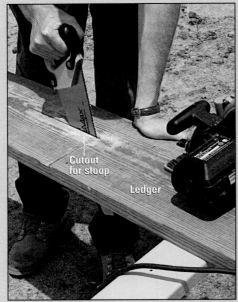

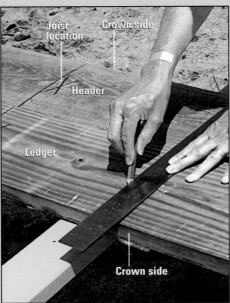

6 Cut the ledger board and the header to length. The header is usually 3 inches longer than the ledger because it's fastened to the ends of the rim joists. If you need to notch the ledger for an obstruction, use a circular saw, stopping just short of the corners. Finish the cuts with a handsaw.

7 Lay the ledger and header next to each other with their crowns (pages 64–65) facing outward and the header overhanging the ledger by 1½ inches on each end. Mark both boards for joists, in this case every 16 inches. Mark a large X on the side of the line where the joist will go.

8 Push a flashing up beneath the siding about an inch. Have a helper or two hold the ledger in place while you drive 3-inch screws to hold it in place temporarily (if working alone, see page 81). Make sure the ledger has its crown side up. Test the ledger for level and adjust if necessary.

WHAT IF...
Your ledger is on masonry?

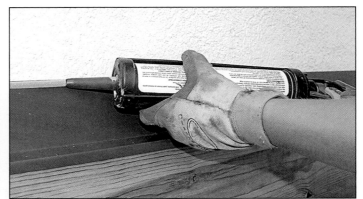

Ledgers installed on masonry surfaces need protection from water. There's no siding on masonry to hold the flashing, so cut a slot for it. Install the ledger and mark the wall about an inch above it (or the width of the flashing less about ⅛ inch).

Tack a level guide board on the ledger so the saw blade will cut on your mark. Using a circular saw equipped with a masonry blade, cut a kerf from one end of the ledger to the other—as deep as the top lip of the flashing. Blow the dust out of the kerf with a shop vacuum and push the lip of the flashing into the kerf until it's seated firmly. Then caulk the top of the flashing with silicone caulk.

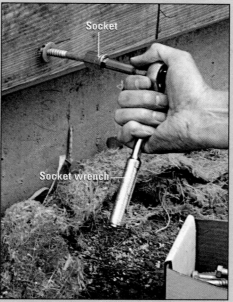

9 Check indoors to make sure lag screws will not hit any gas or water lines or electric cable. Counterbore pilot holes if you want recessed lag screw heads. If possible, avoid your joist marks. Then drill through the ledger only, with a bit slightly smaller than the diameter of the lag screw threads.

10 Use a long bit to bore a smaller hole through the house framing. Slip a washer onto a lag screw and tap the screw partway into the hole. Tighten the screw with a socket wrench, keeping it perpendicular to the ledger.

11 Every few feet along its length, check the ledger's face to see that it is close to plumb. To make adjustments, try tightening one screw. If that doesn't work, loosen both screws, insert a shim at the bottom or top, and retighten.

WHAT IF...
There's a vent in the way?

Almost all homes will present some kind of obstacle where you must install the ledger. The most common will be dryer vents. Before installing the ledger, hold it in place and mark the cutout for the vent. Cut the notch with a jigsaw. Angle the bottom of the cutout so lint doesn't collect.

STANLEY PRO TIP

Check the ledger for flatness

The ledger must be plumb and flat so you can gang-cut the joists. If the joists are all the same length, any waves in the ledger will transfer to the header. If the ledger has no waves larger than ¼ or ½ inch, you can build the outside frame and cut the joists to fit inside it, as shown on pages 120–123. If you have large waves, install the joists, cut them to length, and then install the header as shown on page 166.

LAYING OUT A SLOPED SITE

To locate deck footings when the yard slopes away from the house, you must first measure out from the house along a level line, then down to the ground along a plumb line. This is difficult to do using mason's lines and batterboards. Instead construct the outside frame of the deck, temporarily support and level it, then measure down for the footings.

This method may seem tedious, but actually it will not consume a lot of time. You must build the frame anyway, so you might as well do it now.

Though the supports are temporary, make them sturdy because they need to hold the frame still while you work on it. You will reuse one of the supports later (Step 3, page 142). The 4×4s used as temporary supports can be used later as permanent posts for the deck.

PRESTART CHECKLIST

☐ **TIME**
Four or five hours to build a frame, support it, and measure down to locate the footings

☐ **TOOLS**
Tape measure, framing square, mason's line, hammer, circular saw, drill, sledgehammer, plumb bob, post level, carpenter's level or water level

☐ **SKILLS**
Measuring and cutting boards, fastening with nails or screws, working on a slope

☐ **PREP**
Install the ledger; consult the framing plan to determine the exact dimensions for the outside joists and the header

☐ **MATERIALS**
Joist lumber, 16d galvanized nails or 3-inch deck screws, stakes, 4×4s for temporary supports, 1×4s for bracing

1 Cut the rim joists and the header to length. Lay the pieces on the ground and fasten the rim joists to the header with two or three screws or nails at each joint. Set the frame in position and check it for square, using both a framing square and a 3-4-5 triangle (page 83). To keep the frame from going out of square, screw a 1×4 brace at both corners, driving two screws into each joint. Use scraps of lumber to support the frame near the header so they will be at the same height as the header.

PIER AND BEAM OVERVIEW

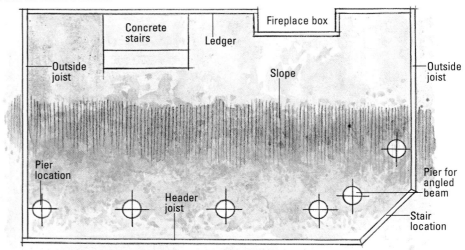

In this plan four posts run in a row parallel to the house. At the angled corner two posts are positioned at a 45-degree angle.

Piers for serious slopes
Codes require at least 7 horizontal feet of soil surrounding the bottom of the footing. If the ground past the footing is strongly inclined, an extra-deep hole may be needed.

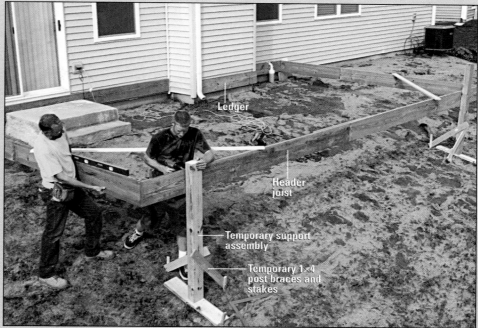

2 To make a temporary support, place a piece of 1× lumber about 2 feet long on the sloped ground. Set a 4×4 post on top of the board, hold it plumb, and use a 2× scrap as a guide to mark its bottom for cutting, as shown. Cut the post and attach it to the board with angled screws.

3 Temporarily brace each support post with 1×4s and stakes. Raise the frame so it is level. Attach the rim joists to the ledger with one screw at each joint. Slide the temporary support assembly up against the header and anchor the support with stakes as shown. Fasten the header to the support post. Estimate the footing locations and install batterboards at both ends of the frame. Attach mason's lines to the batterboards.

STANLEY Pro Tip

Use a plumb bob

Use a plumb bob to position the mason's line so it represents the center of the footings. Measure along the line (or use a spacing jig, page 84) to mark the locations of the footings.

Refresher Course
Installing batterboards

Build batterboards. Make a batterboard out of 1×2 or 2×4 stakes and 1×4 crosspieces. Depending on the hardness of the soil and the slope, cut the stakes 18 to 36 inches long. Assemble the pieces with a single screw at each joint.

Install batterboards and mason's line. Drive the stakes in until solid. Crosspieces should be at least 8 inches above ground. Locate batterboards at 2 to 3 feet beyond the footing locations so they won't get in the way when you dig the holes.

FRAMING

Once you've laid out for the footing holes, follow instructions on pages 112–115 to dig and pour the footings. Footings should be at least 2 inches above grade at all points; on a sloped site they'll stick up higher on the down side of the slope.

Keep things level, plumb, and straight
Take a little extra time to precisely align all the framing members. Double-check posts for plumb and adjust the braces if necessary. When using a mason's line to set a row of posts, keep the line about ⅛ inch away from the posts so the line stays straight. Framing members often get bumped during construction, so go back and check all the posts just before installing the beam, and check the beam just before installing the joists.

PRESTART CHECKLIST

☐ **TIME**
Two days with a helper to install posts, beams, and joists for a medium-size deck

☐ **TOOLS**
Tape measure, hammer, drill, circular saw, handsaw, layout square, chalk line, post level, carpenter's level, mason's line

☐ **SKILLS**
Measuring and cutting boards, checking for level and plumb, following a framing plan

☐ **PREP**
Install the footings with J-bolts and allow the concrete to set; draw layout lines on the ledger and the header

☐ **MATERIALS**
Lumber for posts, beams, joists, blocking, and braces, 16d galvanized nails or 3-inch deck screws, joist hangers, hurricane ties

A. Posts and beams

1 Install post anchors on the footings (page 90). The day before you set the posts, square one end, seal them, and cut them about a foot longer than needed. Install and brace the corner posts plumb in both directions, sealed end down. Align the line posts with the corner posts and brace them.

2 Hold a carpenter's level on top of a straight board. Set one end of the board on top of the ledger and hold the other against an outside post. Draw a mark on the post that is level with the top of the ledger.

FRAMING OVERVIEW

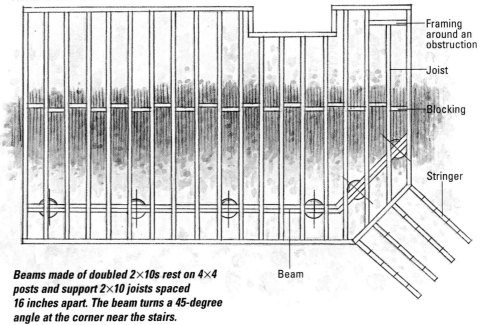

Beams made of doubled 2×10s rest on 4×4 posts and support 2×10 joists spaced 16 inches apart. The beam turns a 45-degree angle at the corner near the stairs.

3 To determine the height at which the post should be cut, measure down twice: Use a scrap piece of joist lumber to measure down the width of the joists and a scrap piece of beam lumber to measure down the width of the beam.

4 Mark the cut line on the corner posts and hold a chalk line between the marks. Then snap the line to mark the interior posts for cutting. For the posts that will support the angled beam, use a carpenter's level to mark for cutting.

5 To cut a post, mark all four sides with a layout square and cut with a circular saw or reciprocating saw. If the post is a 6×6, you'll need to finish a circular saw cut with a handsaw.

REFRESHER COURSE
Beam options

Beams for decks are usually made of 2× lumber rather than a single piece of 4× lumber. (Thick lumber is more prone to crack and warp than two or three 2×s fastened together.)

The simplest method of beam construction is shown on page 94. Just fasten two 2×s together. Drive two or three 10d nails or 2½-inch screws every 16 inches, unless your inspector specifies otherwise. The resulting beam is 3 inches thick, but a post bracket is 3½ inches thick. To make up the difference add a ½-inch plywood shim at the post (page 140).

Beam with spacers. Beams that will be set on posts should have pointed pressure-treated plywood spacers to increase rigidity and allow water and debris to fall through. Locate the spacers 12 to 18 inches apart. Some inspectors prefer a continuous strip of plywood the same width as the 2×s for added strength.

Two-part beam. A two-part beam is made by attaching 2×s to both sides of the posts, then cutting the posts. See pages 163–164 for instructions. Because this method adds lateral stability to the deck, it is often used for second-story decks with long posts.

A. Posts and beams (continued)

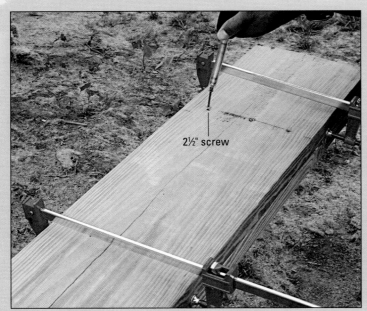

6 Make the beams longer than they need to be (you'll trim them later). Lay one 2× on top of another with the crowns facing the same direction and the cupped sides (page 64) facing each other. To keep the top edges flush, you may need to use clamps. Drive two or three 10d nails or 2½-inch screws every 16 inches unless your building codes have specific fastening requirements.

7 In this deck plan one end of each beam is cut at a 45-degree angle. Cut only this end now; cut the other end after the joists are installed and the frame is squared. Set a circular saw at 45 degrees (test it for accuracy on a scrap). Using a layout square as a guide, cut through one of the boards. Flip the beam over. Use a square to mark the other board with the same angle. Complete the cut.

WHAT IF...
The bracket is wider than the beam?

A beam of two 2×s is only 3 inches thick and the post bracket opening is 3½ inches wide, so add a shim to fill. Set the beams in place and adjust them so they meet properly. At each post, shim with a piece of ½-inch pressure-treated plywood about 4×6 inches.

STANLEY PRO TIP: Brace the beam

You'll prevent problems if you secure the beam as soon as you've plumbed and leveled it— otherwise it's easy to knock it out of position.

Temporarily brace the beam every 6 feet or so. To make a brace, drive a stake about 5 feet away from the beam on the up side of the slope. Anchor a 2×4 brace to the stake. Check the beam for plumb and drive a screw through the brace into the beam.

This is the best time to tighten the nuts that hold the post anchors to the concrete pier. Don't crank down too hard. You might need to refine your adjustments later.

B. Angled corner and joists

Equal distance in both directions

1 The joint where the two beams meet doesn't have to be tight, but the two beams must be on the same level. Wedge a shim above the post of one beam, if necessary. Drill pilot holes and drive screws or nails to fasten the beams to each other.

2 Assemble the outside frame as you did when you laid out the deck (pages 136–137), set it on the beams, and attach the rim joists to the ledger. Check for square, then anchor the rim joists to the beam with screws.

To mark the angled cut line, measure out from the corner an equal distance in both directions. Align a straight 1×4 with both measurements, and mark the header and the rim joist. Transfer the marks to the faces of the boards with a square.

WHAT IF...
Joists must be notched around steps?

Measure from the top of the ledger

Mark for notching joist

2× support

1 If a set of concrete steps is in the way, notch the joists. Cut a joist to length and hold it in place. Level the joist. Steps often slope away from the house, so there may be a gap under the joist. Mark where the joist meets the top of the ledger. Transfer that measurement to the joist where it crosses the edge of the step. Lay out your cut line between these two points.

2 Because the width of the joist has been reduced, it must be reinforced. Cut a scrap piece of 2× lumber to rest on a lower step and come up nearly to the top of the joist. Attach the support to the joist with several screws.

B. Angled corner and joists (continued)

3 Use one of the temporary supports that you made for marking the layout (page 136) to hold up the header; the rim joist rests on a beam. Set a circular saw at 90 degrees and cut the header and the rim joist.

4 Measure between the cuts on the header and rim joist and cut an angled piece to fill the corner. Hold the angle-cut piece in place and drill pilot holes. Attach it with nails or screws.

STANLEY PRO TIP: **Trim beam when framing is complete**

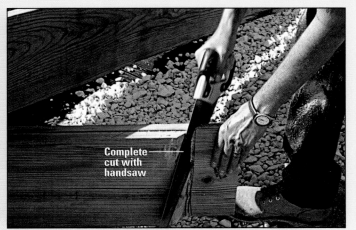

1 Cut partway with a circular saw. Once the framing is complete and you've rechecked it for square, mark the beam ends for cutting. Remove the outside joist so you can make a clean cut. Cut as deeply as possible with a circular saw (this cut is on the angled end of the beam).

2 Complete the cut with a handsaw, because a standard circular saw blade will probably not reach through both boards. If the resulting edge is ragged and unattractive, use a plane or belt sander to smooth it.

5 Cut and install the joists (see pages 122–123) with the crowns up. Attach joist hangers at the ledger. At the header use joist hangers, or drive screws or nails through the header into the joists. To measure for cutting a joist at the angled section, hold it in place and mark it: Have a helper hold one end up against the ledger so that its bottom edge is close to the top of the ledger. While another helper measures to see that the joist is parallel with the next joist, mark the bottom of the joist. Transfer the mark to the face of the joist using a layout square, and cut at a 45-degree angle.

6 Even if you have fastened all the other joists to the header by backscrewing or nailing, use a special skewed joist hanger to attach an angled joist to the header.

WHAT IF...
An obstruction interferes with a joist?

It's common for pipes, vent caps, and other obstructions to stick out of the house at about the same height as the ledger. If a vent falls at the top of a ledger, cut a notch for it (page 135). If the vent falls in the middle of the ledger, remove the vent cap and extend the duct by 1½ inches. Use a hole saw to make a clean circular cut in the ledger, fit the duct through the ledger, and reinstall the vent cap (page 161).

  If the obstacle is in the path of a joist, you'll have to frame around it, as shown at right. Install ledger pieces on either side, taking care that the pieces are at exactly the same height. Install joists on either side of the obstacle, then cut and install a piece of blocking between the joists. Cut a joist to run from the header to the blocking piece.

LAYING THE DECKING

Buy decking boards long enough to span the entire deck so you won't need to make butt joints. If that is not possible, plan the location of the joints. Either place them in an alternating pattern or aim for randomness to hide them. Never place joints side by side. Wherever there will be a butt joint, double the nailing surface by fastening a 2×4 cleat alongside the joist (page 74). To avoid joints consider using a divider strip (below right).

Install the decking with its lengths running wild, but allow enough at the ends for a 1½-inch overhang, 2½ inches if you plan to attach lattice skirting framed by 1× (see pages 178–179).

These pages show installation of cedar decking using nailed spacers. Wet pressure-treated decking (see page 65) will shrink, so install the pieces without spacing. (To install decking at an angle, see pages 124–126; for a pattern that uses a center strip, see pages 168–171.)

PRESTART CHECKLIST

☐ **TIME**
A day to install decking for a 300- to 400-square-foot deck

☐ **TOOLS**
Tape measure, circular saw, chalk line, hammer, nail set, drill, chisel, flat pry bar

☐ **SKILLS**
Cutting with a circular saw, fastening with screws or nails, straightening boards

☐ **PREP**
Check that the framing is completely fastened and that there will be a nailing surface for all decking boards

☐ **MATERIALS**
Decking boards, screws or nails

Crown faces house

Good side up

1 Sort seven or eight decking boards and place them good side up on the framing. Orient each board with its crown facing the house. Choose a straight board for the first one, which in this plan goes up against the house.

2 Snap a chalk line that is the width of a decking board plus ½ inch on the joists. The siding may be a little wavy, so check that the line is at no point closer to the house than the width of a decking board.

Driving nails

Many people like the appearance of a nailhead better than a screw head. However, when driving nails, one wrong swing will make a permanent dent in the decking. Practice on scrap pieces until you get the knack. Aim for a free, easy swing with a fairly loose wrist. Use a hammer with a face that is smooth, not serrated. Finish driving nails with a nail set.

Avoid unsightly joints with a divider strip

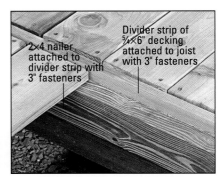

2×4 nailer attached to divider strip with 3" fasteners

Divider strip of ⁵⁄₄×6" decking attached to joist with 3" fasteners

If your deck is longer than 16 feet and you want to avoid unsightly joints, here's a nifty solution: In the center of the deck, attach a piece of decking to the joist using 3-inch fasteners. Attach a 2×4 cleat to the piece of decking. Butt the decking boards up against the divider strip on either side, leaving a ⅛-inch gap for expansion.

3 Cut the first decking board to length; you cannot cut it when you trim the edges (Step 8). Align the board with the chalk line and attach it with only as many fasteners as it takes to keep the board straight; you'll drive the rest later (Step 7). Drive the fasteners into the centers of the joists.

4 Allow succeeding boards to run wild—install them longer than they need to be so you can cut them off later. Use spacers between the boards. Install only as many fasteners as it takes to keep the boards straight; the fewer, the better. Drive the fasteners into the centers of the joists.

5 To bend a warped board, drive a fastener partway into the decking (but not into the joist). Have a helper push the bent board into position and finish driving the fastener. Every seven boards or so, sight along a board or use a line to make sure the decking is straight. Make adjustments if necessary.

Pilot holes near a board end

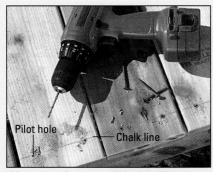

Wherever a fastener will be less than 3 inches from the end of a board, take a few seconds to drill a pilot hole before driving the fastener. Otherwise the board will probably split—a condition that cannot be repaired.

DESIGN OPTION
Invisible deck fasteners

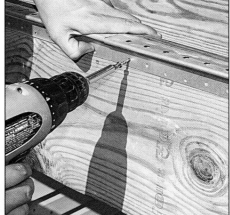

If you don't like the looks of exposed nails or screw heads, deck clips or rail fasteners are made for you. Both of these fastening methods are more costly than screws or nails, and more labor-intensive, but will give you a deck surface that's fastener-free. See pages 72–73 for information on installing these hidden fasteners.

Laying the decking *(continued)*

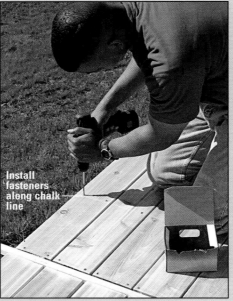

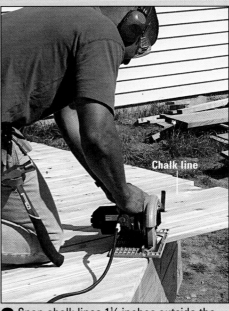

Header

Install fasteners along chalk line

Chalk line

6 When you are within five or six boards of the edge, measure to see whether the last piece will overhang the header an acceptable amount—¾ inch to 2½ inches. If not, you may need to rip-cut the last piece or gradually increase or decrease the spacing to make up the difference.

7 Once all the boards have been installed with the minimum number of fasteners, snap chalk lines over the centers of joists. Drive the rest of the fasteners along the lines. This will produce lines of fastener heads that are straight, with only a few exceptions—a crisp finishing touch.

8 Snap chalk lines 1½ inches outside the framing. Cut the lines with a circular saw. If any waste piece is longer than 16 inches, have a helper support it as you cut. Otherwise it could splinter near the end of the cut. Cut freehand (as shown) or use a guide (see page 126).

Snapping a chalk line

To measure 1½ inches away from the framing, hold a piece of 2× lumber under the decking and mark the decking at both ends of the cut. Have a helper hold the chalk line at one mark while you pull it taut over the other. Lift the line straight up and let go to create a straight line. If the line is incomplete, repeat the process.

WHAT IF...
Your decking needs long notches?

If you have to cut decking to go around a long obstacle, such as a threshold, a step, or the second level of a deck, you may have to cut a long notch.

Begin by holding the board against the outcropping. Mark both sides for the width of the cut. Measure how far the board must travel toward the outcropping (include the spacing between boards). This is the depth of the notch.

To cut the width, make a plunge cut. Set the blade deep enough to cut the board, plus ¼ inch. Retract the blade guard, start the motor, and lower the blade onto the cut line. Cut the face of the board first, just up to the cut lines. Then cut the bottom side, going a little past the cut lines. Finish with a handsaw.

LAYING OUT STAIRWAYS

Designing a stairway can be complicated and confusing. The trickiest part is making sure that all the steps—including the bottom and top steps—are the same height. A professional carpenter might consider the methods shown on the following pages to be slow, but they provide a nearly fail-safe approach for a do-it-yourselfer.

Stair options

The illustration at right shows the components of most deck stairways. A standard set of stairs has rises of about 7 inches and runs of 11 inches, but you may want deeper stairs (see page 101). If the treads will be 2×s, stringers can be spaced as much as 28 inches apart; if you will use decking boards, space stringers 18 inches apart or closer. Interior stringers must be notched; outside stringers may be notched or closed. For each tread use a single 2×12 or 2×10, or use two or more boards spaced as you would decking boards. Risers (see page 173) are not necessary, but they do hide the underside of the deck and offer a more finished look.

PRESTART CHECKLIST

☐ **TIME**
A couple of hours to partially cut a stringer, calculate rise and run, and design a stairway

☐ **TOOLS**
Level, circular saw, tape measure, calculator, framing square with set stops, carpenter's pencil

☐ **SKILLS**
Basic mathematics, measuring and cutting, checking for level

☐ **PREP**
Finish the decking, and decide on the type of landing (if any)

☐ **MATERIALS**
Straight board, 2×12 for the first stringer

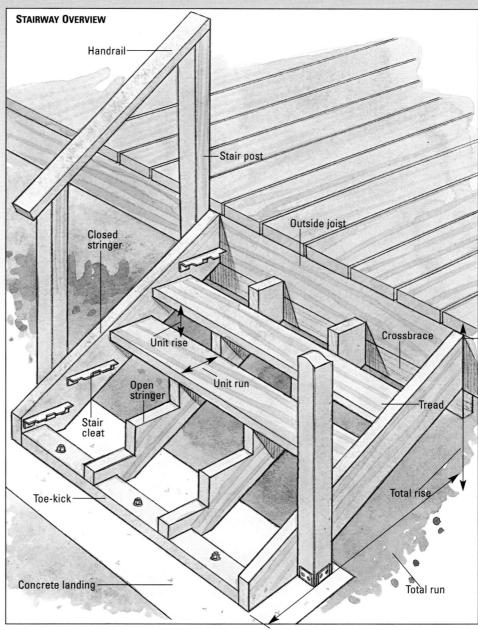

STAIRWAY OVERVIEW

Handrail

Stair post

Closed stringer

Outside joist

Unit rise

Crossbrace

Open stringer

Unit run

Tread

Stair cleat

Toe-kick

Total rise

Concrete landing

Total run

The vertical distance that a stairway travels from the landing pad to the top of the deck is the total rise. The horizontal distance it travels is the total run. The vertical and horizontal distances traveled by each step are the unit rise and unit run.

A landing must be level (even if the yard is not) and may be made of concrete, pavers, or crushed stone. Stringers are the stair's joists,

and these may be either notched or closed, with brackets. Stringers must be firmly attached to the deck; an extra brace (page 172) may be needed. A toe-kick anchors the stringers to the landing pad. Treads— which may be composed of a single board or several pieces—are the parts that you walk on. Optional risers (page 173) cover the vertical spaces between treads.

Laying out stairways *(continued)*

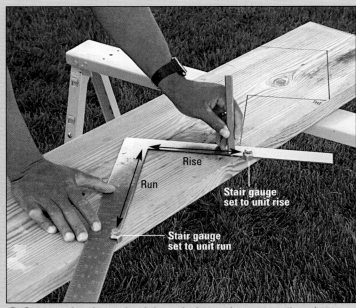

1 If the yard is level, find the total rise by measuring down from the deck to the ground. If the yard slopes, use a level and a long board to extend the deck level out to a point where you estimate that the stairway will end, and measure down from there. Calculate rise and run (page 101). You may decide that you need to move the landing pad closer to or farther from the deck. If so, repeat this step and recalculate.

2 Once you've determined the unit rise and run as well as the number of rises, draw a stringer on a 2×12. A framing square equipped with stair gauges makes this easy. For the top and bottom of the stringer, remember to take the tread thickness into account.

STAIR GAUGES
Marking rise and run

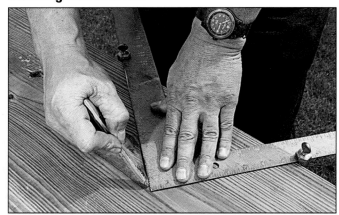

Stair gauges (sometimes called set stops or buttons) clamp to the edges of a framing square. They are especially useful when laying out stringers. Tighten them at the marks for your rise and run and set them against the edge of the stringer. Slide the square up the board as you lay out each step.

WHAT IF...
You want different treads?

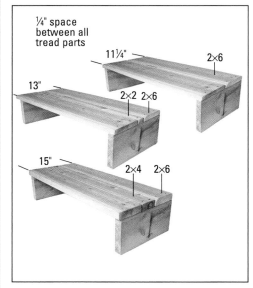

¼" space between all tread parts

11¼" 2×6
13" 2×2 2×6
15" 2×4 2×6

You can use almost any combination of lumber sizes to make treads that meet your specifications. Two 2×6s spaced ¼ inch apart make a tread 11¼ inches deep. Two 2×6s spaced ¼ inch on either side of a 2×4 result in a 15-inch tread. Rip standard sizes for different widths.

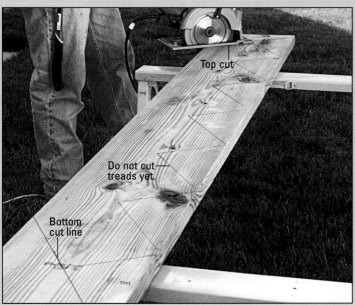

3 Double-check the stringer layout, thinking through how it will go together. The bottom rise should be 1½ inches shorter than the other rises if you are using 2× treads, and 1 inch shorter if you are using ⁵⁄₄ decking for treads. Visualize how the stringer will attach to the deck (see page 153). Cut the stringer at both ends only.

4 Hold the partially cut stringer against the deck in the position where it will be attached. Check that the treads will be level. Mark the ground for the location and height of the landing pad. The landing pad should support the stringers fully and should extend outward a comfortable distance for walking.

WHAT IF...
You want to install the pad later?

If a stairway will not be heavily used, it can end at the yard with no landing pad. Or you can build the stairway first and add a pad under the stringers later. Calculate rise and run as you normally would. Cut the stringers (page 152), keeping them 1 or 2 inches above grade at their bottoms. Temporarily support the stringers at their bottoms, attach them to the deck, and check that they are square to the deck and that their treads are level.

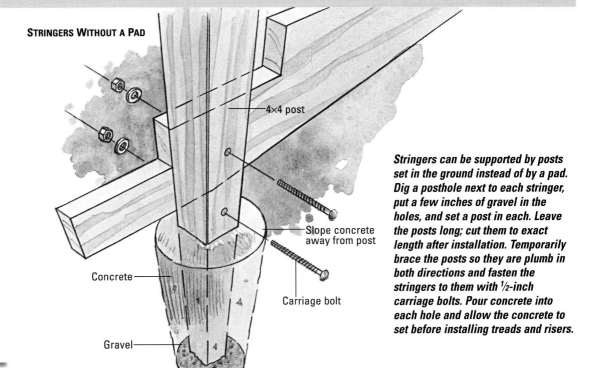

STRINGERS WITHOUT A PAD

4×4 post

Slope concrete away from post

Concrete

Carriage bolt

Gravel

Stringers can be supported by posts set in the ground instead of by a pad. Dig a posthole next to each stringer, put a few inches of gravel in the holes, and set a post in each. Leave the posts long; cut them to exact length after installation. Temporarily brace the posts so they are plumb in both directions and fasten the stringers to them with ½-inch carriage bolts. Pour concrete into each hole and allow the concrete to set before installing treads and risers.

FORMING A CONCRETE PAD

Many concrete patios and sidewalks are less than 2 inches thick and lack metal reinforcing. In areas with freezing winters, they will almost certainly develop cracks. These pages show how to build a long-lasting pad.

A concrete slab may be raised one step height above the yard or an adjacent patio surface, or it can be set just above ground level. If the pad is 75 square feet or smaller, you don't need to worry about drainage. To determine the location and height of a landing for the steps, see page 148. The pad shown here includes two piers to key into its sloped site. Omit the piers for a level site.

Though it may feel solid a few hours after pouring, concrete takes a week or two to achieve full strength. Wait at least three days before exerting heaving pressure on the pad.

PRESTART CHECKLIST

☐ **TIME**
About a day to excavate, build forms, mix concrete, pour, and finish the surface

☐ **TOOLS**
Level, tape measure, circular saw, sledgehammer, drill, hammer, wire cutters, concrete, wheelbarrow, hoe, concrete finishing tools (opposite page)

☐ **SKILLS**
Measuring and cutting, checking for level and square, mixing in a wheelbarrow, smoothing a concrete surface

☐ **PREP**
Determine the location for the pad and remove any sod

☐ **MATERIALS**
Lumber for forms and stakes, gravel, bags of dry-mix concrete, reinforcing wire mesh

1 Excavate topsoil and tamp down about 2 inches of gravel. Cut 2× boards to use as forms for the pad. Fasten them together in a rectangle. Use a framing square to check the corners for square. Fasten the boards to stakes driven into the ground, and check for level and square.

Drive stakes below the top of the form boards

Reinforcing mesh

2 Backfill with soil behind the form boards so wet concrete can't ooze out from the bottom. Cut wire reinforcing mesh to fit and lay it on top of stones so that it will be near the center of the pad's thickness when you pour the concrete.

FORMING AND POURING A CONCRETE PAD

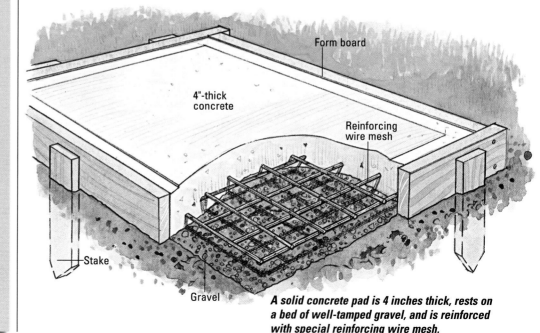

Form board
4"-thick concrete
Reinforcing wire mesh
Stake
Gravel

A solid concrete pad is 4 inches thick, rests on a bed of well-tamped gravel, and is reinforced with special reinforcing wire mesh.

Screed board

3 Mix the concrete (pages 88–89) and pour it into the forms. Using a board long enough to reach from form to form, screed the surface: Drag the board, using a side-to-side motion as you move it across the length of the pad. Repeat until the surface is fairly level and has no low spots.

4 Using a wooden, steel, or magnesium float (shown below left), smooth out the entire area. With the float held nearly flat, lightly scrape across the pad in long, sweeping arcs. As you work, water will rise to the top. Keep smoothing as long as the surface is wet. Once it has started to dry, lightly drag a broom across it to create a nonslip surface.

Concrete finishing tools

Magnesium float

Mason's trowel

Edger

These three tools are all you need to finish a small concrete pad. A magnesium float is easier to use than a steel or wooden float and is more than adequate for smoothing the concrete before giving it a broom finish (see Step 4 above).

5 Slip the point of a mason's trowel between the form and the concrete and slice all around the pad to a depth of 1 to 2 inches.

Edger

6 Run an edger around the perimeter to round off the corners. This will prevent chipping. Press lightly and repeat until the corners are smooth. Let the concrete set for a day, then pry away the forms.

BUILDING THE STAIRS

Once you've determined the rise and run and installed a landing pad, you're ready to build the stairs.

Stairs have to withstand plenty of use, so choose lumber that is straight and free of knots and other defects. Pay extra for Select or No. 1 lumber. Some lumber dealers sell 2×12s specifically approved for use as treads or stringers.

If you accidentally break a step off a stringer, drill pilot holes, apply exterior grade polyurethane glue, and drive screws or nails to reattach it.

The full width of the stringers must be firmly attached to the deck framing. Usually the outside or header joist is not deep enough, so you need to install a 2×6 or 2×8 brace directly below. This may require some improvising. Build out from the beam or from the posts so that the brace is as strong as the joist above it (see pages 172–173).

PRESTART CHECKLIST

☐ **TIME**
Once the landing is finished and the layout calculated, four to five hours to cut and install stringers, a toe-kick, treads, risers, and rail posts for an eight-step stairway

☐ **TOOLS**
Tape measure, level, hammer, drill, circular saw, handsaw, framing square, layout square

☐ **SKILLS**
Cutting 2× lumber at angles, fastening with nails or screws

☐ **PREP**
Complete the crossbrace, lay out and cut either end of a stringer, and install the landing

☐ **MATERIALS**
2×12 for stringers, 2× lumber or decking for treads, 2×4 toe-kick, 4×4 posts, post anchors, angle brackets, screws or nails, masonry screws

1 Test the partially cut stringer (page 149) to make sure it fits between the deck and the landing with the tread lines level. With a circular saw, cut each line. Don't cut farther than the intersection of the tread and riser lines.

2 Finish the cuts with a handsaw or a saber saw. Take care not to bump the resulting teeth of the stringer. Use the first stringer as a template for laying out the others (page 103).

REFRESHER COURSE
Notching for a toe-kick

The bottom of an inside stringer rests partly on the slab and partly on the 2×4 toe-kick (page 147). Use a circular saw and handsaw to cut a notch 1½ inches high and 3½ inches deep.

WHAT IF...
You want a cleated stringer?

To make a closed stringer, make only one cut at the bottom and one at the top. Draw lines indicating both the bottoms and tops of the treads. Drill pilot holes and attach the tread cleats with 1¼-inch lag screws.

3 Attach a crossbrace directly below the rim or header joist and anchor the stringers to the brace. The tops of the notched stringers (and the metal cleats on closed stringers) must line up so a tread can rest across all of them. Square the stringers to the deck with a framing square, and anchor them with angle brackets.

4 Slip a 2×4 toe-kick under the inside stringers and against the insides of the outside stringers. Drill holes through the toe-kick; then drill holes into the landing using a masonry bit. Fasten the toe-kick to the landing with bolts and anchors or masonry screws. Drill angled pilot holes and drive screws or nails to attach the stringers to the toe-kick.

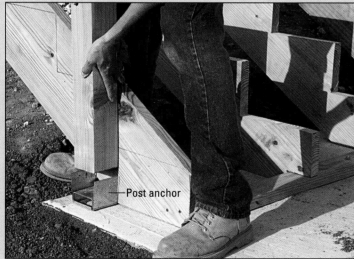

5 Attach a post anchor to the landing where the post is at the full width of the stringer. (Use the epoxy-and-threaded-rod method shown on page 116.) Fasten the post to the anchor. Plumb the post and drill a hole for a carriage bolt through the post and stringer. Be sure the carriage bolt will not interfere with the tread or tread hardware. Tap the bolt through and fasten it with a washer and nut.

6 If the outside stringers are notched, cut the treads so they overhang 1½ inches on each side. If you are using closed stringers, cut treads to fit between them. Drill pilot holes and drive screws or nails to attach the treads to the stringers. Use three fasteners per joint for a 2×12 or 2×10 tread, two fasteners for narrower boards.

ADDING THE RAILING

A railing is one of the most visible parts of a deck, so choose lumber that is free of cracks and splinters. After the railing is installed, sand all the corners smooth.

Assembling the parts

Draw your design and double-check the sizes and measurements. In this railing the post length equals the height of the railing above the deck plus the decking thickness, plus the joist width, minus the thickness of the cap rail. The baluster length equals the height of the railing above the deck minus the gap between the bottom of the railing and the deck (about 2 to 3 inches), minus the thickness of the cap rail.

Check codes for these requirements:
- The minimum height of the railing.
- Allowable baluster spacing.
- How the posts attach to the framing.
- The maximum space between the bottom of the balusters and the deck.

You may be able to buy precut balusters and posts that fit your design requirements.

PRESTART CHECKLIST

☐ **TIME**
Working with a helper, about a day to build a railing for a medium-size deck

☐ **TOOLS**
Tape measure, hammer, drill, circular saw, power mitersaw, jigsaw, clamp, post level, ratchet and socket wrench

☐ **SKILLS**
Accurate measuring and cutting, fastening with nails and screws

☐ **PREP**
Finish the framing and the decking

☐ **MATERIALS**
4×4s for posts, 2×4s for bottom and top rails, 2×2s for balusters, decking or 2×6s for rail cap, screws or nails, carriage bolts with washers and nuts, lag screws

A. Installing the post

Jig for length of post

1" from post side

1 Posts are as long as the height of the railing, plus the width of the joist and the thickness of the decking, minus the thickness of the rail cap. Set up a jig that allows you to cut all the posts to the correct length. A 22½-degree angle cut on the bottom adds a decorative touch.

2 Mark for two holes in the posts that are each 1 inch from opposite sides of the post and 1½ inches from the top or bottom of the joist. Drill holes the same diameter as the carriage bolts you will use (Step 4). Staggering the holes avoids splitting the post along the grain lines.

RAILING OVERVIEW

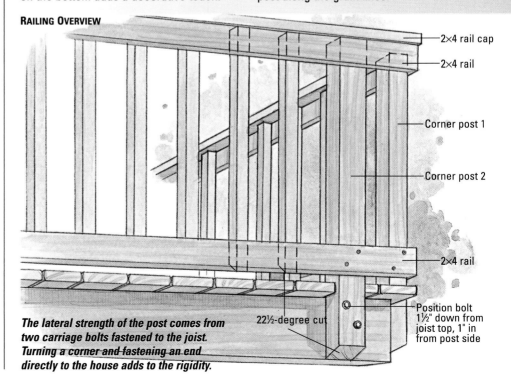

- 2×4 rail cap
- 2×4 rail
- Corner post 1
- Corner post 2
- 2×4 rail
- Position bolt 1½" down from joist top, 1" in from post side
- 22½-degree cut

The lateral strength of the post comes from two carriage bolts fastened to the joist. Turning a corner and fastening an end directly to the house adds to the rigidity.

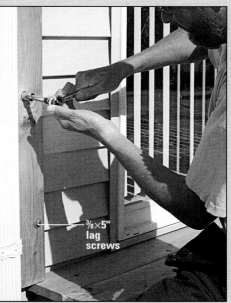

3 For each post cut a notch in the decking so the post can fit tightly against the joist. Use a professional-quality jigsaw for this—it's difficult to cut straight with a cheap model. Cut the notches with ⅛ inch of play to allow for expansion and so you won't have to force the post in.

4 Clamp the post so it is plumb in both directions. Drill into the existing holes and through the joist. Tap carriage bolts all the way through. Under the deck, slip on a washer and tighten a nut for each bolt.

5 Where the railing meets the house, use 5-inch lag screws and washers to firmly fasten a 2×4. This is stronger than a 4×4 post attached to the deck.

WHAT IF...
You want notched posts?

Notched posts take time and experience to cut, but make a pleasing finishing touch for a deck railing. They draw the baluster up closer to the deck edge and make a slightly firmer joint than surface-mounted posts.

Mark the posts for a notch that is 1½ inches deep and as long as the depth of the joist—about 7½ inches for a 2×8 joist, about 9½ inches for a 2×10. (Use a joist scrap to be exact.) Add the thickness of the decking and mark for the crosscut.

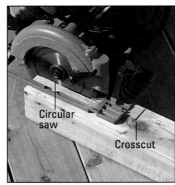

Cut the notch
Make a crosscut where the notch ends. With the saw set to maximum depth, cut the long lines on each side without cutting beyond the crosscut. (For a corner post, set the blade to a depth of 1½ inches and make two long cuts.)

Chisel away the excess
Use a hammer and chisel to crack out the waste—it will neatly pop out as one piece. Then chisel away the remnant where the saw blade could not reach.

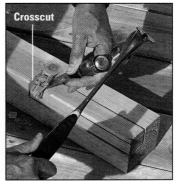

Complete the corner post
Make the long cuts and a shallow crosscut. Chisel toward the crosscut and split out the waste. Chisel down along the crosscut and along the long cuts to remove the remnant of wood remaining.

B. Installing the deck railing

1 Measure and cut pieces for the bottom rail. At an outside corner, hold two pieces in place and mark for a cut. You could miter this corner, but a miter joint might come apart in time. A basic butt joint is safer.

2 Measure and mark the proper space between the bottom rail and the deck (check local building codes). Position the bottom rail; drive two nails or screws into each post. Install the top rails, top edges flush with the post tops. Drive two 3-inch fasteners where rails join at the corner.

3 Make a simple jig that supports the end of the baluster and stops it at the correct length. Test the jig to make sure your measurements are correct, then gang-cut the balusters as needed.

Adding the stair railing

2×4 spacer

3" deck screw

1 For the top stair rail, hold a 2×4 against the top and bottom posts, parallel with the stairway. At the top, mark the rail for an angled cut. Still holding the stair rail in position, mark the lower rail post (Step 2) for an angled cut.

2 Use a layout square and T-bevel to mark lines around the rail post. Set a circular saw blade to a depth about ¼ inch more than the thickness of the post, and cut both angled lines. Have a helper hold the post, gently lifting upward as the cut is finished.

3 Cut the bottoms of the stairway balusters at 22½ degrees—just like the deck balusters. Then hold a baluster plumb against the angled railing, and mark the top angle. Gang-cut the balusters and fasten them in place using a scrap 2×4 spacer.

4 Use a jig like this to space and plumb balusters and position them at the right height. Check for plumb at every fifth baluster. Make incremental adjustments in the next few balusters as needed. Attach each baluster with one 3-inch screw or nail driven into the top and bottom rails.

5 Install the rail cap so it overhangs the top rail and post by equal amounts on each side of the posts. Drive two 2½-inch fasteners into each post and one every 2 feet or so into the top rail.

6 At a corner make a precise miter joint where two pieces of cap rail meet. First, on one of the boards, cut the mitered end only, and let the other end run wild. Check the fit of the miter. If the fit is good, cut the other end of the cap rail. Drill pilot holes and drive screws to draw the joint tight.

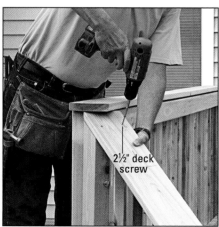

4 Where the stairway rail cap meets the deck rail cap, hold a board in position and mark it alongside the post for a bevel cut. Adjust the angle on a circular saw and experiment on scraps until it is right. Attach the cap rail with 2½-inch screws.

WHAT IF...
Finials will be added?

Typically, finials are placed above each post. Once the cap rail is in place, bore a hole ⅛ inch narrower than the double-threaded screw that comes with the finial. Twist the screw into the predrilled hole in the finial with pliers. Apply exterior-grade polyurethane glue to the bottom of the finial and twist it into the cap rail.

STANLEY PRO TIP

Secret to a tight miter

Corners are seldom perfectly square; that's why even a well-executed miter joint will gap. To close the gap, clamp or tack the mitered cap rail in place. Then cut through the miter as shown. Push the pieces together and fasten for a perfect miter joint.

Two-Level Deluxe Deck

Wide Stairs & Pergola

This deck has attractive features that are easy to build. The decking of the upper level sports an eye-catching chevron pattern. The stairway is extra wide—ideal for party seating. At one end of the deck, a pergola (an overhead trellis) combines with a lattice screen to increase privacy.

Framing
While the basic structure of this deck is similar to the others in this book, one difference is the beam: It is made of two 2×s bolted to both sides of the posts. This type of beam is generally easier to build than the beams shown in the other two decks, which rest on top of the posts.

Decking, stairs, and railing
A single strip of decking runs parallel to the house in the center of the upper level area. The other decking boards run at 45-degree angles and butt against the center strip. This method calls for extra framing—two rows of blocking—but once the center strip is installed, it's fairly easy to lay the rest of the decking.

Wide and deep stairs require more stringers and tread pieces, but the construction techniques are similar to those used in the basic stairs shown on pages 152–153. The attractive paver landing is actually easier to build than pouring a plain concrete slab.

Each railing post is made of four pieces of 2× and 1× lumber. This is more complicated than installing simple 4×4s but requires only basic carpentry skills. The result is a decorative post that is less likely to crack than a solid 4×4. Once the posts are set, the balustrade sections can be built as modules, then attached between the posts for an upgraded look.

Pergola and trellis
A pergola made of several layers of beams, rafters, and top pieces is easy to build as long as you follow the step-by-step instructions. Trellis material comes in easy-to-cut 4×8 sheets and can be fastened in less than an hour.

Extra features often require no special skills and only a little extra time to build.

Chapter Preview

Laying out the site
page 160

Installing the beams
page 162

Installing the joists
page 165

Decking with a center strip
page 168

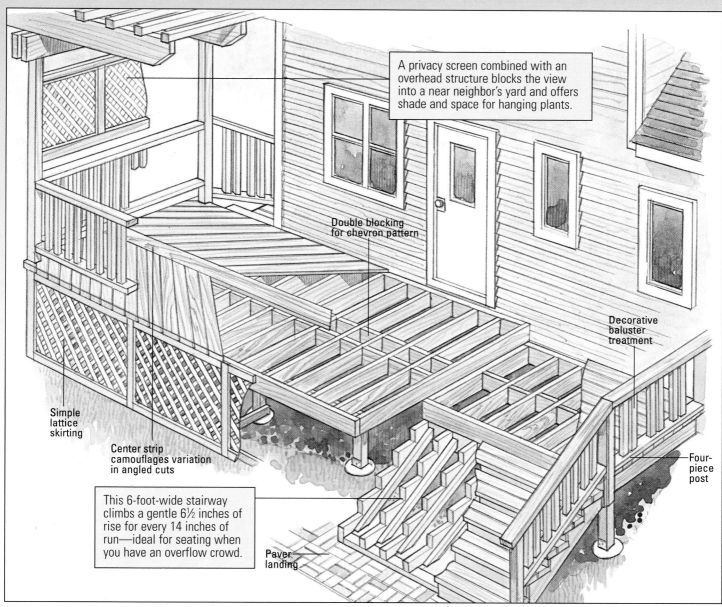

A privacy screen combined with an overhead structure blocks the view into a near neighbor's yard and offers shade and space for hanging plants.

Double blocking for chevron pattern

Decorative baluster treatment

Simple lattice skirting

Center strip camouflages variation in angled cuts

Four-piece post

This 6-foot-wide stairway climbs a gentle 6½ inches of rise for every 14 inches of run—ideal for seating when you have an overflow crowd.

Paver landing

This is the most complicated deck in the book, packed with attractive features such as the extra-wide stairway, chevron-patterned decking, privacy screen with an overhead structure, and decorative skirting. Building these features requires only basic skills and a modest amount of additional time.

Building deep and wide stairs
page 172

Installing the railing
page 174

Building the pergola
page 176

Adding skirting
page 178

LAYING OUT THE SITE

A concrete slab runs alongside this house—a fairly common situation. In some cases you can lay joists directly on top of a slab. However, a slab is probably no more than 4 inches thick, so it cannot support posts.

The first step is to install one ledger for each level. (See pages 132–135 for complete instructions.) Place the ledger 1 inch plus the thickness of the decking below the bottom of the door sill. If the house has beveled siding, cut the siding or shim it with cedar siding so that the ledgers will be vertically plumb (page 133).

The footings and posts for the upper level are set into the ground beyond the slab; see pages 108–111 for using batterboards to lay out the site. The photos at right show layout for the lower-level post, which will be set on piers that go through the slab.

PRESTART CHECKLIST

☐ **TIME**
Once the ledger is installed, several hours to build batterboards, run string lines and check them for square, and mark the slab for the footing locations

☐ **TOOLS**
Tape measure, hammer, sledgehammer, carpenter's level, drill, chalk line, mason's line, a jackhammer if a concrete patio is in the way

☐ **SKILLS**
Building batterboards, measuring, checking lines for square

☐ **PREP**
Install the ledger boards

☐ **MATERIALS**
1×2 and 1×4 for batterboards, a straight board, deck screws

1 Use a plumb bob or carpenter's level to reference down from the edge of the ledger to the slab. (Note that the shims are 1½ inches longer than the ledger to accommodate the thickness of the rim joist.) To draw a line exactly perpendicular to the house, lay a straight board on the slab, and use a 3-4-5 triangle (page 83) to square it with the foundation. Draw a line on the slab along the edge of the board. This line indicates the edge of an outside joist for the lower level.

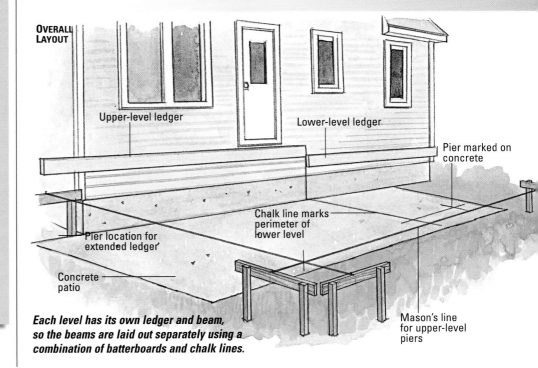

OVERALL LAYOUT

Each level has its own ledger and beam, so the beams are laid out separately using a combination of batterboards and chalk lines.

Plumb from post location marked on ledger

Mason's line

Jackhammer

2 Snap chalk lines on the slab indicating the outside of the joists. Measure from those lines to locate the footings. Check and recheck your work.

Outside of joist

Center of pier

3 Where the ledger runs past the house, reference down with a carpenter's level or a plumb line and use batterboards and mason's line to mark the footing locations.

4 Rent a jackhammer to cut holes in the concrete slab to accommodate the footings. Make the holes a few inches wider than the tube forms.

WHAT IF ...
A vent must go through the ledger?

If a vent must run through the ledger, remove the vent cap and its tailpiece. If the vent does not fall between joists, you may need to frame out to make room for the vent (see page 143). Measure for the center of the hole and use a hole saw to cut the hole. Hole saws can bind and buck; practice with the tool before cutting the ledger board. You may need to attach a longer pipe to the vent cap before replacing it.

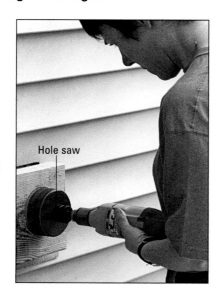

Hole saw

REFRESHER COURSE
Fastening a ledger

Attach the ledger with a pair of lag screws about every 16 inches. The screws must be long enough to go through the entire thickness of the framing member behind the siding (page 135). Place the screws where they will not get in the way of the joists, and counterbore the holes if you want to recess the heads.

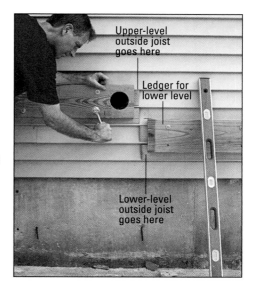

Upper-level outside joist goes here

Ledger for lower level

Lower-level outside joist goes here

INSTALLING THE BEAMS

Form and pour the footings with J-bolts and allow the concrete to cure for 48 hours. Install post anchors and install posts that are a foot or so taller than they need to be (see pages 116–117). Plumb the posts using a post level and brace them firmly with 1×4s so they won't move when they get jostled during beam construction.

Building a two-part beam
Some inspectors prefer an on-top beam made of two 2×s fastened together (pages 118 and 140) because the resulting beam is actually stronger than the sum of the two parts. Others prefer the two-part beam shown on these pages because attaching to the sides of the posts adds stability. Most inspectors will accept either type of beam. Confirm local requirements.

PRESTART CHECKLIST

☐ **TIME**
With a helper, about six hours to measure and cut posts, build two beams, and install the beams

☐ **TOOLS**
Tape measure, post level, carpenter's level, hammer, drill, bit for installing carriage bolts, circular saw, mason's line, handsaw, clamp, layout square, adjustable wrench or socket and ratchet

☐ **SKILLS**
Measuring and cutting, checking for level and plumb

☐ **PREP**
Install and anchor the posts

☐ **MATERIALS**
Lumber for beams, 16d galvanized nails or 3-inch deck screws, 7-inch carriage bolts with washers and nuts

1×2 block

Mason's line

1 Check that the ledger is straight using a mason's line and two 1×2 blocks. If it has waves of ½ inch or less, install the outside joists and header first, then add the inside joists. If the ledger has major waves and you install the header now, you will have to measure joists individually. Also see the method on pages 165–167.

Mark for location of bottom of beam

2 Rest one end of a straight board on the ledger and have a helper check for level as you mark a corner post. From this mark, measure down the width of the joists to mark the top of the beam. Repeat for the other corner post.

BEAM AND LEDGER OVERVIEW

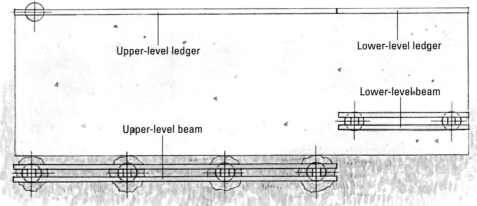

Upper-level ledger

Lower-level ledger

Lower-level beam

Upper-level beam

Four piers sunk into the yard support the beam for the upper level, while two piers cut into the slab support the beam for the lower level.

3 Measure down the width of the beam stock and attach a temporary brace to each corner post to support the beam pieces as you work.

4 Cut two beam pieces to length and mark them for post locations (see below). Put a beam piece on the temporary brace with its crown side up and adjust it until it is level. Temporarily fasten it at the end opposite the brace with a 3-inch screw. Install the second member on the other side of the post. Double-check that the beam is at the correct height to support the joists.

STANLEY PRO TIP: **Mark for post locations**

To avoid awkward measuring as you install the beams, clamp them together and mark the location of each post. Strike a line with a square and mark an X to indicate the location of the posts. Let the end of the beam run long a few inches. It can be trimmed once you are satisfied with the joist locations.

Decorative beam cuts

If the end of a beam will be visible, cut a 45-degree angle in the bottom of each piece for a more attractive look. Before making the cut, make sure the crown side is facing up.

Installing the beams (continued)

Carriage bolt

Socket wrench

Extended bit

5 Clamp the beam members tightly against the posts. Attach the second piece in the same way as the first. Counterbore the inside face of the beam if you want to recess the bolt nuts. Using an extended drill bit, drill two holes for the carriage bolts through the beam members and the post.

6 Tap 7-inch carriage bolts through the holes. Make sure the bolt heads face the outside of the deck; they look more finished than the nuts.

7 Slip a washer and turn a nut onto each bolt. Tighten the nut with a ratchet wrench. It's a good idea to use a deep socket or an extension on the wrench to avoid banging your knuckles on the beam.

STANLEY PRO TIP: **Cutting the post**

Reciprocating saw

Remove nut and washer and drive bolt back to make cut on this side

With a reciprocating saw. Cut the post flush with the tops of the beam pieces. (The decking will be uneven if the post sticks up even a little.) One method is to use a reciprocating saw. Don't worry if you gouge the beam; it will be covered.

Or with a circular saw... Adjust the blade on a circular saw for as deep a cut as possible and cut two sides of the post. Retract the blade guard and use the top of a beam piece as a guide for the blade.

...and handsaw. Finish the cut with a handsaw. If part of the post is a little too high, use a belt sander or file to level it off.

INSTALLING THE JOISTS

The joist installation method shown on these pages—attaching all the joists to the ledger and cutting them to length later—works when the ledger is not straight (see Step 1 on page 162 to check the ledger).

Before attaching a joist to the ledger, check that the end is square and that there are no splits or cracks. If you find a flaw, cut off about an inch or turn the board around and install the other end (if it is square and unflawed) onto the ledger. Make sure each joist is installed with its crown facing up.

If the ledger is straight, install the rim joists and header first and check them for square. Cut all the inside joists to the same length and install them with joist hangers (pages 122–123).

Check with your local building department to see whether codes require hanger nails or screws.

PRESTART CHECKLIST

☐ **TIME**
With a helper, about 4 to 5 hours to install 20 joists and a header

☐ **TOOLS**
Tape measure, hammer, drill, circular saw, chalk line, layout square

☐ **SKILLS**
Measuring and cutting boards, driving screws or nails, and attaching joist hangers

☐ **PREP**
Install the ledger and the beam, check the ledger for straightness, and draw layout lines on the ledger (page 134)

☐ **MATERIALS**
Joists, joist hangers, screws or nails

Temporary cleat

Joist hanger

1 Screw a temporary cleat to the top of a joist, extending outward about an inch. Rest the cleat on the ledger. Align the joist with the layout lines, install a joist hanger on the ledger, and fasten the joist to the hanger.

1×4

2 Check that the outside joists are square to the ledger. Transfer the layout lines on the ledger to a long 1×4. At the other end of the joists, temporarily attach the 1×4 to the joists so they are spaced correctly.

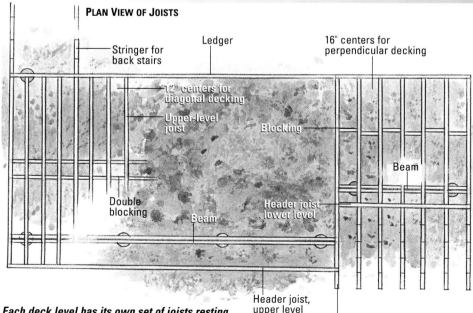

PLAN VIEW OF JOISTS

Stringer for back stairs

Ledger

16" centers for perpendicular decking

12" centers for diagonal decking

Upper-level joist

Blocking

Beam

Double blocking

Beam

Header joist lower level

Header joist, upper level

Stringer, main stairway

Each deck level has its own set of joists resting on its own ledger and beam. It is not necessary to fasten the two levels together; when the decking is installed, the structure will be stable.

Installing the joists (continued)

3 When the joists are installed and evenly spaced, measure out from the house and mark the top of both rim joists for cutting. Remember that the header thickness will add 1½ inches to the length of the framing, and that the decking will overhang the framing by another 1½ inches. Snap a chalk line between the marks. Check that there is a clear line on top of every joist.

Use a layout square to mark a cut line on the side of every joist (see Step 7). Each cut line must meet the chalk line precisely.

4 Cut each joist with a circular saw. Vertical cutting is a bit tricky, so practice on scrap pieces first. You may cut freehand or with a layout square or scrap of 1× clamped on as a guide. Cutting down lets the weight of the saw do the work; cut upward if it seems more comfortable.

STANLEY PRO TIP

Use a header support

It's difficult to hold a header precisely in place while driving screws or nails. Screw a scrap piece of wood to the underside of the outside joists to support the header as you work.

5 Cut the header to length—usually 3 inches longer than the ledger. With a helper, hold it up against the joists and drive 3-inch screws or 16d galvanized nails to attach it to an end joist. Attach to the other joists in the same way. Make sure the top of the header is flush with the top of the joists.

Mark line midway between the ledger and the beam

6 To mark the joists for blocking, snap a chalk line across the top of the joists. Blocking is usually installed midway between the ledger and the beam.

7 At each chalk line, draw a square line down both sides of the joist. Cut blocking pieces 1½ inches shorter than the joist spacing to fit between the joists. For instance, if joists are 16 inches on center, cut 14½-inch-long pieces. For 12-inch centers use 10½-inch blocking pieces.

8 Unless you have a special reason to line the blocking pieces in a straight row (see below left), install the blocking in staggered fashion to make fastening easier. Drive two or three screws or nails through the side of each joist.

WHAT IF...
Blocking pieces double as nailers?

Sometimes blocking is needed to provide a nailing surface for the decking. This deck's design calls for a center decking strip with angled pieces that butt against it. Two straight rows of blocking, 6½ inches apart, are needed to support the ends of the angled decking pieces. When using blocking to support decking, take special care that the top of the blocking is perfectly flush with the tops of the joists; if blocking is even ⅛ inch lower or higher than a nearby joist, the decking surface will be uneven.

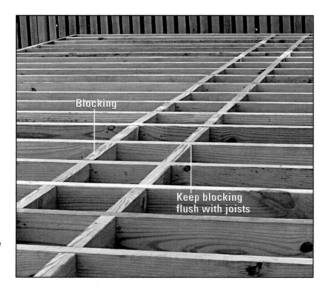

Blocking

Keep blocking flush with joists

STANLEY PRO TIP

Measure blocking

Every few blocking pieces, check that the joists are correctly spaced. You may need to cut a blocking piece a little short or long to bring the joists back into alignment.

DECKING WITH A CENTER STRIP

If you attempt to install angled decking boards that meet at their miter cuts, expect a struggle. Decking boards may vary in width by as much as ¼ inch, making it very difficult to maintain perfect joints. If the spacing between boards varies or one board bows slightly, the joint will gap. The project is much more manageable if you install a center strip and butt the miter cuts against it.

This pattern has another advantage: Because you end up with two relatively narrow sections of decking, most of the boards that run between the house and the center strip will be exactly the same size. The boards that run from the center strip to the outside of the deck can be miter-cut on one end only; let the other end run wild, then snap a chalk line, and cut the ends.

PRESTART CHECKLIST

☐ **TIME**
About eight hours to cut and install angled decking with a center strip for a 300-square-foot deck

☐ **TOOLS**
Tape measure, hammer, drill, circular saw, layout square, power mitersaw, chalk line

☐ **SKILLS**
Making consistently accurate 45-degree miter cuts, fastening with screws or nails

☐ **PREP**
Install framing with two parallel rows of blocking

☐ **MATERIALS**
Decking boards, nails or screws

¼-inch plywood spacer

Center strip

1 Temporarily attach a strip of ¼-inch plywood against the house to act as a spacer. Choose a particularly straight decking board to use as the center strip. Position it midway between the rows of blocking and measure at various points to make sure it is exactly parallel to the house. (If the deck section between the strip and the header is slightly narrower or wider than the section between the strip and the house, that will not be noticeable.) Double-check that the board is straight, and fasten it with two screws or nails driven into each joist.

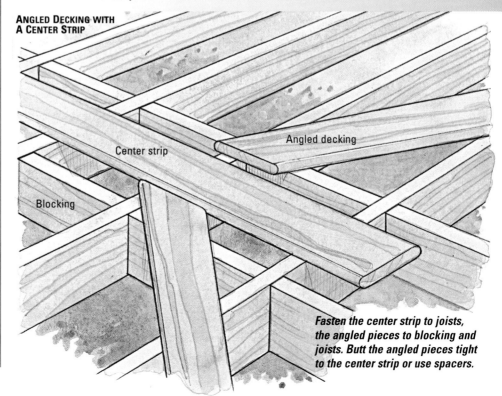

ANGLED DECKING WITH A CENTER STRIP

Angled decking

Center strip

Blocking

Fasten the center strip to joists, the angled pieces to blocking and joists. Butt the angled pieces tight to the center strip or use spacers.

Distances are equal when board is at 45 degrees

2 Practice with a power mitersaw (shown above) or circular saw until you are sure you can make precise 45-degree cuts in all the decking boards. Set up the work site for comfort and ease so that making these cuts is routine.

3 Miter-cut the end of one board and hold it in position on the deck with one end resting on the center strip. Measure from the corner of the resulting triangle in two directions, as shown above. When the measurements are equal, the board is at 45 degrees to the house. There should be a space of about ⅛ inch between the center strip and decking. Subtract the ⅛ inch when marking the boards or just cut to the good side of the mark instead of the waste side. The saw blade will remove about ⅛ inch.

Cut miters with a circular saw

With practice and a professional-quality circular saw, you can make accurate 45-degree miter cuts with little trouble. Test your skills on scrap pieces of wood and don't try cutting actual decking boards until you are sure of your skills. First, try holding a layout square with one hand while cutting with the other hand. If you find that the blade guard refuses to retract, try clamping the square as shown at right so you can retract the guard as you work.

STANLEY PRO TIP

Make a 45-degree cutting jig

A jig like this makes it possible to cut accurate 45-degree miters with a circular saw. Cut off the corner of a piece of plywood so that you have an equilateral triangle with each side of the triangle about 11 inches long. Drive three screws to fasten the cut side of the triangle to a piece of 1×. Use clamps to help hold the jig firmly on the board to be cut.

Decking with a center strip (continued)

4 Place the decking board in position with one end pressed against the plywood spacer at the house and the other end against the center strip. Use nails to space the miter-cut piece slightly away from the center strip. Measure again to see that the board is at a 45-degree angle to the house. Sight down the length of the board to see that it is straight. Fasten it with as many nails or screws as needed to keep the board straight.

5 For boards on the other side of the center strip, miter cut one end only. Use a layout square to make sure that the first board on this side is directly across from a board on the house side. Check that the board is straight and fasten it with as many fasteners as needed to keep it straight.

REFRESHER COURSE
Check the boards

Before purchasing decking, make a scale drawing to plan the most efficient use of available lengths (page 124). Make a list of the lengths needed, adding 10 or 15 percent for waste and rejects. You can cut back that margin if you handpick the decking, but allow at least 5 percent for mistakes and defects that you might miss. If you handpick the boards, look for defects such as crooks, twists, splits, loose knots, wane, and cupping (page 64). Confirm that at least one side is smooth and shows minimal defects. On the site, store the decking flat, away from moisture—in a sheltered area if possible.

DESIGN OPTION
Trimming the edges

1 Trim along the edges of the deck adds a decorative detail with just a little extra work. Make your own trim by ripping ¾-inch pieces from your decking stock.

2 Fasten the trim to the ends of the decking with two 8d finish nails into each decking board. Countersink each nail with a nailset. Cut scarf joints where two pieces meet.

6 Once some full-length pieces are installed, measure for the shorter pieces on the house side; these must have miter cuts on both ends. For each piece, cut one end at a 45-degree miter. Place the board in the position where it will go, with one end pressed against the plywood spacer and nails used as spacers along its length. Mark the board for the miter cut on the other end.

7 Let the boards on the other side run wild. Once all the boards are installed with as many fasteners as needed to keep them straight, snap a chalk line 1½ inches out from the header joist and cut along the line. Tack a long, straight board as a guide to ensure a straight cut. Once the decking is trimmed, strike a chalk line at each joist and drive the rest of the fasteners (page 146). Drill pilot holes before adding fasteners near the ends of boards (page 145).

3 Whenever you get to the end of a trim piece predrill it, or insert the nail in your cordless drill and drill the nail in.

4 At the corners of the deck, miter the trim at 45 degrees and fasten it with finishing nails in predrilled holes.

WHAT IF...
You need to eliminate small pieces on a step?

Despite the best-laid plans, you may end up with an awkward piece at the wrong spot—like a step. If varying the spacing won't solve the problem, make a large piece of decking using a biscuit joiner or dowels and exterior adhesive. Rip-cut the decking edges for a smooth joint.

BUILDING DEEP AND WIDE STAIRS

Stair treads that are 14 inches wide make a graceful transition to the lawn and provide comfortable places for people to sit and relax.

For advice on calculating and building a stairway, see pages 100–103. Stairs with 14-inch runs (tread widths) should have rises of between 5½ and 6½ inches.

The wider the treads, the more total run the stringers have to span. When you notch stringers, you weaken them. After the notches are cut out of these 2×12 stringers, about 5½ inches of uncut width is left for strength—in other words, the stringers are as strong as 2×6s. These stringers have to span a distance of about 9 feet, which is close to the limit for a 2×6 joist (see the chart, page 68). So 2×4 cleats were added for extra strength (Step 7).

PRESTART CHECKLIST

☐ **TIME**
Most of a day to install a set of stairs like those shown

☐ **TOOLS**
Tape measure, circular saw, handsaw, hammer, drill, framing square

☐ **SKILLS**
Calculating rise and run for a stairway, measuring and cutting with a circular saw, fastening with nails or screws

☐ **PREP**
Review pages 100–103 of this book

☐ **MATERIALS**
2×12 for stringers, pavers, sand, and edging for the landing pad surface, decking for the treads, 2×4 toe-kick, lag screws with masonry anchors

Crossbrace

1 Install a crossbrace directly beneath the joist to provide adequate surface for attaching the stringers. Connect the brace firmly to posts or the beam so it is just as strong as the joist above it.

Framing square

Stair gauge set to unit rise

Stair gauge set to unit run

2 Calculate rise and run and mark a stringer using a framing square. Cut the top and bottom of the stringer and hold it in position to determine the location and height of the landing pad (page 101).

STAIRWAY OVERVIEW

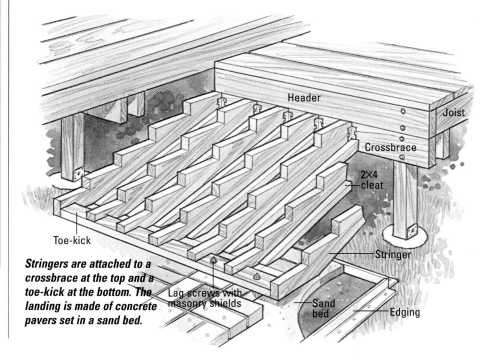

Header

Joist

Crossbrace

2×4 cleat

Toe-kick

Stringer

Lag screws with masonry shields

Sand bed

Edging

Stringers are attached to a crossbrace at the top and a toe-kick at the bottom. The landing is made of concrete pavers set in a sand bed.

Crushed
limestone

Edging

3 To construct a paver landing pad, excavate the site. Install several inches of crushed limestone and tamp it firm. Install edging and check that the corners are square.

Sand

4 Spread 1 or 2 inches of sand over the limestone and screed it with a straight board to form a level surface that is lower by one paver's thickness than the finished height of the pad.

Paver

5 Set the pavers on top of the sand. If you need to cut any pavers, use a rented masonry saw. You may be able to avoid cutting pavers by adjusting the position of the edging. When the pavers are laid, sweep extra-fine sand into the joints; tamp firm and repeat.

Inside stringer notched around toe-kick

6 Cut the stringers. Notch the inside stringers for the toe-kick. Attach the stringers at the top to the crossbrace. Anchor the toe-kick to the pad using lag screws and masonry anchors.

2×4 cleat

2×4 overhang gauge

7 Attach the stringers to the toe-kick by toe-fastening with 3-inch deck screws. To add extra strength, attach a 2×4 cleat to the side of each stringer. For each step install the riser board first, then the tread boards. Clamp a scrap 2×4 to the side of an outside stringer to help maintain a consistent 1½-inch overhang. For treads you can use two full-width decking boards and one board rip-cut to a narrower width.

INSTALLING THE RAILING

For a small amount of time and money you can build a distinctive and handsome railing. This railing design is a variation on the one shown on pages 154–157; see those pages for complete instructions on planning and assembling a basic railing.

None of the steps in building this railing requires special woodworking tools or skills. All the pieces can be cut with a circular saw, though a power mitersaw or a radial-arm saw will make the job easier. The pieces are attached with screws or nails; fancy joints are not needed.

The post is made of 2×4s and 1×4s that in combination are much less likely to develop cracks than a standard 4×4 post. A built-up post also lends a handcrafted appearance to the deck.

Consult local building codes to determine the required overall height of the railing and how far apart the balusters must be.

PRESTART CHECKLIST

☐ **TIME**
Working with a helper, a day to construct about 60 feet of railing

☐ **TOOLS**
Tape measure, hammer, drill, circular saw, layout square, post level, ratchet and socket wrench

☐ **SKILLS**
Measuring and cutting boards, laying out for consistently spaced balusters, fastening with nails or screws

☐ **PREP**
Determine post locations and notch the decking to accommodate (page 155)

☐ **MATERIALS**
2×4, 1×4 for posts; 2×4 for top, bottom rails; 2×6 or ⁵⁄₄ decking for rail cap; 4-inch lag screws; 2- or 3-inch deck screws or nails; angle brackets

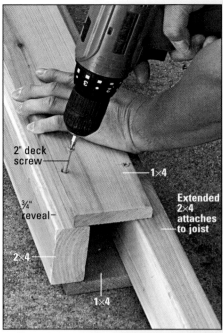

1 To make a regular post, cut two 1×4s and one 2×4 to the height of the railing, minus the thickness of the rail cap. Cut another 2×4 to the same length, plus the combined width of the outside joist and the decking thickness. Fasten by drilling pilot holes and driving screws or nails.

2 Make a corner post with three 2×4s and one 1×4. Use a scrap of 1×4 as a guide for the ¾-inch reveal along the edges of the boards. Join 2×4s with 3-inch deck screws.

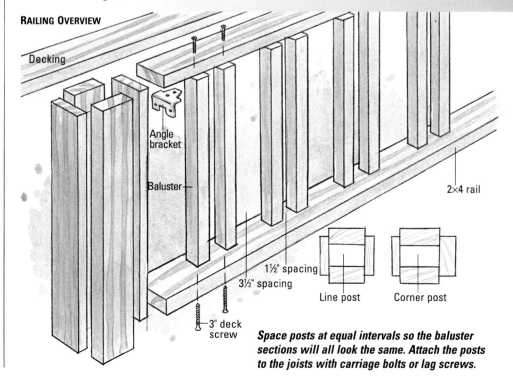

RAILING OVERVIEW

Space posts at equal intervals so the baluster sections will all look the same. Attach the posts to the joists with carriage bolts or lag screws.

3½" spacing

1½" spacing

Post
level

¾ decking to
center
balusters

3 For each post, notch the decking so the longer 2×4 can attach tight to the joist. Position the post with the short boards resting on top of the decking. Hold the post plumb, drive pilot holes, and attach with lag screws or carriage bolts.

4 Measure the distance between the posts and cut two 2×4 rails to fit. Mark on the rails for balusters that are evenly spaced; you may choose a paired pattern as shown— an alternating spacing of 1½ inches and 3½ inches. Set the rails on a flat surface, and lay two pieces of decking as spacers next to them so that the 2×2 balusters will be centered within the width of the rail. Attach the balusters to the rails with one screw or nail driven into each joint.

Toe-fasten
bottom rail

Two 2×4 scraps
hold section 3"
above deck

Angle
bracket

5 Set some 2×4 scraps on the deck to temporarily hold the baluster section up so its top is flush with the tops of the posts. Slip the baluster section into place and clamp it. Drill angled pilot holes and drive nails or screws as shown.

6 Reinforce the top rails with angle brackets. Attach a rail cap to the top of the railing as shown on page 157. One advantage of this approach is that the whole railing section can be removed for future maintenance—especially helpful if you choose to paint it.

BUILDING THE PERGOLA

This structure may look complicated, but taken step-by-step it is easy to build. The most difficult part is working above your head, so have a pair of stable stepladders on hand and enlist a reliable helper.

Because only one row of posts is used in this design, the pergola can be no wider than 6 feet. For more shade install at least two rows of posts with beams. Use 2×6s for beams and rafters that span up to 8 feet, and 2×8s for beams or rafters with spans of up to 11 feet.

The detailing of the pergola can be changed easily to suit your taste. Choose a simple or ornate design for the ends of the beams and rafters (see box on opposite page). Position the top pieces closer for more shade, farther apart for less shade.

PRESTART CHECKLIST

☐ **TIME**
Working with a helper, most of a day to build a three-tiered overhead with a lattice panel

☐ **TOOLS**
Tape measure, hammer, drill, circular saw, post level, carpenter's level, layout square, ratchet and socket wrench, sandpaper

☐ **SKILLS**
Measuring and cutting boards, checking posts for plumb, fastening while working on a ladder

☐ **PREP**
Notch the decking so that posts can go tight up against the outside joist

☐ **MATERIALS**
4×4 posts, 2×6 rafters, 2×8 beams, 1×2 for top pieces; lattice, 2×4 and 2×2 frame for lattice; hurricane ties; 1½-inch, 3-inch screws

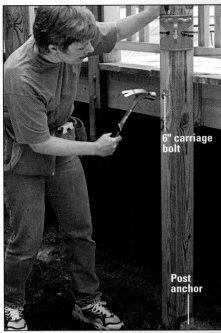

6" carriage bolt

Post anchor

1 Cut posts to the desired height, and anchor them so they have lateral strength. In this case, posts are bolted to a joist and attached to a post anchor on a concrete patio. If you set posts in holes, cut them to height after the concrete sets.

Mark for positioning rafters

Overhang mark

2 Cut the rafters to the same length, and mark them for the distance they will overhang. Clamp them together with their crowns facing up; lay out and mark them for the installation of top pieces.

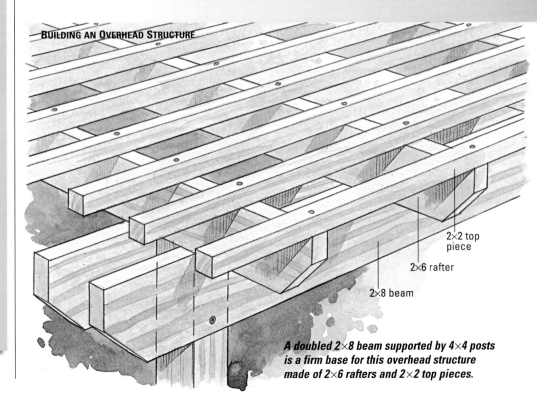

BUILDING AN OVERHEAD STRUCTURE

2×2 top piece

2×6 rafter

2×8 beam

A doubled 2×8 beam supported by 4×4 posts is a firm base for this overhead structure made of 2×6 rafters and 2×2 top pieces.

3 Cut two 2×8 beams to the same length. Hold them together with their crowns facing up, and lay out on their tops for rafters that are evenly spaced. To hold the rafters, install hurricane ties on one beam where they will be least visible. Attach the beams to the posts with 3-inch deck screws.

4 Center each rafter on the beams, using the overhang mark made in Step 2. Attach each rafter with a hurricane tie on one beam and by toe-fastening screws into the other beam. Cut 2×2 top pieces to length. Mark for a 6-inch overhang at each end. Attach the top pieces to the rafters with 3-inch screws or nails. Sand any rough edges with medium-grit sandpaper.

WHAT IF...
You want an ornamental touch?

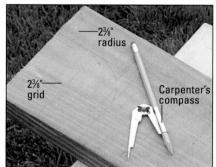

Experiment with a compass to come up with two or three curves as shown. If you wish to mimic an element of your house, you may be able to trace the design on a piece of cardboard and then transfer the design to the board. Cut one board and use it as a template for marking the others.

5 Cut 2×4s to span from post to post, and install them by drilling angled pilot holes and driving screws or nails. To provide a nailing surface for the lattice, attach a 2×2 nailer flush with the inside edges of the 2×4s and the 4×4 post.

6 Cut a lattice panel to fit inside the frame and attach it to the nailers with nails or screws. Cut pieces of 2×2 and install them tightly to the lattice so that the lattice is sandwiched between two pieces of 2×2.

ADDING SKIRTING

If a deck is raised high enough that you can see under it, you may want to cover the framing and footings with skirting.

Unless you live in a dry climate, make sure the skirt provides enough ventilation that the area underneath can dry out between rainfalls. If you install skirting made of solid 1×s instead of lattice, leave at least ½-inch spaces between the boards. The vinyl lattice shown here is ideal—it won't rot and it requires no painting.

Making it strong enough

If the skirt will be less than 2 feet high and in a low-traffic area, attach it to the joist leaving its bottom edge unsupported. For a skirt that can withstand bumps from a lawn mower or errant soccer ball, frame along the bottom: Tie the horizontal piece at the bottom to the posts under the deck, keeping it at least ¾ inch above grade. Use only pressure-treated lumber.

If you want to use the space under a deck for storage, frame one of the skirt sections with 2×4 or 1×4. For occasional access attach the section with screws that can be removed. If you need access often, install hinges and a latch.

PRESTART CHECKLIST

☐ **TIME**
About a day to frame and install about 40 feet of lattice skirting

☐ **TOOLS**
Tape measure, post level, drill, hammer, circular saw, handsaw, square, string

☐ **SKILLS**
Improvising a framing plan, cutting boards, fastening with screws or nails

☐ **PREP**
Choose a skirt material that suits your needs, estimate materials for framing

☐ **MATERIALS**
2×4 for framing, lattice panels or other skirt material, 1×2 or 1×4 for trim, ⅞-inch roofing nails, 2- or 3-inch deck screws or nails

Doubled 2×4 vertical skirting support

Facing 2×4

Rear 2×4 support

2×4 horizontal support

Spacer, ¾" above grade

1 Make a vertical support by cutting one 2×4 so it reaches from behind the joist down to ¾ inch above grade. Cut a facing 2×4 to extend from the bottom of the joist to the top of the horizontal support. Plumb the support; attach the pieces with 3-inch screws. Install the horizontal pieces.

2 Attach outriggers to the horizontal framing members. Notch each outrigger so it fits over the horizontal 2×4. Use a mason's line to check that the horizontal 2×4 is straight. Install all the outriggers with two 3-inch screws or nails in each joint and into the posts.

OVERALL SCHEMATIC OF SKIRT AND FRAME

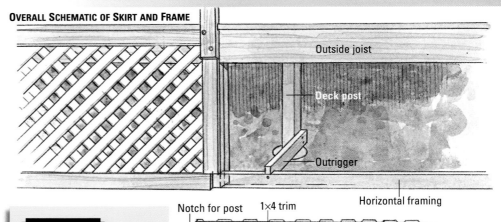

Outside joist

Deck post

Outrigger

Horizontal framing

Notch for post   1×4 trim

STANLEY PRO TIP

Add screen to keep pests out

To help prevent wasps and other insects from building nests under the deck, staple window screening to the back side of the lattice before installing it.

Framing pieces will show through the lattice, so place the vertical 2×4s where you can attractively cover them with trim boards.

1×4 trim

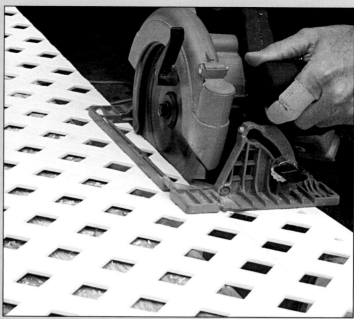

3 At an outside corner, attach two outriggers to hold the horizontal 2×4s firmly. Cut the end of a horizontal piece with a handsaw. The 1×4 trim will overlap at the corner. If the horizontal 2×4 follows the grade, decide whether the lattice and trim also should follow the grade. It may be best for appearance to level the lattice and trim even if some of the horizontal 2×4 will show. (Hide it with plantings.)

4 Lay the lattice on scrap pieces of lumber so you have a stable edge for cutting. Mark the lattice for cutting using a chalk line or a framing square and pencil (a drywall T square is even better if you have one). Cut the lines with a circular saw, setting the blade so it extends ¼ inch beyond the lattice.

5 Notch the lattice to fit tightly along the sides of the railing posts. All other lattice edges will be covered by 1×4 trim, so cut the lattice about ¼ inch short for easy installation. Buy ⅞-inch galvanized roofing nails to fasten the lattice in place. Use just enough nails to keep the lattice from sagging—the 1×4 trim will actually support it.

6 Install the trim of your choice. In this example, 1×4 is used—1×2 would work as well. Start by installing the horizontal trim, fastening it into the bottom 2×4 frame and the outside joist with two 2-inch fasteners every 18 inches. Beneath the deck posts, add trim to cover the vertical skirt frame. Finally add trim under the decking. Just a portion of the joist will show through the lattice.

CUSTOM TOUCHES FOR YOUR DECK

Building any of the basic decks featured in this book will provide an outdoor living space that you can enjoy for years. You can go one step (or a couple of them) further, however, and increase the usefulness of the deck and your enjoyment of it.

Almost every aspect of deck structure can be added to, modified, or improved to make it more stylish and useful. Take a pergola, for example, which provides both shade and an attractive visual accent. It's shown in its most basic form, attached with two posts to one of the deck joists, on pages 176–177. On a larger structure this construction method may not be adequate. You might need more shade, your design or site might prohibit a side-mounted structure, or you might just want something more elaborate. The four-post overhead on page 182 fills the bill.

Perhaps your site doesn't offer enough privacy. The screen on pages 186–187 might solve your problem. Maybe you can't find commercial seating and furnishings that meet your tastes and help you separate one deck space from another. In that case look at the built-in benches on pages 188–189.

Those projects and others in this chapter will help you customize your deck, providing you with design elements and structures that will enhance the appearance and practicality of your outdoor living space.

Like all aspects of good design, it's best to integrate these projects into your new deck from the start. But you can build almost all of these projects as retrofits if you want to upgrade an existing deck. You may have to remove some decking boards to add a four-post overhead,

or dig footings and add additional posts for a privacy screen, but the extra effort will be worth it.

What's most important in both a new deck and an upgrade of an old one is that you build your enhancements so they appear to be an integral part of your deck and the landscape, reflecting your tastes and lifestyle. Details that define the overall style of your deck should be carried into the new structures. If you use cedar for your decking and railings, use cedar for your seating, too; pressure-treated lumber will look out of place. You can hide the new look of fresh wood in a retrofit by staining and sealing it to match the old. And if an old railing never looked quite right in the first place, you can replace it with a new style and use the old lumber elsewhere in your landscape for planters or benches.

These enhancements will make a new or old deck more useful and enjoyable.

CHAPTER PREVIEW

Four-post overhead
page 182

Privacy screen
page 186

Built-in benches
page 188

Outdoor kitchen
page 190

Low-voltage deck lighting
page 192

A four-post overhead shades the deck and looks great at the same time. You could add a pair of sturdy beams across the top to provide hanging points for a porch swing if you like, or enclose three sides with lattice panels to make a cozy nook.

Framing for special circumstances
page 194

Other decking patterns
page 197

Custom railings
page 198

Access ramp
page 202

Expanding a deck
page 204

Storage and hatches
page 205

FOUR-POST OVERHEAD

If your deck is small and your overhead will span its entire surface, you can support its upper structure with posts extended from the railing system. In this configuration use through posts supported in footings (pages 162–164). To simplify construction and save time and money, use a single-post corner instead of a double-post design. In all other cases a four-post overhead will have at least two posts supported by the decking and the framing under it.

In a new deck, plan the location of the posts and include specific details of the support structure in your detailed plans. Retrofitting an old deck requires some forethought too. You'll have to remove a portion of the decking (page 211) to gain access to the joists.

Overhead structures do not have to support a live load, but use the live-load span tables (page 68) when computing the size of the lumber anyway. That way you won't have to worry that the upper structure will sag under its own weight. Many overheads use a doubled 2× beam fastened to the sides of the posts. This construction is strong enough to support the structural load and avoids unattractive framing connectors. Use carriage bolts and countersink the nuts for a better look.

PRESTART CHECKLIST

☐ **TIME**
About 12 hours for a 10×12-foot overhead, more with decorative cuts

☐ **TOOLS**
Tape measure, speed square, circular saw, framing square, framing hammer, chisel, ladder, cordless drill

☐ **SKILLS**
Measuring, cutting, fastening

☐ **MATERIALS**
2×, 4×, and 1× lumber, carriage bolts, machine bolts, washers, nuts, fasteners

Supporting interior posts

1 Mark the centerline of the post on the top edge of both joists that will hold the post support. Measure the space between the joists and cut a 4×4 brace to fit. Set the brace in place, flush with the top of the joists and centered on the lines. Keep it on the marks by clamping the joists against it. Drill lag-screw pilot holes through the joists and slightly into the center of the brace. Then drive the lag screws in with a socket wrench. Cut 2×4 cleats (4 to 5 inches wide) and screw them into both joists on either side of the 4×4 brace. The cleats add stability to the brace. Retighten the lag screws.

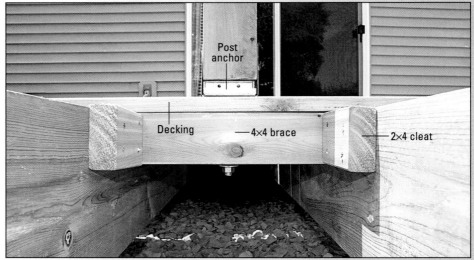

2 Mount the interior posts after installing the decking board that covers the 4×4 brace, but before the adjacent board. This allows you to reach the nut on the bottom of the bolt. Drill through the decking at the post location (or through the center of the 4×4 brace from below) with a bit the same size as the machine bolt. Set the post anchor in place and push the bolt through the hole. Tighten the bolt fingertight. Install, plumb, and brace the post and tighten the nut. Then finish attaching the decking up to the next post location.

Mounting the posts

Let post height run wild

1×4 bracing

Carriage bolts

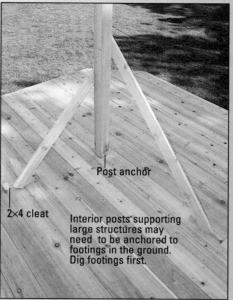

2×4 cleat

Post anchor

Interior posts supporting large structures may need to be anchored to footings in the ground. Dig footings first.

1 Snap chalk lines on the decking to outline the layout. Set corner posts unless you already have through posts. Notch the posts and decking if necessary (see page 155), or set the post flush with the corner. Fasten the post to the outside joist with carriage bolts, and brace it plumb.

2 Set interior posts into the post anchors and brace them temporarily with 1×4s fastened to the joists on open decking or 2×4 cleats tacked to the deck surface. Square the post with a 3-4-5 triangle (page 83), tapping the anchor to adjust it. Tighten the anchor and plumb the posts.

3 When the posts are plumb and braced securely, mark a corner post for the top of the beam (in a sandwiched-beam construction) and mark the height on the other posts with a level. Transfer the marks to adjacent sides of the posts and cut them with a reciprocating saw.

WHAT IF...
You want ornamental rafters or beams?

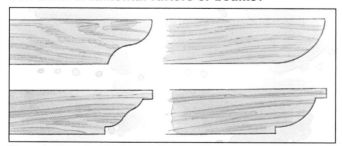

The ends of overhead rafters and beams have a great potential for helping you express the personality of the structure. Experiment with the pattern by sketching designs.

When you've settled on a design, draw it carefully to full scale on graph paper. Use french curves, the bottom of a can or jar, coins, or a compass (page 177) to draw curves. Trace the curves onto the ends of a rafter or beam, and cut the ends with a jigsaw. Smooth the contours with a rasp or similar tool, then use the cut rafter or beam as a template to draw the curves on the remaining pieces. Cut the ends, and sand them smooth.

DESIGN OPTION
Add gussets for strength and looks

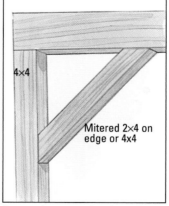

4×4

Mitered 2×4 on edge or 4x4

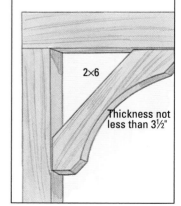

2×6

Thickness not less than 3½"

Gussets have two functions: They help stabilize the structure and add to its appearance. How you design and cut your gussets will have a great deal to do with the style of your overhead. You can mount the gussets on the interior surfaces of the framing or miter them for a cleaner look.

Mounting the posts (continued)

Bolt

Temporary cleat

Fasten corners with brads

1×4 trim

Spread thin bead of construction adhesive here

4 Measure down both sides of the post to the depth of the beam and mark this point. Tack a temporary cleat onto the post at the line to help you steady the beam as you raise it. Or miter 2×2 collars and finish-nail them at the marks. Counterbore one beam to recess the bolt nuts. Clamp the beams together and predrill both of them for the bolts. Clamp the beams to the posts, drill the holes through them, and fasten the bolts. Then install the remaining roof structure.

5 Add trim around the post bases to hide the anchors. Miter-cut one end of a 1×4 trim piece and hold it in place against the post and anchor. Mark the intersection of the other post face on the opposite end of the trim, and miter-cut the end. Apply a thin bead of construction adhesive along the miters, and finish-nail the trim to the post. Drive 1½-inch brads into the mitered corners, then countersink the nailheads and fill the holes. Sand the filler smooth when it dries.

DESIGN OPTION
Notched-roof arbor

2×2 collar

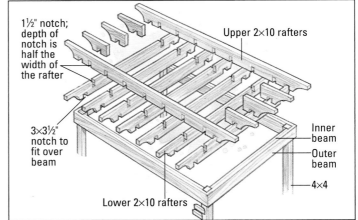

1½" notch; depth of notch is half the width of the rafter

Upper 2×10 rafters

3×3½" notch to fit over beam

Lower 2×10 rafters

Inner beam

Outer beam

4×4

Construction of this arbor is simple, relying on decorative end pieces to enhance its design. The lower rafters should span no more than 80 inches between the beams. Top the rafters with lattice to increase shade. Climbing vines will increase the shade, too, and will soften the edges.

Notched 2×10 rafters span the arbor in one direction, tied together by two perpendicular rafters slipped into notches near the figured ends. Short notched decorative sections balance the design.

Lattice-roofed shelter

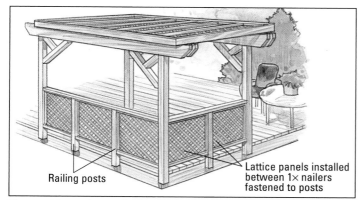

Railing posts

Lattice panels installed between 1× nailers fastened to posts

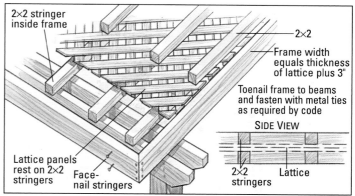

2×2 stringer inside frame

2×2

Frame width equals thickness of lattice plus 3"

Toenail frame to beams and fasten with metal ties as required by code

SIDE VIEW

Lattice panels rest on 2×2 stringers

Face-nail stringers

2×2 stringers

Lattice

The post-beam base of this arbor supports a framed lattice roof, offering plenty of shade to a deck in harsh sunlight. The lattice filters the sunlight and casts patterns whose shapes change as the sun moves across the sky. Lattice railing panels increase privacy and unify the design. Lattice comes in two thicknesses— ¼ inch and ¾ inch. The thicker stock resists warping.

Set the posts first. For a small arbor, build the roof frame, hoist it, and fasten it to the rafters. On a large structure, miter-cut the frame pieces and toenail the side frames to the beams. Then fasten the frame ends to the sides. Cut 2×2 stringers to fit inside the frame and face-nail them to the frame with their bottom edges on the beams. Cut lattice panels to fit, and fasten them in place with 2×2 stringers across the top.

You want to attach the overhead to the house?

Through-posts double as railing posts on a small deck

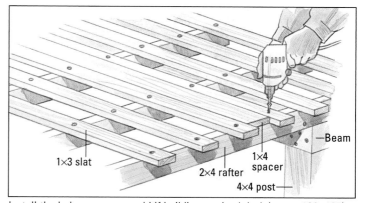

1×3 slat

2×4 rafter

1×4 spacer

4×4 post

Beam

This slat-roofed awning uses a 2×4 ledger to support one end and posts at the other. You can attach the posts to the header as shown here, or to the field of the decking if you only need to cover part of your outdoor space. This design allows more flexibility in the use of space, effectively creating what feels like a separate area under its roof.

Install the ledger as you would if building a raised deck (pages 132–135). Then plumb and brace the posts to the header or deck surface. Face the posts with 1×4 trim or leave them unfaced. Install the beams. Toenail the rafters to the ledger and the beams at 16-inch intervals (closer if you want more shade). Screw the 1×3 slats to the rafters, using a 1×4 as a spacer.

PRIVACY SCREEN

The easiest privacy structure to build is a lattice screen. Lattice blocks the view but is open enough to keep you from feeling closed in. You can grow vines on it and it fits into almost every landscape.

You can construct a lattice screen as a deck railing or as a fence in the yard.

As a deck railing, attach posts to the deck—either with through-posts at the corners and taller rail posts in between, or tall rail posts throughout. You'll need to dig post holes and set posts for a detached lattice fence. Just make sure that the fence line is square to the landscape feature of your choice. If its function is to provide privacy to the deck, it should be square to the deck, no matter how far away it is.

Lattice is prone to warping, so buy the thicker ¾-inch stock and support sections 6 feet long and longer with vertical battens fastened at half the width of the bay (the space between posts). Lattice frames look better in smaller 4- to 6-foot bays.

PRESTART CHECKLIST

☐ **TIME**
About three hours per 6-foot bay

☐ **TOOLS**
Tape measure, framing square, speed square, cordless drill, circular saw, 4-foot level, concrete tools for fence

☐ **SKILLS**
Measuring, cutting, fastening, digging

☐ **PREP**
Lay out and set footings for a fence

☐ **MATERIALS**
Posts, lattice, nailers, fasteners, concrete and forms for fence footings

1 Square the bottom of the posts and fasten them to the rim joist or header, making sure they are secure and plumb. Measure the width of the bay at the bottom (it might be different from on top) and toenail the bottom rail in place between the posts. Make sure it's level. Install the remaining bottom rails. On bays 6 feet and wider, fasten 4×4 braces to the rim joist to support the bottom rail and keep it from sagging. Measure the length of the top rail, scarf-cutting it so joints are centered on the posts. Fasten the top rail to the top of the posts and a cap rail to the top rail.

WHAT IF. . .
You want to dress up the railing?

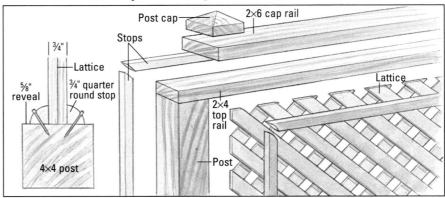

A few details will make your lattice installation look snappier. Use ¾-inch quarter round for the stops instead of square stock. For a smaller reveal use 5/4 stock for the stops; it will leave a ⅜-inch reveal on a 4×4 with ¾-inch-thick lattice. No matter what you use, miter-cut the stop corners and put a construction adhesive on the miters before you nail them. Add a 2×6 cap rail and post cap. Or install the top rail between the posts (the same as the bottom rail) and a little below the tops, then top the posts with post caps (option not shown).

2 Mark the posts ⅝ inch from each edge at the top and bottom inside the bays and snap a chalk line between each set of marks. Also mark the top and bottom rails on the insides at the same points and snap chalk lines. Finish-nail 1× stops with their outside edges on the lines on one side of the posts and rails. 1× stops will leave a ⅝-inch reveal on both sides when a ¾-inch lattice panel is installed (see illustration on opposite page bottom).

3 Brush sealer on the edges of the lattice and paint or stain the panels before you hang them. Cut the panels to fit the bays and set them against the nailers. Hold the lattice in place and install 1× stops with finish nails. Do not drive fasteners into the lattice—only into the posts and rails.

DESIGN OPTION
Building a louvered screen

Louvered screens offer the same benefits as lattice screens, but they fit better in some landscape styles.

Louvers partially block the view and let in cooling breezes. They are an effective design element where strong vertical lines are needed; they are an excellent contrast to the predominately horizontal lines of a deck. This holds true whether you fasten the louvered frame to the deck or set a louvered fence out in the yard.

The privacy created by a louvered design, however, is somewhat limited; the perpendicular view is completely blocked, but the angular view is not. If a viewer is moving—walking or riding in a car—the fence is less effective at blocking the view.

If you build a frame of 4×4 posts and 2×4 rails, the corners of 1×6 louvers angled at 45 degrees will extend slightly past the edges of the rails. If you don't like the appearance, you can place the louvers at a greater angle or rip-cut them to 4⅞ inches.

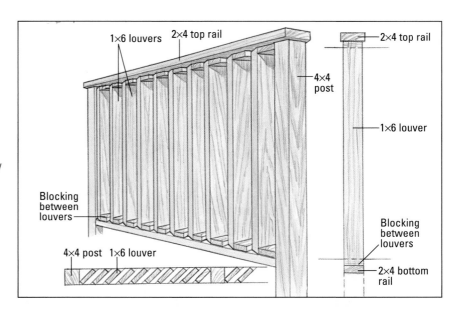

BUILT-IN BENCHES

Built-in benches bring more to a deck than a place to sit down. They can help define space at the edges of the deck or within its perimeter, accent the deck, or double up as storage units.

You can incorporate a bench between permanent planters like the design shown on pages 128–129, you can build movable freestanding benches (although 2× furniture can get heavy), or you can take advantage of the strength of dimension lumber and your deck framing and build these permanent benches.

Whatever bench you design, build it from the same lumber as your decking and railings. Otherwise it will stick out as a displaced design element.

If your built-ins are perpendicular to the joists, the joist spacing will affect the length. Benches built parallel to the joists can be any length. And of course, you can build both types on the same deck. It's easiest to frame built-in benches before the decking goes on. Bench seats should be about 18 inches above the decking and 15 to 30 inches deep.

Built-in perimeter benches help define the edge of a deck in addition to increasing the seating. For continuous seating, cut enough supports to install one every 4 to 5 feet. Most building codes permit perimeter seating without a railing on ground-level decks; on an elevated deck leave enough space for a railing behind the seating.

PRESTART CHECKLIST

☐ **TIME**
About six hours to cut and assemble a 5-foot bench

☐ **TOOLS**
Tape measure, speed square, clamps, circular saw, cordless drill

☐ **SKILLS**
Measuring, cutting, fastening

☐ **MATERIALS**
2× lumber and fasteners

A. Framing a bench perpendicular to joists

Mark the locations of the 2×10 legs on the joists. Keep the outer edges of all legs the same distance from the edge of the deck. Cut the legs to length, predrill them for three lag screws or bolts, and fasten them to the joists. Install blocking between the joists adjacent to the legs. Cut the seat rails to the width of the seat and screw them to the legs. Attach a cleat to the outside of each leg as a nailing surface for the decking. Install the decking before you screw the bench to the seat legs.

Building a bench on through-posts

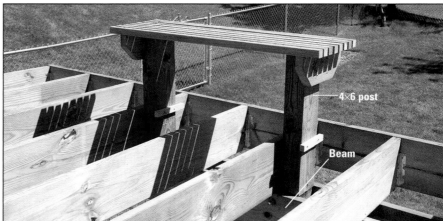

1 You can build a bench on posts that extend through the deck like these 4×6s. Instead of cutting the posts flush with the beam, leave them long until the joists are in place. Then you can determine the height of the posts above the deck surface and trim them. You can build a bench shorter than the post spacing by supporting one end on a through-post and the other end on a short piece of post bolted to the beam and joist. If you are building this kind of bench on an elevated deck, make sure the deck overhang is sufficient to build a railing behind the bench.

B. Framing a bench parallel to joists

1 Mark the locations for the 2×10 legs on the joist. Attach the legs to the joists with lag screws or bolts through predrilled holes, and attach blocking between the joists to keep the seat from rocking. Cut the seat rails to length—about 16 inches for a bench seat that is 19 inches deep—and screw them to both seat legs.

2 Attach cleats to both sides of the legs to provide a nailing surface for the ends of the decking. You can install the seat slats before or after the decking. But if your slats will overhang the seat rails by more than 6 inches, install the decking first so you won't bump your head against the seats while driving the decking screws.

2 Cut the 2×6 seat rails to the width of the seat and screw one to the outside face of each post. Install cleats on the posts with their top edges flush with the tops of the joists to provide a nailing surface for the decking.

3 Clamp a 2×4 to each seat rail as an overhang guide. Align the end and edge of the first 2×2 seat slat and screw it to one seat rail. Square the slat to the rails and attach it at the other end. As you screw down the remaining seat slats, space them with pieces of ½-inch plywood. If your slats are straight you won't have to square each one.

OUTDOOR KITCHEN

Ever since outdoor barbecuing became popular in the 1950s, the technology of grills and accessories has improved dramatically. If you've never left the outdoor cooking craze or are thinking about joining it for the first time, installing an outdoor kitchen requires some planning.

The scope of an outdoor cooking area is best determined by answering the question "How do I want to use it?" You may want a place for full-scale outdoor dining, for small gatherings of family or a few guests, or merely for occasional weekend cookouts.

An outdoor kitchen requires a structure to house a grill. The unit illustrated here does so with little cost and effort. You can add a prep sink, under-the-counter refrigerator, rotisserie, and any number of storage areas by building additional bays.

PRESTART CHECKLIST

☐ **TIME**
24 to 30 hours

☐ **TOOLS**
Framing hammer, measuring tape, framing square, speed square, cordless drill, circular saw, carpenter's level, chalk line

☐ **SKILLS**
Measuring, sawing, fastening

☐ **PREP**
Draw plans

☐ **MATERIALS**
2×4 framing lumber, siding, cement backerboard, 1× trim stock, fasteners

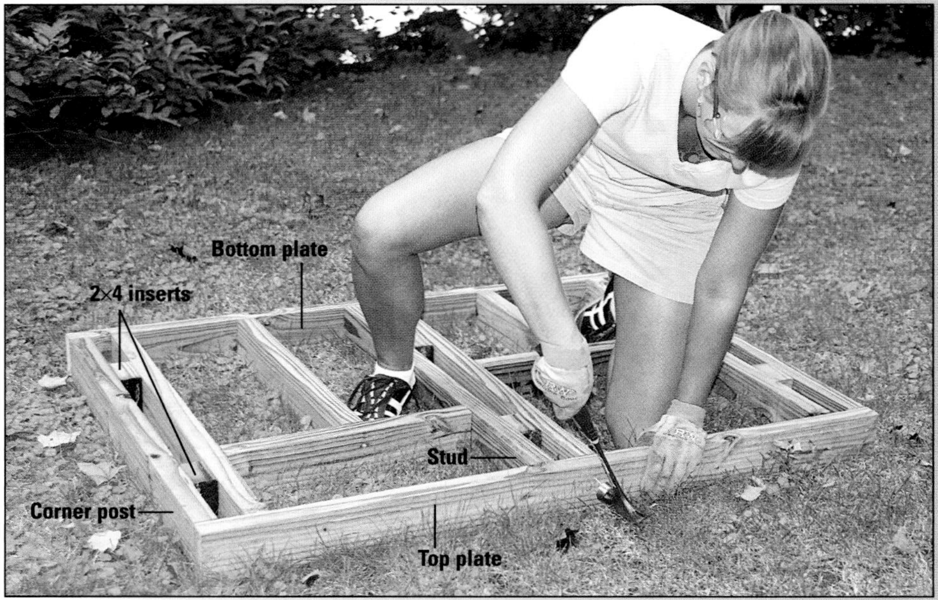
Bottom plate
2×4 inserts
Stud
Corner post
Top plate

1 Cut all the framing members to length and lay out the pieces for the left wall on the deck. Put them in their approximate positions so you'll have them handy when you need them. Assemble the corner posts for this wall first, inserting 6-inch lengths of 2×4 between the corner post studs and driving 3½-inch screws from both sides. Line up the bottom plate and face-nail it to the studs, spacing them correctly. Face-nail the top plate to the studs, keeping the studs properly spaced and square in the frame. Assemble all the walls in this fashion.

FRAMING PLAN

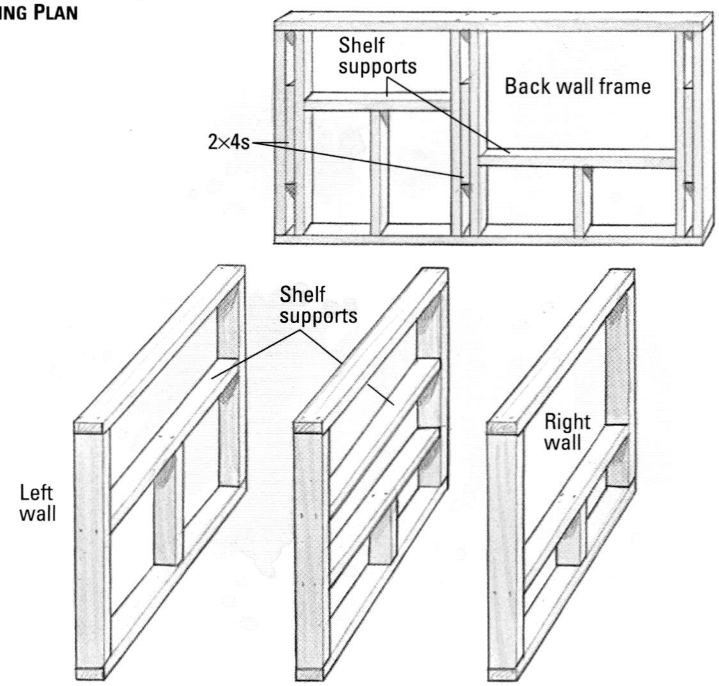
Shelf supports
Back wall frame
2×4s
Shelf supports
Right wall
Left wall

2 Snap chalk lines on the deck to locate the positions of the walls. Make sure the footprint of the frame is square to the deck. Square the corners with a framing square. Set the left wall on its chalk line and fasten one end of the bottom plate to the decking by driving 3-inch screws into the bottom plate. Line the bottom plate up on the chalk line and fasten the other end. Then go back and secure the middle of the bottom plate.

3 Fasten the remaining walls to the deck with the same techniques, pulling the walls together with screws through the rear studs into the corner posts. Cut the front frame members and toenail them in place. Measure and cut the plywood countertop base and fasten it to the frame. Cut and fasten plywood for the remaining top plates and the shelves. Line the grill bay with cement backerboard. Install the siding, tile the countertop and top plates, and install the grill.

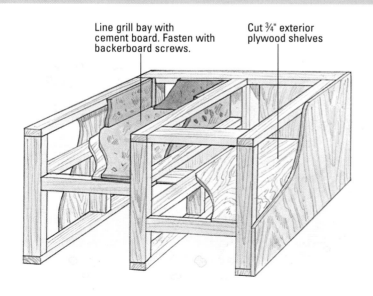

LOW-VOLTAGE DECK LIGHTING

For path lighting to your deck, buy a low-voltage kit with lights on stakes that stab into the ground. Wires run from the lights to a transformer that plugs into an outlet. Easier yet are solar-powered path lights. A solar panel charges an internal battery, so these lights don't need wires. They don't produce a great deal of light, though.

On-deck lighting requires planning, especially if some (or all) of your fixtures are recessed. Recessed lights require some extra work, but the results can be dramatic.

Add up the wattage of the lights you are installing and purchase a transformer with a built-in timer that will deliver adequate power. For example, eight 18-watt lights and five 20-watt lights add up to 244 watts. A 250-watt transformer will handle the load, but won't allow you to add more lights in the future—something you're almost sure to do. Buy a transformer with 20 percent more capacity than you initially need.

PRESTART CHECKLIST

☐ **TIME**
About eight hours to wire and install lighting on a 12×16-foot deck, depending on the lighting plan

☐ **TOOLS**
Tape measure, hammer, cordless drill, jigsaw, screwdriver, wire stripper, diagonal cutters, crimpers

☐ **SKILLS**
Measuring, cutting, drilling, fastening, cutting and stripping wire

☐ **PREP**
Determine light locations

☐ **MATERIALS**
Low-voltage fixtures and wire, cable staples, GFCI receptacle

1 Mount the low-voltage transformer near an existing receptacle, or install a new ground-fault circuit interrupter (GFCI). Be sure to place both units in locations that will stay dry and won't allow them to be damaged. Install the GFCI receptacle in a box rated for outdoor use.

2 Mount all the fixtures in their proper locations, using your dimensioned plan as a guide. Connect the cable to the fixtures with the snap connectors supplied by the fixture manufacturer.

Fixtures of many styles are available for low-voltage systems so you can mount a light in almost any deck location. Run cable for path lighting in a shallow trench. Wire the system, then cover the trench.

Fixture wires

Thread wiring through hole drilled in framing

Transformer

Terminals

3 Fasten the cable to the deck framing, running it alongside posts and under rails, or wherever it will be the least visible. Fasten the cable with exterior wire staples. Use rounded staples for round cable, flat staples for flat wire.

4 Wherever the wiring has to cross a framing member, drill a hole in the board and pass the cable through it.

5 At the transformer, strip the ends of the wires about ¾ inch and connect them to the terminals on the transformer, following the manufacturer's instructions. Plug the transformer into the GFCI receptacle and check all the lights to make sure they're lit.

DESIGN OPTION
Recessed fixtures

Recessed fixtures work well in stair risers, deck skirts, and other vertical surfaces. To install one, mark the fixture outline on the framing member, drill a starter hole for a jigsaw, and cut the hole with the saw.

WHAT IF...
There's a HI/LO switch?

HI/LO switch

A HI/LO switch allows you to change the amount of current flowing to the lights. First try running the lights with the switch set to LO. If some of the lights do not come on, or if they are too dim, flip the switch to HI.

Turning on the lights

Many low-voltage systems turn the lights on automatically when it gets dark and also give you the option of setting the lights on a timer. Follow the manufacturer's instructions for setting the lighting program.

FRAMING FOR SPECIAL CIRCUMSTANCES

Many alterations in the design of a basic deck can't be accomplished without modifying the framing. For example, you can visualize a wraparound deck as two decks with common framing, but each side will require its own ledger. Curves will add style to a deck, but will need joists cut in a contour. And if your proposed deck site has a tree or large rock that looks like it's in the way, don't be dismayed—incorporate it into the decking with modified framing.

The techniques used to modify joist plans to accommodate an obstacle can also be put to another use. They make properly supported holes in the decking so you also can use them to inset a small pond or fountain, sandbox, fire pit, or barbecue. You also can apply these alternate framing methods to support removable panels for access to water faucets or for storage areas under the deck.

PRESTART CHECKLIST

☐ **TIME**
Three to four hours, depending on the special circumstance

☐ **TOOLS**
Framing hammer, measuring tape, framing square, speed square, cordless drill, circular saw, carpenter's level, chalk line

☐ **SKILLS**
Measuring, cutting, fastening

☐ **PREP**
Varies with circumstances

☐ **MATERIALS**
Varies with circumstances

A. Wraparound

A wraparound deck needs support along two sides of the house, and that means two ledgers. Lay out both sides of the deck as single units (pages 82–85) and install the ledgers with the techniques shown on pages 80–81. Put the ledgers on different planes for a step-down design.

B. Inside corner

Most decks on the inside corners of a house will need two ledgers. But before you lay out the site, check the corner for square. If the house is badly out of square, install one ledger, but treat the other as a rim joist—which will require posts and footings set close to the house.

ALTERNATE FRAMING PATTERNS FOR WRAPAROUND DECKS

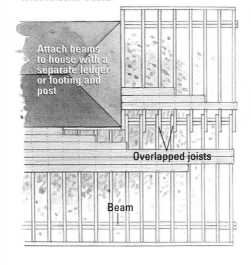

Attach beams to house with a separate ledger or footing and post

Overlapped joists

Beam

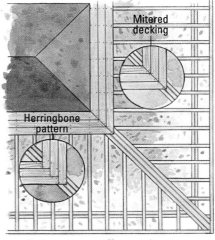

Mitered decking

Herringbone pattern

Framing for a wraparound deck will almost always be determined by the decking pattern you choose. Pick the pattern when you plan your deck, and install the framing accordingly.

C. Curve

Angle of intersection with framing scribe

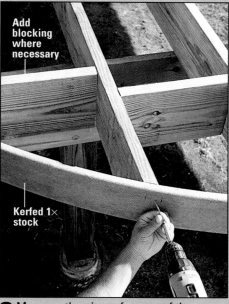

Transfer angled mark to both sides of joist

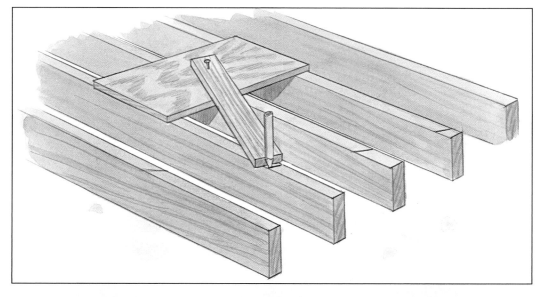

Add blocking where necessary

Kerfed 1×
stock

1 Lay out the site and set posts, beams, and joists, keeping them at the proper spacing with a 1×4 tacked to their top edges (pages 96–97). Make a framing scribe, fasten it in place, and mark the outline of the curve on each joist. Duplicate the angle of the scribe where it intersects each joist.

2 Using a speed square, transfer both ends of the angled marks to the sides of each joist. Cut the angled end with a reciprocating saw, making sure the blade does not wander away from either line.

3 Measure the circumference of the arc and either cut benderboard or 1× stock to fit. Saw kerfs in 1× stock every ⅜ to ½ inch so the board will bend around the curve. Fasten the benderboard or kerfed stock to the ends of the joists, adding perpendicular blocking where necessary.

MAKE A FRAMING SCRIBE
Lay out large curves

Before you make a framing scribe, be sure to make a scaled drawing of your deck plan so you will know exactly where the center point of the curve falls on the framing.

Using your dimensioned plan, fasten a rectangular piece of plywood over the location of the center point. Mark the center point on the plywood and fasten a 1×4 scribe with one nail, centering the nail on the scribe and the center-point mark on the plywood.

Measure from the nail out to the end of the 1×4 and cut it at the length of the radius of the curve. Move the end of the scribe from one joist to the next, marking each with the angle at which the 1×4 crosses it.

Enclosing an obstacle

1 Install double joists in double joist hangers on both sides of the obstacle and at a sufficient distance from it (allowing room for the mature size of a tree, for example). Install a double header in hangers on both sides of the obstacle.

2 Measure the spacing for the remaining joists and install them in hangers. Make sure you have at least one joist fastened at the same spacing as the rest of the deck.

3 Attach the decking to the joists, cutting the boards so you leave an edge overlapping the framing by an equal amount on all sides.

WHAT IF...
You want a round opening?

1 Set up your framing plan in a configuration similar to that above, but add perpendicular and corner blocking to support the circumference of the circle.

2 Install the decking, cutting the ends so they overhang the framing. Using a cardboard template equal to the arc of the opening, mark the circle on the decking and cut it with a jigsaw. Smooth the edges with a rasp.

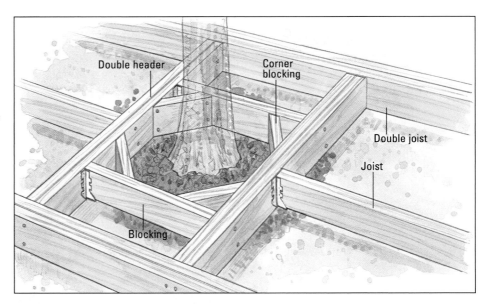

Double header

Corner blocking

Double joist

Joist

Blocking

OTHER DECKING PATTERNS

The primary concern with any decking pattern is that the framing under it supports it adequately.

Both herringbone and chevron patterns will require a thickened joist to accommodate the fasteners at the ends of the boards.

Framing for a modular pattern is similar to standard framing except that the joists are interrupted at right angles and at a length equivalent to the decking section.

For framing for other decking patterns see pages 124–126 and 168–171.

Framing for deck patterns

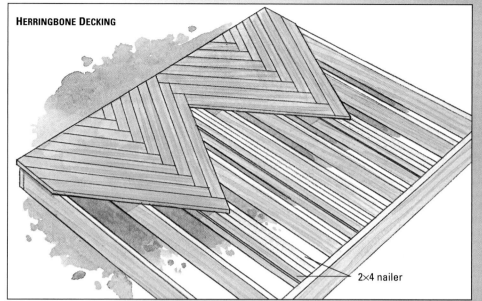

HERRINGBONE DECKING

2×4 nailer

To install herringbone decking, position joints symmetrically on the deck. At each joint, triple the width of the joist by fastening a 2×4 cleat on either side. Install full-length decking pieces first, then the shorter pieces.

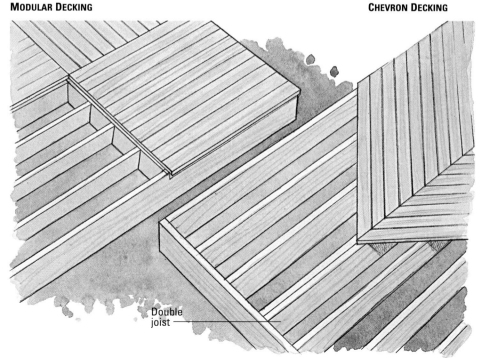

MODULAR DECKING

CHEVRON DECKING

Double joist

A modular pattern (above) is easy to build—the framing is not complicated and all the decking boards are the same length.

A chevron pattern calls for a doubled joist in the center of the framing. Work carefully to maintain consistent, tight joints.

CUSTOM RAILINGS

Railing designs offer hundreds of ways to personalize your deck, and each design calls for particular construction techniques, shown on these pages.

Even the method used to mount the rails will affect the style of your deck: Bottom rails can be placed flat or on edge inside the post bays or on edge on the faces of the posts; long rails can be placed on edge in notched posts; and top rails can be installed inside the bays or continuously on top of the posts. You can insert 2×2 balusters, alternating slats and battens, or panels in the bays. Even the most common beveled baluster design will look different than others with a 2×6 rail cap, finials, and post caps. Check local codes for railing height and baluster spacing.

PRESTART CHECKLIST

☐ **TIME**
About a day to build a railing for a medium-size deck

☐ **TOOLS**
Tape measure, hammer, drill, circular saw, chisel, post level, ratchet and socket wrenches

☐ **SKILLS**
Measuring, cutting, fastening with screws and nails

☐ **PREP**
Complete deck framing

☐ **MATERIALS**
Posts, rails, balusters

Notched-post designs

Notch cut in decking · Full-thickness post

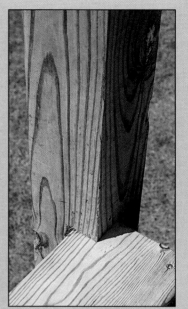

You can install rail posts without notching them if your decking is cut flush with the joists. But flush-cut decking is not as attractive as decking that overhangs the framing by about 1½ inches.

With overhanging decking you'll have to notch either the decking or the posts. Notching the decking results in a stronger railing because it doesn't reduce the thickness of the post.

Installing a notched corner post creates a clean, contemporary look and saves time and lumber too. Cut deck or post notches with a jigsaw. See opposite page for instructions for cutting corner notches.

STANLEY PRO TIP

Strengthen notched posts

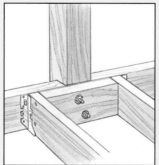

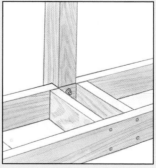

Railing posts often take a lateral beating. People lean up against the rails, pushing them slightly outward, and even though top rails and cap rails will reduce this stress, you may want to install additional framing, especially on notched posts that

support an overhead. For posts on a header, add 2× blocking between the joists. This creates a thicker base for the carriage bolts. On rim joists add blocking between the interior joists to reduce flexing.

REFRESHER COURSE
Fastening rails

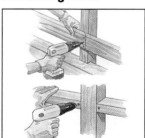

How you fasten the posts to the rails will differ with different railing styles. Face-nail (or screw) flat rails to the the posts, using scarf joints centered on the post when necessary. Toenail flat rails through the edges or support them on 2× cleats inside the posts. Predrill all holes first.

Installing through-posts

Notch decking boards at posts

Machine bolt

Through-post is supported in footing

2× cleat adds support

Header

Interior joist

Carriage bolts

Header

Through-posts extend from a footing above the height of the decking to support railings or overheads. Such support is needed for large, heavy overhead structures but through-posts are often employed in designs without overheads.

Most often installed with the framing hung on their outside faces, through-posts require a notch in the decking boards. Cut the notches a little oversize to allow drainage.

This design will also keep the remaining posts inside the framing. If post spacing allows it, attach the remaining posts where

a joist meets the header. Otherwise add perpendicular blocking to keep the post from tilting under stress.

Because you need only one post at the corners, this design will save a little on lumber costs, but finding long 4× stock that's straight may prove difficult.

REFRESHER COURSE

REFRESHER COURSE
Cutting notched posts

Notched posts take time and experience to cut, but make pleasing finishing touches for a deck railing. They draw the baluster up closer to the deck edge and make a slightly firmer joint than surface-mounted posts.

Mark the posts for a notch that is 1½ inches deep and as long as the depth of the joist—about 7½ inches for a 2×8 joist, about 9½ inches for a 2×10. (Use a joist scrap to be exact.) Add the thickness of the decking and mark for the top of the notch.

Circular saw

Crosscut

Cut the notch
Make a crosscut where the notch ends. With the saw set to maximum depth, rip-cut the lines on each side without cutting beyond the crosscut. (For a corner post, set the blade to a depth of 1½ inches and make two long rip-cuts on adjoining faces.)

Area blade didn't reach

Waste

Chisel away the excess
Use a hammer and chisel to crack out the waste—it will neatly pop out as one piece. Then chisel away the remnant where the saw blade could not reach.

Crosscut

Make a corner post
Make the long rip-cuts and a shallow crosscut between them. Chisel toward the crosscut and split out the waste. Chisel down along the crosscut and along the long cuts to remove the remaining wood.

Designing custom railings

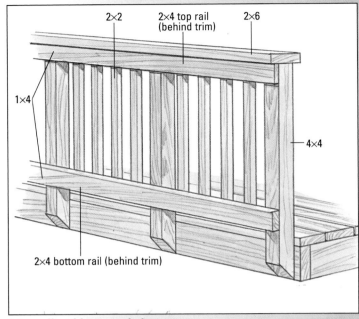

Edge rails with square balusters

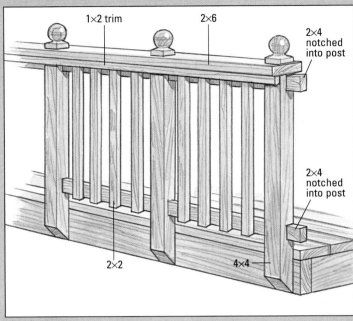

Notched rails

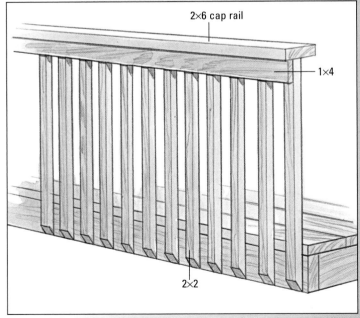

Railed baluster (low rails on low decks only)

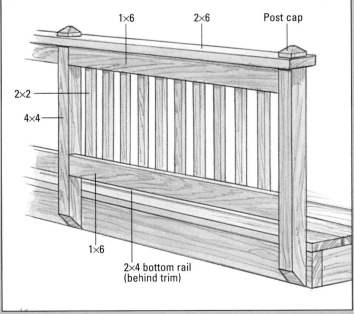

Hooded balusters

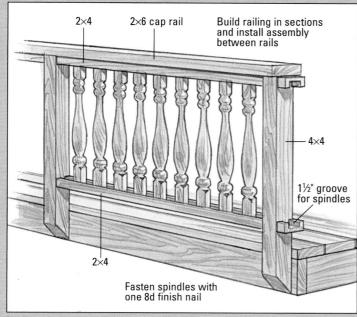

2×4 2×6 cap rail Build railing in sections and install assembly between rails

4×4

1½" groove for spindles

2×4

Fasten spindles with one 8d finish nail

Inset spindles

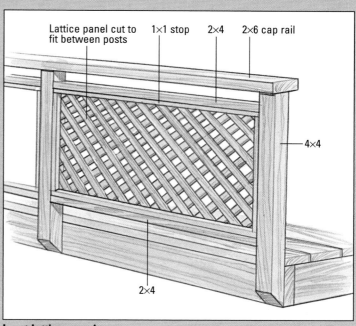

Lattice panel cut to fit between posts 1×1 stop 2×4 2×6 cap rail

4×4

2×4

Inset lattice panels

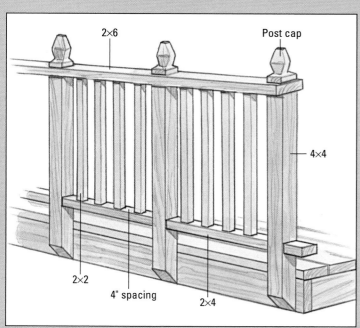

2×6 Post cap

4×4

2×2

4" spacing

2×4

Inset flat rails

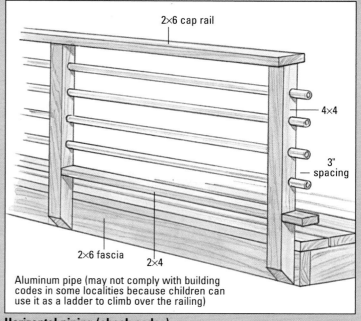

2×6 cap rail

4×4

3" spacing

2×6 fascia 2×4

Aluminum pipe (may not comply with building codes in some localities because children can use it as a ladder to climb over the railing)

Horizontal piping (check codes)

ACCESS RAMP

An access ramp could be viewed either as an angled deck or flat stairs, and it shares construction techniques with both. Place the ramp for the most convenient and unrestricted access to the deck.

Keep the maximum pitch (the number of feet the ramp rises for every foot of horizontal run) to 1 in 12, and if possible, build it 42 or 48 inches wide. (The minimum width is 36 inches.) Have the building inspector review your plans before starting construction on the project.

Construct a single-tiered ramp—one whose entire rise is on a single stringer—as shown here. To build longer ramps, set posts on footings at equal intervals along both sides of the run. Mark the angle of descent on the posts, and cut and install stringers with angled ends. Install handrails on ramps and landings.

PRESTART CHECKLIST

☐ **TIME**
10 to 12 hours for a 10- to 12-foot ramp

☐ **TOOLS**
Tape measure, speed square, hammer, carpenter level, small sledge, circular saw, jigsaw, cordless drill, trowels, concrete tools

☐ **SKILLS**
Measuring, marking patterns, cutting, fastening, working with concrete

☐ **PREP**
Remove sod and install landscape fabric and gravel

☐ **MATERIALS**
Lumber, fasteners, concrete, framing hardware

 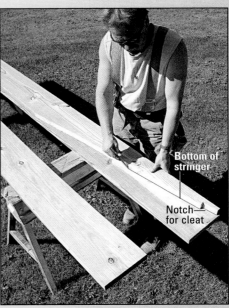

1 Measure the rise of the ramp (page 101) and adjust the run to comply with pitch requirements. Drive stakes at the location of the landing pad. Lay out the landing pad with a sheet of plywood or batterboards. Remove the sod; excavate, form, and pour the landing pad (pages 150–151).

2 Spread landscape fabric and gravel on the site, then lay out the stringers. Mark the angle of descent on the bottom of the stringer and a $3/4 \times 4$-inch notch at the bottom end. This notch will fit over a cleat fastened to the landing pad. Cut one stringer and use it as a template for the others.

5 Predrill and screw the beveled strip to the ends of the stringer (wide face to the stringers).

3 Cut a pressure-treated 1×6 to the outside width of the ramp. Then set your circular saw to cut a 5-degree bevel on one edge of the 1×6. Reset the saw to 0 degrees (or 90 degrees) and cut a 1½-inch strip from the bottom of the 1×6.

4 When the concrete is cured, mark the stringer positions on the joists and fasten the stringers to the joist (page 153). Drill ⅜-inch holes in the cleat at the locations for threaded studs (page 116) and slide the cleat under the stringers. Square the whole assembly to the deck and drill locator holes into the pad with a masonry bit. Remove the cleat, drill holes for the studs, epoxy them in place, and reinstall the cleat with nuts and washers.

6 Cut the decking to length allowing a 1-inch overhang, and attach it to the stringers. Space the boards with a spacing jig (page 125).

7 To ease the transition between the pad and the ramp, brush a latex bonding agent on the existing concrete and trowel on a 6- to 8-inch-wide transition strip at the bottom edge of the decking. Tack scrap from the stringers to the outside edges of the ramp to form the concrete. Force the concrete under the first decking board and trowel the concrete at the same angle as the scrap forms.

EXPANDING A DECK

If your house came with a deck that's simply not big enough to accommodate your gatherings, you can tear out the old one and build a new structure. Attaching a deck extension is a simpler solution.

An extension is not difficult to build. It is essentially an added deck section supported by part of the existing structure.

Your choice will be to either build up or build down. Both techniques are shown here. Consider the extensions as separate decks and lay them out, set posts, and install decking with the methods shown earlier in this book.

An old unused slab patio can be restyled as a deck. If the concrete is not powdery or breaking into chunks, you can install sleepers (shown below) and fasten down decking in a weekend.

Framing a deck extension

To frame an extension that rises one step from the existing deck, lay out the post locations (pages 82–85) and cut the posts so the joists rest on the surface of the old deck. Build the frame and toenail it to the old deck. Design your extension to use 2×6s, if possible. That way you'll have about a 7-inch step to the new deck.

To frame a step-down deck extension, treat the old beam as a ledger for the new frame. Mark the joist locations on the beam and lay out the site with batterboards and mason's lines (pages 82–85). Hang the joists in joist hangers. Refer to the decking plan below for framing ideas.

UNUSED SLAB PATIO
Decking with sleepers

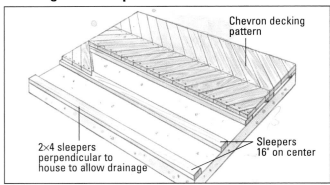

Decking laid over concrete must be raised from the surface of the concrete with 2×4 pressure-treated sleepers. Snap chalk lines 16 inches on center on the surface of the slab to mark sleeper locations. Install the 2×4s flat. Fasten them with masonry nails or a powder-actuated tool. Cut and install the decking. Consider patterns other than parallel decking—the flat 2×4s provide a sufficient nailing surface for many patterns.

DECKING PLAN

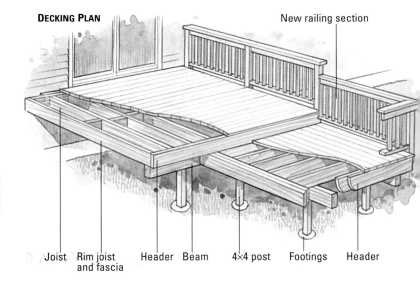

STORAGE AND HATCHES

Adequate storage sometimes is not considered in deck design. But there are opportunities to make space, including on-deck storage, such as boxed seating frames with hinged lids. The most natural space for storage is under the deck.

A space at least 2 feet high under the deck offers plenty of storage space. Grade-level access—through a door—isn't very handy with a 2-foot space because you would have to crawl under the deck. It's easier to build an access hatch, a larger version of the hose-bib access panel at right, so you can lower things into the storage space from the deck.

You can attach a storage box to the joists before you install decking, and make the hatch from decking cut to fit the recess. Cut a hole in one of the decking boards or install flush lifting handles so you can lift the hatch out.

With a deck raised 4 or more feet off the ground, entry through a door becomes practical. Build removable skirting sections or hinged siding panels.

Hinged skirting

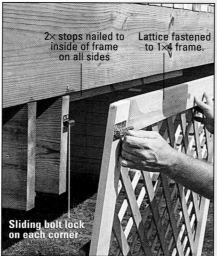

2× stops nailed to inside of frame on all sides

Lattice fastened to 1×4 frame.

Sliding bolt lock on each corner

Construct latticed skirting (pages 178–179), but make one or more of the sections removable. Fasten the lattice to the back of a 1×4 frame cut to fit the section. Install 2× stops inside the opening for the lattice to rest against. Fasten sliding bolts to the panel at the corners and the shoes on the bottom frame. Slide the bolts to keep the panel in place.

Hose-bib hatch

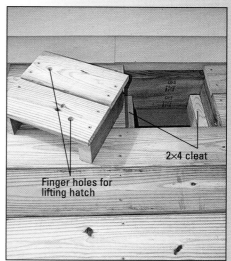

2×4 cleat

Finger holes for lifting hatch

To make an access panel for a hose bib or electrical outlet, cut the decking on either side of it flush with the inside of the joists. Cut two pieces of decking to fit in the opening and cleat them together with wood scraps. Drill 1-inch holes near one end of one board and the opposite end of the other. Nail 2×4 cleats to the joists to support the hatch.

HANGING A STORAGE DOOR

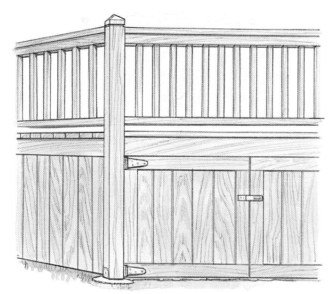

Build a skirting frame as shown on pages 178–179, using solid panels or siding that matches the house instead of lattice. Build framing to support a door.

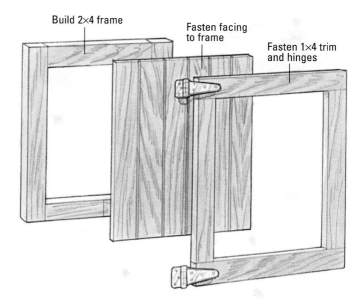

Build 2×4 frame

Fasten facing to frame

Fasten 1×4 trim and hinges

Trim the siding to improve its appearance. Build a door of the style shown above. Glue and nail the joints for durability. Add hinges and a latch to keep it closed.

FINISHING & REPAIRING

A deck is usually in an exposed location where it is subject to the ravages of the elements. Many older decks are built of nontreated or poorly treated lumber, making them easy targets for rot.

Exposure to the sun causes untreated wood to turn gray. In the case of redwood, this is an attractive silver color. If the wood is pressure-treated, the color is less attractive. Either way, the gray can be removed by washing with a deck cleaner.

Overexposure to the sun dries out the wood, opening the grain and turning tiny cracks into major splits. Sun-dried boards will curl and twist if they are not securely fastened every 16 inches or so.

If moisture is allowed to sit on wood surfaces for long periods, wet rot can be the result. Wet rot usually starts in crevices and joints where water collects and is slow to dry out. If a board is substantially rotted it should be replaced. Pages 208–213 show how to diagnose rot and shore up or replace damaged boards.

Moisture may also lead to black, slimy mildew. Fortunately you can quickly treat mildew by washing the affected area.

Once you've finished building a deck—or when it's time to refinish your old deck—protect your investment by applying sealer or stain or both. Check with a lumber supplier to find out which product works best for your wood and in your area; pages 214–217 will help you choose.

CHAPTER PREVIEW

Proper care, use of stain or sealer, and simple repairs keep a deck looking good for many years.

Diagnosing deck problems
page 208

Repairing decking
page 210

Repairing framing
page 212

Selecting finishes
page 214

Applying a finish
page 216

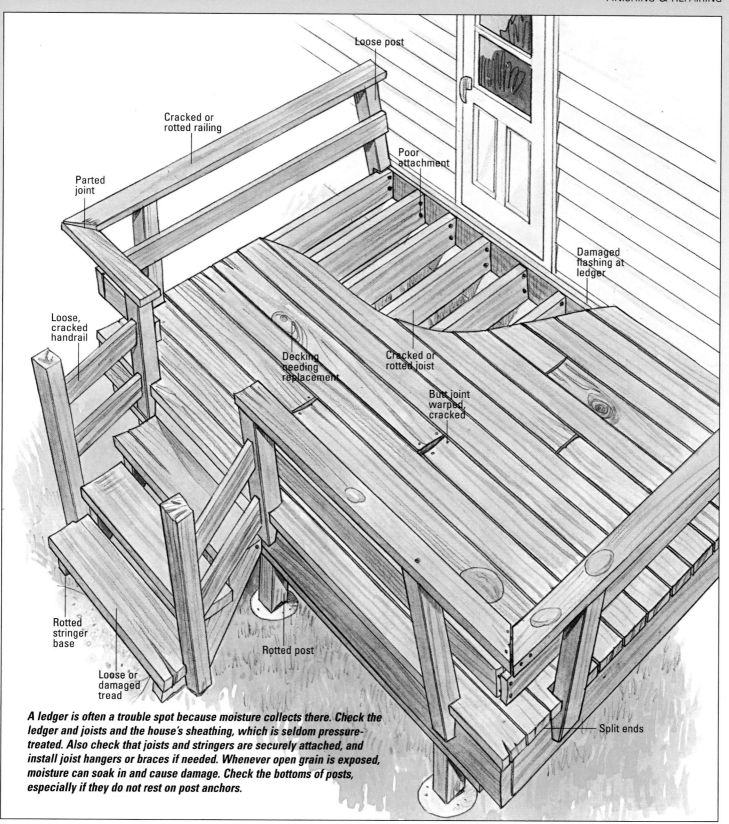

Loose post

Cracked or
rotted railing

Poor
attachment

Parted
joint

Damaged
flashing at
ledger

Loose,
cracked
handrail

Decking
needing
replacement

Cracked or
rotted joist

Butt joint
warped,
cracked

Rotted
stringer
base

Rotted post

Split ends

Loose or
damaged
tread

*A ledger is often a trouble spot because moisture collects there. Check the
ledger and joists and the house's sheathing, which is seldom pressure-
treated. Also check that joists and stringers are securely attached, and
install joist hangers or braces if needed. Whenever open grain is exposed,
moisture can soak in and cause damage. Check the bottoms of posts,
especially if they do not rest on post anchors.*

DIAGNOSING DECK PROBLEMS

If a deck is in serious trouble you can often feel it before you see it. Some boards or sections feel spongy when you walk on them. Railings feel wobbly.

Don't wait for these symptoms of wood rot to manifest themselves before you take action. A quick tour of your deck, screwdriver and flashlight in hand, enables you to spot trouble before it takes its toll.

Determine the type of lumber used in your deck. If the boards are untreated fir, pine, or hemlock, apply generous coats of sealer even if you find no symptoms yet; these woods can develop rot in a few months.

Probe the boards with a screwdriver. If it sinks in easily, rot is present. Chances are if one board is rotted, the boards attached to it are rotted as well. If the rot is shallow, clean the area, let it dry, and apply plenty of sealer. You may want to add a cleat for extra strength (page 210). Take steps to ensure that the spot will not remain wet after a rainfall. If the rot is deeper than an inch or so, the board should be replaced.

PRESTART CHECKLIST

☐ TIME
About an hour to make a fairly thorough inspection of a medium-size deck

☐ TOOLS
Screwdriver, flashlight, putty knife

☐ SKILLS
Attention to detail

☐ PREP
Remove skirting, if any, so you can get at the underside of the deck

☐ MATERIALS
None needed

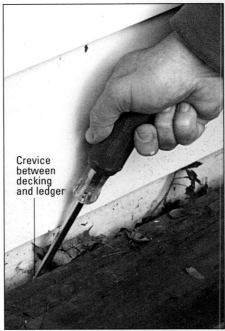

Crevice between decking and ledger

Check the ledger first. Stick a screwdriver into the top and side of the ledger. (Don't jab at a metal flashing; you could poke a hole in it.) If the wood feels spongy, rot is present. There also may be rot on the underside of decking boards or in the house's sheathing.

Check each post where it abuts decking, where it attaches to a joist, at its top, and at its bottom. Poke with a screwdriver to find any areas of rot.

Grasp posts or railings and give a good shake; if the railing feels loose it could be dangerous. Check for rot, but the problem may be loose fasteners. Sometimes bad design is the culprit—there may not be enough fastening surface for the post.

Rail caps are among the most exposed parts of a deck. Check the entire railing for looseness, and refasten as needed by drilling pilot holes and driving screws or nails. Balusters are often attached with only one fastener at either end, so some may come loose in time.

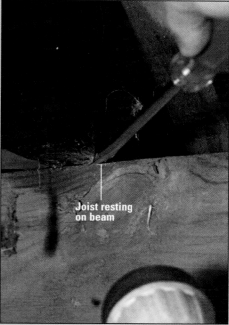

For decking that is generally cracked and split, sand the surface, then apply several coats of sealer. If decking boards are cracked at the ends, consider snapping a chalk line and cutting them off (page 146) if the decking overhangs the edge sufficiently. Apply sealer to the cut ends.

If dirt or leaves collect between decking boards or in other crevices, moisture will remain for weeks at a time. This almost certainly will lead to rot unless the wood is well treated. Keep a deck clean to forestall rot. Try to clean between decking on an annual basis.

View from below: Put on old clothes, grab a flashlight and screwdriver, and venture below the deck. Check the undersides of decking boards, around the ledger, posts, stringers, treads, and any joints or crevices.

Hammer popped nails back into place, or better yet pull them and replace them. Redrive loose screws. If decking is severely cupped or rotting, replace it.

Crawl under stairs if you can, and check for overcut notches in the stringers. Such overcuts seriously weaken the stringer, hold water, and can rot quickly, resulting in a broken stringer and injuries.

Got bugs?

If termites, carpenter ants, or other wood-boring insects are a problem in your area, your deck may be on their menu. Pressure-treated lumber rated at .40 CCA or labeled for ground contact (page 60) is probably safe, but nontreated wood, including redwood and cedar, is at risk.

A primary infestation of wood-boring insects means that the colony (with its queen) lives in the ground, where it can find moisture, and makes daily forays to find wood.

A secondary infestation occurs when the wood itself provides enough moisture that the pests can encamp right inside a board.

These creatures don't like sunlight, so they tunnel inside boards where you can't see them. Once you see the damage, it's probably too late to save the board. If you see tunnels running inside a board, usually following the grain, you've got bugs. Consult with a professional exterminator.

REPAIRING DECKING

It's not unusual for several decking boards to be damaged on a deck that's otherwise in good condition. Replacing a board or two is not difficult. New boards, if they are of the same type as the old ones, may blend in color with the old boards after a year or two. If you clean and refinish the entire deck, the new boards typically will blend in right away.

To refasten boards, it may help to use deck screws that are 3½ or 4 inches long.

Opening the gaps
Decking boards should have gaps between them, about ⅛-inch wide, so that water can seep through and dry out after a rainfall. If a gap is filled with debris, clean it out with a stiff broom. If that doesn't work, use a putty knife. If cleaning isn't enough, widen a gap by cutting with a circular saw.

PRESTART CHECKLIST

☐ **TIME**
An hour or two for most deck repairs

☐ **TOOLS**
Hammer, drill, flat pry bar, taping knife, cat's paw, circular saw, jigsaw or reciprocating saw

☐ **SKILLS**
Making straight cuts in boards that are fastened, fastening with nails or screws

☐ **PREP**
Inspect the deck for damage to framing, and plan to make additional repairs, if needed

☐ **MATERIALS**
Decking boards, nails or screws

A. Cutting to replace part of a board

1 If only part of a long board is damaged and you don't want to replace the entire board, replace a section at least three joists long. Use a jigsaw to cut on the waste side of the joist. Begin the cut between the boards and curve into a perpendicular cut; reverse cut to finish.

2×4 cleat

2 Install a 2×4 cleat to provide a fastening surface for the new board. Fasten the new board in place with 2½-inch deck screws. Allow the new board to run past the end of the deck and cut it to length after the board is fastened.

WHAT IF…
Decking is warped upward?

Warped board

Draw it down with a screw…
Warped boards can often be tamed with a stronger fastener. If you don't mind the appearance of an extra fastener head, drill a pilot hole and drive a screw next to the existing fasteners. For a neater look remove the old fasteners and drive screws that are at least 1 inch longer than the old ones.

…or hold it with an angled screw
Force the warped board down and drill a pilot hole at an angle. Drive the fastener.

If a board does not lie down all the way after refastening, wait a week for it to become partially flattened and try driving the fastener (or an even longer one) again.

B. Removing decking

1 If a nail head is partially popped up, pry it out using a flat pry bar. Protect soft decking (cedar or redwood is softer than pressure-treated lumber) with a taping knife placed under the pry bar (see Step 3).

2 If you will be throwing out the board anyway, use a cat's paw to dig in under the nailhead and pry the nail partway out. Finish prying with the claw of a hammer.

3 To remove a board without damaging a neighboring piece, start at the end where the board overhangs the deck. If that is not possible, use a flat pry bar and a taping knife to shoehorn the damaged board out.

STANLEY PRO TIP: **Dealing with stubborn screws**

Increase the turning power: Screw heads often get so rusty or stripped out that the bit can't get a solid hold. Instead of cranking away with the screwdriver bit, clamp a pair of locking pliers onto the screwdriver shaft. Press firmly on the screwdriver and turn the pliers.

Deepen the phillips head: If that doesn't work, drill a ⅛-inch hole into the center of a phillips head. This sometimes allows the tip of a screwdriver to bite in and grab.

Cut the screw: If you can get to the area below, cut through the shank of the screw using a reciprocating saw equipped with a metal-cutting blade.

REPAIRING FRAMING

If you find several framing members that are substantially rotten, it's time to consider tearing down the deck and starting over. However, if the boards are not severely damaged or if you are certain that only a few are rotten, repairs may solve the problems. Consult with a professional deck builder if you are not sure.

Keeping it strong
If a deck feels spongy when you jump on it, it may be underbuilt, with joists or beams that are too small for their spans (page 68). If you have room to work underneath, it may be possible to shore up a weak deck by installing a new beam with posts and footings. However, this is slow, tedious work. To add a modest amount of extra strength, install a row of blocking in the middle of the joists (page 167) and support it with a post or two.

PRESTART CHECKLIST

☐ **TIME**
A couple of hours for most repairs

☐ **TOOLS**
Drill, hammer, circular saw, reciprocating saw, flat pry bar, cat's paw

☐ **SKILLS**
Fastening with screws or nails while working in awkward positions

☐ **PREP**
Inspect the entire deck to make sure the repairs will fix all the problems

☐ **MATERIALS**
Joist material, 2×4 for braces, screws, nails, carriage bolts with nuts and washers

A. Railing repairs

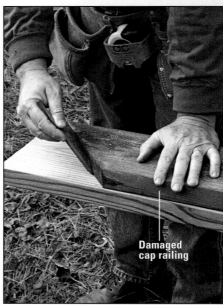

Damaged cap railing

1 If a cap railing is partially rotten but mostly sound, clean out the joints where moisture and debris collect, let the piece dry, and apply sealer. If the damage is severe, remove the cap and use it as a template for cutting a replacement piece.

2 When installing the new piece of cap railing, begin at a corner joint. Clamp a scrap in place to hold the old and new pieces even. Drill pilot holes before using a 3-inch screw to snug up the joint. Apply two fasteners at each post.

Shoring up a joist

Splint

Carriage bolt

Temporary support

Base for support

A joist that is cracked and sagging can be splinted with a piece of pressure-treated lumber of the same size. Begin by placing a scrap of 2× lumber or a couple of layers of plywood on the ground beneath the damage. Cut a 2×4 long enough to be wedged beneath the joist—it should be long enough to require a few whacks with a hammer to get it nearly upright. Cut a splint so it extends 2 feet on either side of the damage and set it in place above the support. Continue to tap the support upright until the cracked joist is even with the splint.

Fix the splint in place by drilling holes for two ½×8-inch galvanized carriage bolts at each end. Pound the carriage bolts in place, attach the washer and nut, and tighten. Remove the temporary support.

B. Post repairs

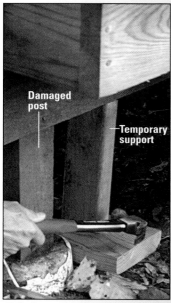

1 Before removing a damaged deck post, install a temporary support to hold up the deck while you work. Lay a 2×6 or 2×8 on the ground below. Cut a 2×4 or 4×4 to fit tightly, and hammer it into place.

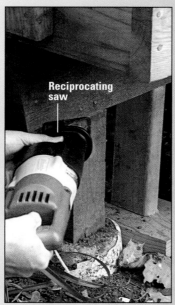

2 Remove fasteners or cut through them using a reciprocating saw equipped with a metal-cutting blade.

3 Use the old post as a template for cutting a new one. Mimic any notches and angle cuts precisely.

4 Slip the new post into position and fasten it with deck screws, lag screws, or carriage bolts.

Repairing a stringer

1 Stringers often develop rot in the open grain where they were cut. To remove one, take off the posts, railing, and treads. Remove or cut through the nails or screws that hold the stringer in place.

2 Remove the stringer. Lay it on top of a new pressure-treated 2×12, crown side up. Use the old stringer as a template for cutting the new one.

3 Anchor the new stringer securely. Attach it with angle brackets and check for square. Reinstall the treads using 3-inch deck screws.

4 Take the opportunity to replace any damaged stair railings and posts—some may split in the process of dismantling the stairs. Use the old pieces as guides for cutting the new.

SELECTING FINISHES

Finishes do more than make the wood look good. The right finish will protect your deck and help it seem a natural extension of your landscape design.

When you're out shopping for finishes, or while you're still in the early planning stages, think first about the color you want, for example, brown, red, or green. Then consider what shade of that color your deck should be—dark brown, tan, pale red, or dark green. Then give some thought to what sheen (flat or glossy) will look best. Decks generally look best with a flat sheen, but a contemporary design scheme might call for something different from the norm.

Then look for information that tells you how durable the finish is and how easy it will be to apply. Generally sealers are the easiest to apply, followed by stains, with paint taking the most time and effort. Consider the wood too. A clear finish is a good choice for redwood and cedar. It allows their natural colors to show through. Pressure-treated lumber usually requires staining or painting.

Sealer

Clear or lightly pigmented sealers protect the wood from water damage and don't change its color much. Look for additives that will ward off mildew, insects, and fungi. Ultraviolet (UV) blockers are a must—they reduce damage caused by the sun's rays. Pigmented sealers do all of the above, but the pigment is designed to change the color of the wood slightly. All-purpose sealers contain water repellents, preservatives, and UV blockers. You can apply sealers over or under stains and under primer and paint.

Stain

Stains are primarily formulated to transform the appearance of the wood—some slightly, some dramatically. Certain formulas are designed to offer some protection to the wood, but this is a job best done with a sealer in conjunction with a stain.

What kind of stain you use will depend on how much of the original wood tones you want to retain. Semitransparent stains allow more wood grain to show through, but wear away more quickly; they are particularly suitable for highlighting wood grains. Heavy-bodied stains contain more pigments and hide the grain. All stains (both oil- or water-base products), including those not designed to penetrate the fibers of the wood, tend to retain the wood's natural look far more than paint. Apply oil-base stains on redwood and red cedar.

Stains are somewhat less expensive than paints, take less time to apply, and go on easily over rough and smooth surfaces.

Paint

Paints conceal some defects and tend to last longer and look better than stains on smooth surfaces. Exterior alkyds (oil-base products) are more costly, more difficult to clean up, and slower-drying. Water-base latex paints cost less, clean up easily, and dry quickly. Each comes in a range of colors and sheens (gloss, semigloss, and flat or matte). New, unpainted surfaces need to be primed first. Oil-base primers provide better protection on raw wood than water-base primers. Add stain blockers to stop bleed-through from redwood and cedar. A good-quality acrylic-latex top coat applied over an alkyd primer makes a durable finish.

STANLEY PRO TIP: **Enough sealant?**

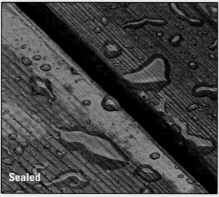

Sealed

Needs sealant

Is your deck sealed properly? In some cases the answer is obvious. Old wood with a dried-out look clearly needs a stiff dose of sealer. But boards that look OK may also be in danger of drying out. So do a quick test once or twice a year. Sprinkle a little water onto the surface.

If the water beads up and does not soak in within two minutes, the board is sealed well enough. If water soaks in within two minutes, apply additional sealer.

The weathered look

If you like wood with a gray, weathered look, don't finish, seal, or paint the deck. Let nature weather the wood naturally. Natural weathering works best with all-heartwood grades of durable species, such as cedar, cypress, and redwood.

The aging time varies with the species and its exposure. Generally cedar and cypress weather to a light silver-gray and redwood turns dark gray. Pressure-treated lumber turns a soft gray, but sometimes retains a hint of its green or tan coloring.

Safety gear

Wear rubber gloves and safety glasses or goggles when you work with finishing materials. Many stains, paints, and sealers contain solvents and other volatile organic compounds.

What will it look like?

All finishes will alter the appearance of all woods. The photos give some idea of the range of appearances different finishes will effect on the same wood (here, untreated Douglas fir). The colors and tones shown in the photos are only representative of degrees of change. Different brand names and various changes in the wood grain, even within the same board, will produce different results.

OIL-BASE CLEAR SEALER

LATEX CLEAR SEALER

SEMITRANSPARENT STAIN

HEAVY-BODIED STAIN

PAINT

DIFFERENT FINISHES
Sample finishes first

Before applying any finish—staining or painting especially—you'll want to know how the final color will look. The only way to really be sure is to see the color when the finish is dry.

Test the final color by applying a small amount in an out-of the-way spot on your deck. Let the finish dry to make sure it produces the color you want. Paint usually dries darker than when wet. Stains usually dry lighter.

WHAT IF...
You want to lighten the wood?

Bleaching agents change the appearance of wood by altering the chemical composition of the surface fibers. They offer a way to tone down the jarring look of a brand-new deck. They soften the raw-wood look and help the varying shades of natural wood to blend in. You get the effect of two seasons of natural weathering in one application, because like the sun, the treatments strip color from the wood fibers. Sealers stop the bleach from working, so if you plan to bleach the wood, don't seal it first. Wait two months after applying the bleach to seal the wood.

APPLYING A FINISH

Home centers offer a wide array of deck cleaners, sealers, and finishes. Check with deck owners in your area to see which products work best and how often they need to be applied. If the deck is exposed to hot sun for extended periods, you may need to apply a fresh coat of sealer every year.

A deck that has turned gray can usually be made to look like new if you wash it and apply a finish. Even grayish-green pressure-treated wood can be stained to resemble cedar or redwood.

It may be worth the cost to hire a professional to finish or refinish your deck. Look through your phone directory for companies that restore, finish, and maintain a deck's appearance. Check out their prices and examine some of the decks they have worked on. Compare the cost with the time and expense it will take you to do it yourself.

PRESTART CHECKLIST

☐ **TIME**
Several hours to clean, and several hours to apply a finish the next day

☐ **TOOLS**
Scrub brush, power washer, pole sander, pump sprayer, paintbrush

☐ **SKILLS**
Attention to detail, applying a smooth coat of finish

☐ **PREP**
Consult with a supplier to find the best products for your wood and your climate

☐ **MATERIALS**
Deck cleaner, deck sealer and/or finish

1 Lightly sand the deck using a pole sander, then sweep it thoroughly. Mix a batch of deck cleaner according to manufacturer's directions, apply it, and scrub with a stiff brush.

Pole sander

2 Use a garden hose or a power washer to rinse the cleaner completely from the deck. If you use a power washer, use the fan or 40-degree nozzle. Be careful not to hold the nozzle too close to the wood; the pressure spray can damage the surface.

FINISH INGREDIENTS AND THEIR USES

Choose a finish that contains all the ingredients you need: water repellent to seal out moisture; preservative to protect against mildew, wet rot, and insects; and UV blockers to stop the sun from turning the wood gray.

Finish	Uses
Clear sealers	These products use oil or waxes to keep moisture from soaking in. Some contain preservatives to keep bugs away and prevent mildew.
Semitransparent stain	Though some products claim to block UV rays without adding color to the wood, the only reliable way to avoid damage from the sun is to add at least a slight pigment. Some finishes dramatically change the color, while others are more subtle.
Resinous finish	This typically comes in two parts and is expensive. The resin gives a deck a permanent wet look. It provides superior protection against water, but may need to be reapplied every year.
Solid stain and porch and deck paint	A solid stain completely changes the color of a board, but allows its grain to show through. Paint covers the color and texture of a board. Oil-base products can be long-lasting; water-base products will wear away quickly.

3 Allow the deck to dry completely. Use a pump sprayer to spread sealer/stain onto the deck. Cover a strip about 3 feet wide— an easy reach for brushing.

4 Immediately brush the surface with a 5- to 6-inch brush so there will be no puddles. Move the brush in one direction only, always with the grain.

5 For detail work, use a smaller brush. Pay attention to the edges of boards, so you don't end up with brush strokes that run across the grain.

STANLEY PRO TIP: **Rent a power washer**

Use a power washer to clean a deck with water only or use it to rinse a deck after scrubbing with deck cleaner. Be sure to use a nozzle that fans out; a focused spray can create dents and carve channels, especially in soft cedar or redwood.

Apply with a roller

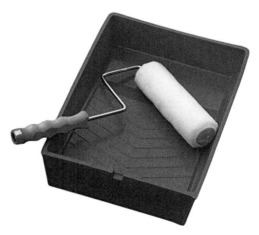

You can apply sealer with a paint roller instead of a pump sprayer. Work carefully to avoid blobs and streaks. Brush the wood within a couple of minutes of applying with the roller.

MASTERING BASIC SKILLS

Precise measurements, straight cuts, and solid joints do not happen by accident. Even though these tasks are themselves relatively uncomplicated endeavors, achieving a level of craftsmanship with any one of them comes only from constant practice.

If you're new to construction or just a little rusty, this chapter can help. It contains all the information you'll need to learn how to use both the hand tools and power tools utilized in building a deck. Start slowly. Take your time. And practice each skill until you feel proficient.

Learn the techniques that lead to professional results, then perform them over and over again until they become second nature.

Fortunately, decks are built from the ground up, and that means you might be able to afford a little imprecision when building the framing—an area that will ultimately be out of sight—as long as the fudge factor doesn't impair the structural integrity of the framing.

Make the job easier
Learning new skills or using old ones in a new project can seem a little daunting. You need to keep distractions and nonproductive actions to a minimum so you can focus on the task at hand. A few simple ideas will help you do that.

First set up an outdoor work station that's removed from the primary work area, but close enough so you don't waste time moving back and forth. Build a sturdy work surface from sawhorses and 2× lumber, and keep clamps handy so your material doesn't move around when you're measuring or cutting.

You'll do most of your cutting with a circular saw, followed by a power mitersaw. Mount the miter to the work surface and install block supports about 3 feet on either side of the saw table.

Invest in accessories that can make your work go quickly. A magnetic drill holder or quick-change sleeve will save hours wasted in changing bits and tips in your cordless drill. An inexpensive drill guide will keep holes at the correct angle to the surfaces. Metal or homemade wood guides will speed accurate cutting.

It helps to have a predictable routine. Strap on a comfortable tool belt and keep basic tools—tape measure, pencil, knife, layout square—in assigned pockets. Jot down measurements rather than trying to memorize them. That way you can think about important things rather than looking for tools or trying to remember a number.

Keep tools in good shape
Keep sharp blades in your saws and maintain a collection of sharp bits for the drill. If a measuring tool is damaged, replace it to ensure accuracy.

Learning the basic skills to build a deck requires a little time and a lot of patience.

CHAPTER PREVIEW

Measuring and marking
page 220

Square, level, and plumb
page 222

Using a circular saw
page 224

Cutting with a handsaw
page 227

Accurate measuring and marking are essential for success when you build your deck. This chapter shows those skills and other carpentry fundamentals that will help you build a strong, beautiful deck.

Cutting with a tablesaw and mitersaw
page 228

Fastening
page 230

MEASURING AND MARKING

Measuring and marking are basic to all other carpentry skills. They don't require complicated or expensive equipment, just concentration.

If you don't already own a quality tape measure, buy one. Get one with a 25-foot-long blade that's 1 inch wide and a blade lock to keep the blade extended. The wide blade extends a long way without buckling.

If possible get a tape measure with the first few inches not divided into 32nds. These fine markings are rarely needed in a carpentry project and can be distracting. Learn to spot the ¼- and ⅛-inch markings instinctively. They're good benchmarks for other measurements.

If you're a bit rusty, practice marking and cutting scrap. That way you won't ruin an expensive piece of lumber.

Even though you've drawn precise plans, take on-site measurements. Your plans may be perfect, but the work site won't be. What matters is that the boards fit where they're supposed to go, not whether they're cut to the precise size on your plan.

STANLEY PRO TIP

Gloves or no gloves?

Gloves protect your hands from splinters and pressure-treated wood. But wearing them makes it difficult to measure and mark precisely, and loose-fitting gloves can be dangerous when using a circular saw. A solution: Keep a pair of high-quality leather gloves in a pocket so you can put them on when handling heavy lumber and take them off when using tools.

A. Marking for crosscuts

Point of the V indicates the precise spot

V marks the spot

Layout square

Waste side mark

Before cutting a board make sure the end that you won't cut is square. If it's not, cut it square and remeasure. Hook the tape measure on the end of the board and extend the tape until you reach the length for the crosscut. Mark the measurement with a V, not a straight line.

Hold the pencil tip on the point of the V, and slide a layout square over until it touches the pencil tip. Mark a straight line, then draw a large X to indicate the waste side of the cut.

Taking inside and outside measurements

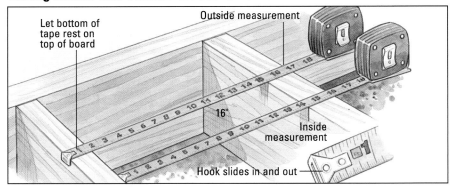

Let bottom of tape rest on top of board

Outside measurement

16"

Inside measurement

Hook slides in and out

To make an outside measurement hook the tape over the edge of one board and read the measurement at the outside edge of the other.

To take an inside measurement push the hook against the inside edge of one board and read the measurement at the inside edge of the other. You can bring the back of the case up to the opposite side of an inside measurement, then add the length of the case to the tape reading. This is less accurate, especially if the back of the case is not square.

Always keep the tape straight and at a right angle to the surfaces you're measuring.

B. Marking rip cuts

Mark the width of the cut on both ends with a tape measure or square. Hook a chalk line tightly on the marks and snap the line. If the cut runs parallel to the edge of the board, scribe a line by holding a pencil against a square at the proper width. Draw the square and pencil down the length of the board.

C. Marking miter cuts

Miter cuts are angled crosscuts most often at 45 degrees. For a 45-degree cut, measure to the long end of the miter, and set your combination square or layout square on the mark. Draw the cut line.

Using a T-bevel

To mark angles other than 90 and 45 degrees, use a sliding bevel gauge, or T-bevel. Set the blade and handle on the inside or outside edges of the boards and lock the blade. Then move the tool to the piece you want to cut, and mark the line along the blade.

Tapes don't always agree

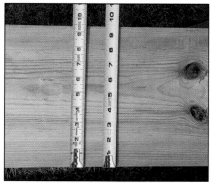

Measurements may not match. Two tape measures, especially if made by different manufacturers, can vary by as much as ⅛ inch from one another. To keep all your measurements consistently accurate, always use one tape on a project.

REFRESHER COURSE
Measuring on-site

Mark actual length on-site whenever possible. No matter how accurately you take measurements with a tape measure, there's no substitute for an on-site measurement. Any number of factors can throw a measurement off, and even a small discrepancy can make a difference. Lumber dimensions may not be exact—the actual dimension may be off by 1/32 inch, which your tape may not show, or you may forget which side of a marked line to cut. Position the stock to be cut as shown—with the cut end as close to the edge as possible, without slipping off—and mark the cut line with a carpenter's pencil.

SQUARE, LEVEL, AND PLUMB

Carpentry projects must be square, level, and plumb. Square means corners are 90 degrees. Level is always gauged by a device, such as a carpenter's level; level is not always parallel to the ground. Plumb is vertical, most accurately gauged by a plumb bob. Levels can show when posts are plumb.

Assuring that your deck elements are square, level, and plumb increases the structural integrity of your project. Make sure your squaring and leveling tools are in good shape, and protect them from damage at the work site. If you suspect a tool is inaccurate, check it against a known good one. If you can't repair or adjust it, purchase a new one.

Using a framing square

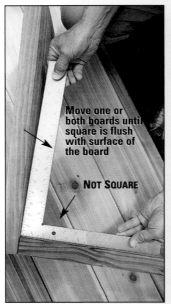

Move one or both boards until square is flush with surface of the board

NOT SQUARE

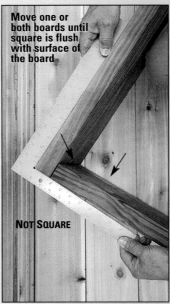

Move one or both boards until square is flush with surface of the board

NOT SQUARE

SQUARE

Position the framing square on an inside or outside edge of the joint and look along the lengths of both the tongue (short side) and the blade (long side). The tongue and blade should fit flush against the surfaces along their entire lengths. If you see light anywhere along either edge of the square, reposition the boards, pulling or pushing one or both of them until the framing square fits snugly. Don't be satisfied if only the corner of the square is tight. The corner is not true unless the square fits snugly along the entire lengths of the tongue and blade.

Square the ends

Before making a crosscut, make sure the end of the board you measure from is square—otherwise one edge of the board will be longer than the other. Check the end with a layout square or combination square on narrow stock; hook a framing square on the outside edge of wider boards. Mark the end and cut it square if necessary.

Squaring corners in the layout

Corners of your layout have to be square or the deck will be out of square.

On small sites, such as a concrete pad at the bottom of stairs or a small deck extension for a barbecue, you can lay out square corners with a 4×8 sheet of plywood. For larger sites use the 3-4-5 triangle based on the Pythagorean theorem: The square of the length of the longest side of a right-angle triangle equals the sum of the squares of the lengths of the other two sides. The longest side of a triangle with sides 3 and 4 feet long is 5 feet long.

To check a corner angle, mark a point 3 feet from the corner along one side and another point 4 feet from the corner along the other side. Measure the straight distance between the points; if it's 5 feet, the corner is square. See page 83 for an illustration of this method in use.

Plumbing posts

Post level

Posts have to be plumb in two directions, and you can use a carpenter's level on both sides to plumb them. Make this job easier by strapping on a post level. It's specifically designed to plumb posts in both directions at once.

Using a carpenter's level

Check level with center vial

Bubble centered between lines in vial

Check plumb with end vial

Use a carpenter's level that is 4 feet long to level and plumb your construction whenever you have room for its length. Shorter levels may be affected by warps or waves in the boards themselves and might not prove as accurate. Boards are level or plumb when the bubble is centered in the appropriate vial.

Leveling on-site

Carpenter's level

Straight board

Mark on post is level with top of ledger

Extend the length of your level with straight boards when working on-site. Get in the habit of checking each piece as you install it and use the widest board possible—narrower boards (like 2×4s) may flex and give you a false reading. Center the level on the board to minimize the effect of flexing or crowning.

WHAT IF . . .
You need to level surfaces that are far apart?

When you need to level objects or surfaces within 6 to 8 feet of each other, a carpenter's level set on a straight board will do. But you can make almost any leveling task easier and more accurate with a water level (available at many hardware stores). Essentially two pieces of clear plastic tubing that fasten to the ends of a hose filled with water, this tool relies on the principle that water will seek its own level over any distance. Hold the ends of the level against both surfaces, and mark each board at the water line.

High-tech levelers

Technology has improved leveling devices so much that they make the task virtually goofproof. For a modest investment you can purchase an automated water level—it beeps when the water is stabilized in the tube. Or you can buy a laser level that indicates level and projects a visible level line across long distance. A few years ago tools like these were only for the pros. Today's prices put them within reach of the average homeowner.

USING A CIRCULAR SAW

You'll probably use a circular saw more than any other tool for deck building. A saw with a 7¼-inch blade and a motor that draws 10 to 13 amps is powerful enough to cut effortlessly through 2× stock, even at a 45-degree angle.

Most saws will come equipped with a combination blade for making crosscuts and rip cuts. If yours has a standard steel blade, replace it with a carbide-tipped combination blade. Inexpensive steel blades will be dull after about four hours of heavy cutting. A moderately priced carbide blade will last a long time and make cleaner cuts throughout its life.

You can accomplish many of your cuts (especially framing cuts) freehand, but for more precision support the workpiece solidly and employ jigs or guides for cuts. Supporting the board will minimize dangerous kickback and splintering along the bottom face as the waste falls away. For all cuts, start the saw off the cut and push the blade into the board with a steady forward motion.

Cutting freehand

Sight on the guide or on the blade as you cut

Rest the edge of the board on a solid surface and tilt it up 30 to 45 degrees, keeping the saw guide or the blade visible. Line up the blade with your cut line, start the saw, and let gravity pull it down the line. Keep the saw plate flat on the stock as you cut.

Crosscutting with a guide

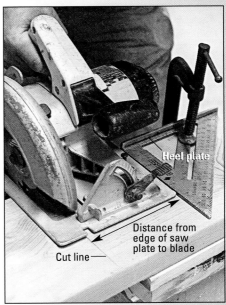

Heel plate

Distance from edge of saw plate to blade

Cut line

Clamp a layout square with its heel plate against the edge of the board, positioned to put the saw blade just on the waste side of the cut. Most saw plates are marked with the distance from the edge to the blade. Put the saw plate flat on the board, start the saw, and push it forward.

SAFETY FIRST
Eye, ear, face protection

Cutting lumber, especially pressure-treated stock, calls for protection. Protect your eyes from flying chips and sawdust with safety glasses. If you are sensitive to pressure-treated lumber, use a facemask. When making frequent cuts, wear ear protectors.

Squaring the blade

Bevel gauge

Don't trust the bevel guide on a circular saw; it could be off by several degrees, producing nonsquare cuts. Check the blade angle with a square, and adjust the plate until it's 90 degrees to the blade. Unplug the saw anytime you adjust the saw.

Changing a blade

Unplug the saw and retract the blade guard. Set the teeth of the blade firmly into a piece of scrap or the top of your outside work surface. Make sure the board won't move. Remove the bolt and tilt the blade out. Reverse the procedure to install the blade.

Cutting miters

Blade guard retracted

Cut line

Heel plate

Plate-to-blade distance

Clamp a layout square to the board as a guide. (Experiment to find the right distance away from the cut line.) Retract the blade guard before starting. The saw might work hard in a miter cut—don't push too hard. Cut the miter before you cut the board to length so you can recut if you make a mistake.

Rip cutting

Rip guide

To make a rip cut, fit the saw with a rip guide. If the cut is not parallel to the edge of a board, either cut it freehand or clamp a long straightedge as a guide. Don't force the saw away from the cut— the rip guide might flex with it.

Bevel cutting

Bevel gauge

Bevel cuts will make the saw work harder, so clamp the board firmly to a work surface using a guide set so the blade will cut along the waste side of the line. Set the bevel gauge to the correct angle and check it with a protractor. Start the saw and ease it into the cut with a slow but constant speed.

Setting the cutting depth

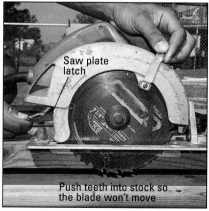

Saw plate latch

Push teeth into stock so the blade won't move

Set the blade to extend no more than ¼ inch through the thickness of the stock. Release the saw plate latch to position the plate to the proper depth.

SAFETY FIRST
Minimizing kickback

When the teeth on the rear of a circular saw blade catch or the blade binds in the kerf, the saw can kick back out of its cut line, ruining the cut and endangering the carpenter. Here are some ways to avoid kickback:

■ Don't try to change directions midcut. If your saw veers off the cut line, stop cutting, back up, and start again. Don't run the saw as you back it up—that also causes kickback.

■ Keep your blades clean and sharp. If you have to push hard to make a cut, chances of kickback multiply.

■ Support the work securely. If the board bends down in the middle or if a heavy piece of waste falls away, it may pinch the blade and cause dangerous kickback.

■ Sometimes a knotted or twisted board, or one with twisted grain, can grab the blade suddenly. Be prepared for this.

■ Operate the saw safely. Never wear loose sleeves or other clothing that could get caught in the blade as you cut. Never bring your face close to the blade as you cut. Keep the power cord clear of the blade.

Good side down
A circular saw blade exits the cut upward and will splinter the top of the board. Where appearance matters, cut with the good side of the board down.

Cutting long stock

Spacer

Work support

Workpiece

Support the board so the saw won't bind or kick back and to keep the board from splintering as the waste falls away. If the waste side is longer than 2 feet, support the board in four places. That way both sides of the cut will stay put and you can make a straight, neat cut.

Cutting thick stock

Cut line transferred to adjacent sides

Mark the cut on one side of the piece and transfer the mark to the adjoining sides with a square. Position the saw to the waste side of the line and against a layout square. Push the saw through the cut from one end to the other. Turn the stock and cut each adjacent side.

Keep saw shoe against wood throughout the cut

Use a blade long enough to cut through stock

Transfer the cut line to two adjacent sides, and keeping both lines visible, position a reciprocating saw with the saw shoe against the stock. Keep the blade in line with the waste side of the cut and off the wood. Start the saw, and rock it back and forth through the lines.

Cutting laps and notches

1 Mark the dimensions of the recess on your board, transferring them to adjacent sides. Mark the depth of the notch on opposite sides. Set your circular saw to the depth of the notch and cut a series of kerfs about ¼-inch apart.

2 Break off the cut pieces with a hammer, starting at the most accessible end and removing a broken section to give you more room at the end of the cuts.

3 Remove the waste with a wide, sharp chisel (bevel side down), clearing away the ridges until the surface is flat.

CUTTING WITH A HANDSAW

Although you'll do most of your cutting with power saws, there are times when cutting with a handsaw will be quicker or necessary. For example, when you have only a few cuts to make in thin or narrow stock, using a handsaw might be faster than getting out the circular saw and setting it up. Then, too, there are certain cuts, such as cutouts for stair stringers, that you can start with a circular saw but need to finish with a handsaw.

Using a handsaw properly is part art, part science. The trick is to change the angle of the saw after you have started the cut. With the proper technique, cutting with a handsaw will turn out to be less difficult than you might expect.

If you don't have a handsaw, buy one with teeth that are beveled to cut in both directions. Most of these are shorter than the traditional handsaw, but they cut faster because they cut on both the upstroke and the downstroke.

Back-cutting a corner cutout

Notching the corner of a thin board is one job that may go more quickly with a handsaw. Start each of the cuts as illustrated on this page, then finish them by holding the saw perpendicular to the board, reversing the position if necessary. Use the same technique to finish cuts on a stair stringer that you started with a circular saw.

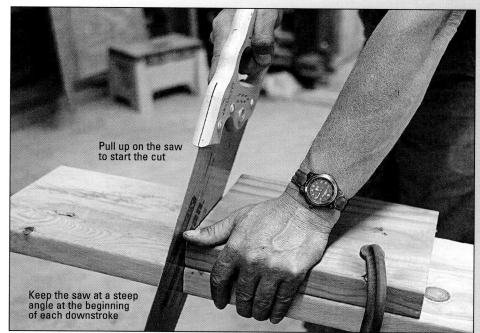

Pull up on the saw to start the cut

Keep the saw at a steep angle at the beginning of each downstroke

1 Begin the cut by setting the teeth on the waste side of the cut line and the heel of the blade (the part closest to the handle) at about 45 degrees to the wood. Put your thumbnail next to the blade so it doesn't wander. For the first few strokes, pull the saw toward you (don't push it) until you have the cut started.

Rock the saw to a flatter angle at the end of each downstroke. Pull back straight.

2 Keeping the saw straight with the cut line, push it down and pull it back, rocking it from a steep angle at the beginning of the downstroke to a flatter angle at the end. Let the weight of the saw do the work. Pushing will only wear you out and cause the saw to wander. When you get within about an inch of the other end of the board, support the waste with your free hand. Hold it firmly to keep the kerf from binding the saw. Hold on to the waste as you continue cutting. Change to a slightly faster downstroke for the last few strokes to sever the waste from the board.

CUTTING WITH A TABLESAW AND MITERSAW

Although you can build a deck without a tablesaw and power mitersaw, these tools can help you do the job more quickly and accurately. If you need to rip long boards, make notches or dadoes, cut accurate mitered corners, or chamfer your post corners, these tools are invaluable.

Buy tools rugged enough to do the work, and they will more than return their cost in saved time and convenience. And a tablesaw and mitersaw will prove handy for other home improvement projects you may take on.

Critical to the quality of both tools is the bed, the fence, and the angle scale. Take along a straightedge and check the bed. It should be absolutely flat. The rip fence on a tablesaw should lock down smoothly and stay put. The same goes for the angle scale on a power mitersaw.

Wear ear and eye protection whenever you use either saw. Power saws are noisy, and throw chips and splinters.

SAFETY FIRST
Power saw safety
Power saws are dangerous. Approach them with plenty of respect.
- Avoid cutting warped wood; it's more likely to bind and kick back.
- Stand to one side of a tablesaw blade, not directly behind it.
- Extend a tablesaw blade a maximum of ¼" above the thickness of the work. More blade means more risk.
- Never remove the blade guard, and keep blades sharp.
- Use a push stick on tablesaw rip cuts narrower than 5 inches to keep your hands away from the blade.
- Attach your mitersaw to a waist-high surface; don't operate it on the ground.
- Keep one hand on the trigger and the other on the work; freehand pieces can quickly become unguided missiles.

Using a tablesaw

Blade guard removed for clarity

To make a crosscut with a tablesaw, first move the rip fence beyond the end of the board. Mark the board for the cut line. With the power off, set the stock on the table and raise the blade ¼ inch above the thickness. Insert the miter gauge in the slot and set the board with a true edge squarely in the gauge. Pull the board back about an inch from the blade and turn the power on. Hold the board securely in the miter gauge (not on both sides) and push the board smoothly into and completely beyond the blade. Shut off the power. When the blade stops spinning, remove the stock.

STANLEY PRO TIP: **Squaring the blade**

Both tablesaw and mitersaw blades need periodic checking to make sure they are square to their tables. A blade that's out of square will produce an unintended bevel cut.

On a tablesaw raise the blade to its limit and set the tilt scale to 0 degrees. Place one side of a square on the table and the other against the blade, between two teeth where the blade face is flat. The vertical leg of the square should meet the blade face without any gaps. If any light is visible between the square and the blade, adjust the blade tilt to eliminate the gap. Adjust the zero stop on the tilt control, and lock the adjustment.

The procedure on a mitersaw is similar. Retract the blade guard, and lower the head to cutting position. Then gauge the angle between the blade and the table. It should be 90 degrees.

Also measure the angle between the blade and the fence; it should be 90 degrees. Adjustment procedures vary; see your saw's operating manual for specific information.

Blade guard removed for clarity

Miter cuts are a form of crosscut, and procedures are essentially the same. Mark the board at the correct angle (so you can see immediately if the cut is correct) and set the miter gauge at the same angle. Raise the saw blade ¼ inch above the stock and line the waste side of the cut line up with the left edge of the blade. Turn the power on and feed the stock slowly past the blade. The saw will work a little harder in miter cuts than straight crosscuts.

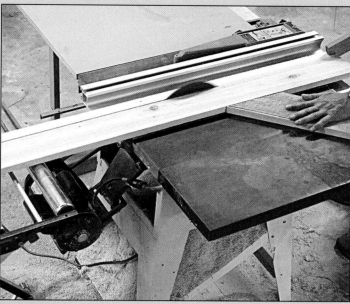

Rip cuts are a tablesaw's forte. If the stock is longer than the table, set up outfeed rollers to support the cut end. Then lock the width of the cut on the rip fence guide. Set the board (good side up) flat on the table and snug against the rip fence. Turn the saw on and feed the work steadily into and completely past the blade, using a push stick at the end of any cut less than 5 inches wide. Turn off the power. When the blade stops spinning, remove the boards.

Using a mitersaw

To cut miters on a mitersaw, mark the cut line on the workpiece and set it square on the table, with the cut line about ¹⁄₁₆ inch away from the blade. With one hand, hold the work snugly on the fence, and with the other grasp the handle of the saw and squeeze the trigger. Let the saw come to full speed, then lower the blade into the work. Reposition the work, and make successive cuts to the cut line.

To cut bevels, set the miter scale at 90 degrees or, for compound miters, the angle of the cut. Tilt the blade to the angle of the bevel and lock it. Holding the work firmly against the fence, lower the saw to check the position of the cut line. Then raise the saw and bring it to full speed, lowering the blade slowly into the stock. Let the blade come to rest before removing the cut piece.

FASTENING

A high-quality hammer and a cordless drill/driver make your deck project go more smoothly and reduce fatigue.

For framing use a 20-ounce framing hammer. The heavier hammer will drive nails with less effort than a lighter hammer. For trim work use a lighter (16-ounce) carpenter's hammer.

A cordless drill/driver is the best tool for drilling holes and driving screws. Buy an 18-volt (or higher) drill/driver with a spare battery so you can work with one battery while the other charges. A 14.4-volt model will do the work, but a lower-voltage tool probably will not be adequate.

When using a cordless drill/driver to drive screws, set the clutch so it disengages when the screw head is flush with the surface of the wood. A magnetic screw holder makes it easy to start screws. Keep the screwdriver tip perpendicular to the head and firmly in the recess. Start slowly with moderate pressure on the drill/driver, increasing both motor speed and pressure until the screw is driven home.

Nailing

Nail set

To start a nail press the point into the board and hold it with one hand while tapping with a hammer. Once the nail stands by itself, remove your hand and pound. Swing the hammer with a fluid motion and a flexible wrist, ending each stroke with a snap.

To set a nail pound until the nailhead is flush with the wood surface. Practice this until you can do it consistently without marring the surface of the wood. Use a nail set, which allows you to force the nailhead into the wood without marring the surface.

Driving screws

Pilot hole

Joist hanger

Drill a pilot hole to protect against splitting the wood whenever you will drive a nail or screw less than 2 inches from the edge of a board. Use a drill bit slightly smaller than the fastener, and drill only through the board to be fastened, not the one beneath.

Equip the drill with a magnetic sleeve and a drill bit that matches the head of the screws you will drive. The magnetic feature holds the screw. A sleeve slides down to hold the screw straight for starting.

Attach with angle-driven screws when you can only get at the end of the board to be fastened. Drill pilot holes at a steep angle and drive the screws until the heads start to bite into the board.

Toenailing

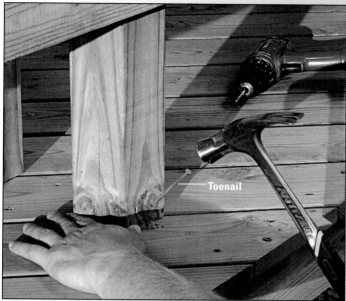

Toenailed fasteners are driven at an angle to connect boards that are at a right angle to one another. Start a nail at a steep angle and reduce the angle as you drive it. As an alternative, drill pilot holes at a steep angle and then drive the nail or screw. When using a nail, finish by using a nail set to drive the head slightly beneath the surface of the wood.

Fastener patterns

Nailing pattern over posts and vertical framing

When making perpendicular joints, stagger the fasteners throughout the grain to minimize splits

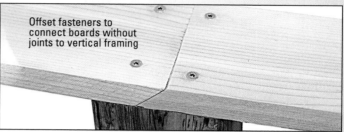

Offset fasteners to connect boards without joints to vertical framing

Fastener patterns can affect both the appearance and the strength of a joint whether you are using nails or screws. You can increase the hold of a fastener by driving it at a slight angle to the surface of the wood. Wherever you drive multiple fasteners close together, stagger their locations if possible to avoid splitting the surface, predrilling the hole for additional protection.

Lag screws and bolts

For extra-strong fastening, use lag screws or bolts. Temporarily support the board so it will not move as you work. Drill a pilot hole. Slide a washer onto the lag screw and tap it partway into the hole. Drive it home using a socket and ratchet wrench.

To attach with a carriage bolt temporarily support the board so it will not move as you work. Drill a hole the same diameter as the bolt's shaft through both boards. Tap the bolt all the way through. Slip on a washer and tighten the nut.

REFRESHER COURSE
Fastener length

Many theories pertain to the length of fasteners, but one you can count on consistently is to use a fastener that penetrates about two-thirds of the way into the bottom board.

Using a power nailer

Lock-out safety tip — Nail strip

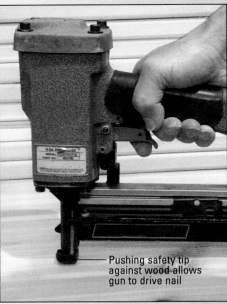

Pushing safety tip against wood allows gun to drive nail

1 Keep the lock-out safety tip off the surface of the wood to disable the trigger when you load the nail strip into the magazine. Slide the nails in until the clip locks securely.

2 Hold the nail gun firmly with your finger lightly on the trigger. Push the tip of the nail gun against the wood where you want to drive the nail, then pull the trigger.

3 Release the trigger, raise the gun, and reposition it for the next fastener.

REFRESHER COURSE
Counterboring

Spade bit same diameter as washer

Bore ⅛ inch deeper than thickness of bolt head or nut

Twist drill same diameter as bolt shank

Although you can leave the heads of lag screws, machine bolts, and carriage bolts on the surface of the wood, the heads and the bolt nuts will look better if they are countersunk.
To counterbore a hole, start with a spade bit the diameter of your washer and drill a hole about

⅛ inch deeper than the thickness of the bolt head or nut. Then center a twist drill bit the diameter of the bolt shank in the counterbore and drill completely through the stock. Slide a washer onto a lag screw or machine bolt before you insert it, and place a washer under the nut too.

DESIGN OPTION
Recessed deck clips

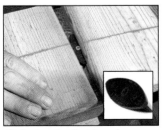

1 Lay out your decking boards on the joists or a flat surface and line up their edges. Snap chalk lines across the boards at intervals equal to your joist spacing. Using a biscuit joiner, cut recesses for the clips into the decking. Make sure to cut slots in both edges of the boards, except the first and last ones.

2 Fasten the first board as prescribed by the manufacturer. Then center the clip on the joist and push it into the biscuit recess. Holding the clip in place, drive in the fastener (generally but not always at 45 degrees). Complete the installation of clips across the deck. Push the next board into place and repeat.

Installing hidden deck clips

Scrap 2×4

1" from edge of decking

1 Lay out your decking boards loosely on the joists. Having them at hand will speed your installation. Predrill and fasten the first row of decking to the joists by surface nailing or screwing (or with the method prescribed by the manufacturer).

2 Push the corner of the clip firmly against the edge of the joist and the decking board. Fasten a clip to each joist and the edge of the first decking board with the fastener recommended by the manufacturer (usually screws).

3 Pull the next decking board into place, just touching each of the clips. Drive the decking board onto the clip points, using a scrap 2×4 to protect the edge. Install the fasteners. Install the remaining boards the same way. Toenail or face-nail the last one.

DESIGN OPTION
Hidden track system

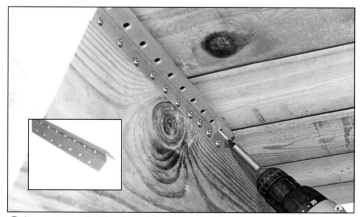

1 Hidden track systems are usually installed on alternate sides of the joists along their entire length. Fasten the track pieces to the sides of the joists, making sure the top plate is flush with the top of the joists. Lay a 2×6 across the joists to help keep the edges flush. Cut the track with aviation snips when necessary.

2 Lay out your decking boards on the top of the joists so they are at hand. With the aid of a helper who will keep the decking properly aligned, fasten the decking to the track with the fasteners provided or recommended by the manufacturer.

GLOSSARY

For terms not included here, or for more about those that are, refer to the index starting on page 237.

Actual dimension: The dimension of a board or masonry unit as measured. See *Nominal dimension*.

Anchor: Metal device set in concrete for attaching posts to footings or piers.

Baby sledge: A small sledgehammer, usually 2½ pounds, used for a variety of construction tasks and repairs where more weight is needed than can be supplied by a carpenter's hammer.

Backfill: To replace earth excavated during the construction process. A material other than the original earth may be used to improve the drainage or structure of the soil.

Baluster: The smaller vertical members of a railing, usually spaced at regular intervals between posts.

Batterboard: A layout fixture made of two stakes driven into the ground, with a crosspiece connecting them at the top. Layout strings are stretched between batterboards to mark edges and corners of a layout.

Beam: A large horizontal framing piece, usually made of 4× or doubled 2× lumber, which attaches to the posts and supports the joists.

Bevel cut: An angle cut along the edge of a piece of wood.

Blocking: Short pieces of lumber, usually the same dimension as the joists, cut to fit between joists. Blocking prevents the warping of joists and adds strength.

Bracing: Diagonal crosspieces nailed and bolted between tall posts, usually those more than 5 feet tall.

Broom finish: A slip-resistant texture created by brushing a stiff broom across fresh concrete.

Bull float: A large, long-handled float used for reaching into the center and smoothing a large slab of wet concrete.

Bubble plan: A plan that includes such nonstructural considerations as view, landscaping features, and traffic patterns.

Building codes: Community ordinances governing construction or modification of structures. Most codes concern fire safety and health, with separate sections relating to electrical, plumbing, and structural work.

Building permit: A license authorizing specified construction work. The permit requires that the work be done in accordance with building codes and requires one or more inspections. In most municipalities, building a deck requires a building permit.

Butt joint: The joint formed by square-cut ends or edges; the easiest carpentry joint, but also the weakest.

Cantilever: A framing member that extends beyond a post or support, typically more than 2 feet. Cantilevers help hide some posts, giving the deck the appearance of floating.

Carpenter's level: A tool for establishing level over short distances.

Chamfer: An angle cut along one corner of an edge, not the entire edge.

Cement: A powdered mix of gypsum and other materials that serves as the binding element in concrete and mortar.

Check: A crack on the surface of a board. If the check runs more than halfway through the thickness of a board, structural integrity is diminished, and the board should not be used.

Cleat: A length of board attached to strengthen or add support to a structure.

Concrete: A mixture of portland cement, fine aggregate (sand), course aggregate (gravel or crushed stone), and water. Concrete becomes harder and stronger with age.

Countersink: To drive the head of a nail or screw so that its top is flush with the surface of the surrounding wood.

Crook: A bend along the length of a board, visible by sighting along one edge. With decking, a slight crook—no more than ¾ inch in an 8-foot board—can be corrected when the board is fastened down.

Crosscut: To saw lumber perpendicular to its length or its grain.

Crown: A slight edgewise bow in a board. In framing, the crown edge is placed upward so gravity will in time force it down.

Cup: A curve across the width of a board. Unless it is severe, cupping is not a problem for framing lumber. Slight cupping in a decking board can be taken out by screwing down each side of the board. Reject any boards with cupping more than ⅜ inch deep.

Darby: A hand tool with a long sole made of smooth wood or metal, used for smoothing the surface of a concrete slab after initial leveling.

Decking: The boards used to make the walking surface of a deck. Decking is usually made of 2×6, 2×4, or ⁵⁄₄×6 lumber.

Dimension lumber: A piece of lumber that has been dried and cut to modular dimensions. Refers to boards at least 2 inches wide and 2 inches thick.

Durable species: Wood species such as heart redwood, heart cedar, tidewater cypress, and some locusts that are naturally resistant to decay and insect damage; sometimes refers to pressure-treated lumber.

Earth-wood clearance: Distance required between wood and the ground; some pressure-treated lumber or durable species can contact the ground.

Elevation drawing: A drawing that shows the vertical face of a deck, emphasizing footings, posts, railings, and any built-in planters, benches, skirting, or overhead structures.

End grain: The ends of wood fibers exposed at the ends of boards.

Fascia: Horizontal trim that covers the ends of deck boards and part or all of the rim joist or header joist.

Finial: An ornament attached to the top of a post or the peak of an arch.

Finish: A coating, such as water repellent or paint, applied to a surface to protect it against weathering.

Flashing: Bent strips of sheet metal, usually galvanized steel or aluminum, that protect lumber from water. On a deck, flashing is often used to protect the ledger and the sheathing behind it.

Flush: On the same plane, or level with, the surrounding or adjacent surface.

Footing: A small foundation, usually of concrete, that supports a post. See *Pier.*

Frost heave: The upthrust of soil caused when moist soil freezes. Posts and footings that do not extend below the frost line are subject to frost heave.

Frost line: The maximum depth to which the ground freezes during winter.

Galvanized nails: Nails dipped in molten zinc (hot-dipped galvanized) to resist corrosion; preferred over electroplated zinc nails for outdoor construction.

Grade: The surface of the ground.

Grading: Altering the surface of ground to permit drainage, prepare an area for construction, or generally smooth the ground near a structure.

Header: A perimeter framing member that runs parallel to major beams and the ledger and to which the ends of inside joists and rim joists are attached.

Heartwood: The center and most durable part of a tree, often marked by a deeper color than the surrounding wood.

Joist: Horizontal framing members that support a floor or ceiling. An *inside* or *common* joist is a nonperimeter joist.

Joist hanger: A metal connector that joins a joist to a ledger or header so that their top edges are flush.

KDAT (kiln dried after treatment): Pressure-treated lumber that has been dried after being treated with preservative; more expensive than undried pressure-treated lumber but less likely to warp.

Lag screw: A screw, usually ¼ inch in diameter or larger, with a hexagonal head that can be driven with a wrench or socket.

Landscape fabric: Woven synthetic fabric that allows water and air to pass, but prevents weeds from growing.

Lap joint: The joint formed when one member overlaps another.

Lattice: A horizontal surface made of crisscrossed pieces of wood or vinyl.

Ledger: A horizontal strip (typically lumber) that's used to provide support for the ends or edges of other members.

Level: The condition that exists when any type of surface is at true horizontal. Also a tool used to determine level.

Load: Weight and forces that a structure is designed to withstand; includes dead load (the structure itself) and live loads (occupants and furnishings, snow, wind uplift, and earthquake forces).

Mason's line: Twine used to lay out posts, patios, footings, and structures. Preferred because it does not stretch and sag like other string.

Miter joint: The joint that is formed when two members meet that have been cut at the same angle (usually 45 degrees).

Modular: A term describing a unit of material or a structure with standardized proportional dimensions.

Nominal dimension: The stated size of a piece of lumber, such as a 2×4 or a 1×12. The actual dimension is slightly smaller.

On-center (OC): A phrase used to designate the distance from the center of one regularly spaced framing member to the center of the next.

Outside joist: A joist that is part of the perimeter framing structure, other than a ledger, of a deck. See *Rim joist.*

Pergola: An open overhead structure designed to provide shade or to support hanging or climbing plants.

Pier: A block of concrete that serves as a footing to support a post. A pier can be poured concrete or a ready-made concrete pier. See *Footing.*

Pilot hole: A small hole drilled into a wooden member to avoid splitting the wood when driving a screw or nail.

Plan-view drawing: An overhead view of a deck that shows locations of footings and framing members.

GLOSSARY *(continued)*

Plumb: The condition that exists when a member is at true vertical. See *Level.*

Plumb bob: A tool that indicates a true vertical line.

Plunge cut: A circular-saw or jigsaw cut where the blade enters the wood through the surface to avoid continuing the cut to an edge or end of a board.

Post: A vertical framing piece, usually 4×4 or 6×6, that supports a beam or joist.

Pressure-treated wood: Lumber or sheet goods impregnated with one of several chemical solutions to resist rot.

Rafter: In deck building, a framing member that supports the uppermost material that makes up a pergola.

Rail: A horizontal framing member of railing that spans between posts to support balusters and sometimes the cap rail.

Ready-mix concrete: Wet concrete that is ready to pour, transported in a truck from a concrete supplier.

Reinforcing bar: Steel rods for reinforcing concrete, sometimes called rebar or rerod.

Rim joist: A term sometimes used to describe an outside joist.

Rip: To saw lumber or sheet goods parallel to its grain or length.

Rise: The total vertical distance a stairway climbs. Also the vertical distance between the topmost surface of two sequential treads.

Riser: A board attached to the vertical surface of a stair stringer to cover the gap between treads and to provide additional tread support.

Run: The total horizontal distance a stairway spans from the structure to finished grade level. Also the horizontal depth of a tread cut made in a stringer.

Sapwood: The lighter-color more recent growth of any species of wood.

Screening: Maximum opening allowed between railing members; distances vary by code.

Sealant: A protective coating (usually clear) applied to wood and metal.

Set-back: The minimum distance between a property line and any structure, as specified by local codes.

Shim: A thin strip or wedge of wood or other material used to fill a gap between two adjoining components or to help establish level or plumb.

Site plan: A map of your property, showing where the deck will be located on your yard.

Skirt or skirting: Horizontal pieces of lumber installed around the perimeter of a deck to screen the area below the deck. Skirting may be made of vertical or horizontal solid boards, or it may be made of lattice.

Sleeper: Horizontal wood member laid directly on ground, patio, or roof for supporting a deck.

Slope: Ground with an inclined surface, usually measured in vertical rise per horizontal distance.

Span: The distance traveled by a beam, joist, or decking board between supporting structures.

Spindle: Small-dimensioned baluster.

Square: The condition that exists when two surfaces are at a 90-degree angle.

Stringer: A diagonal board used to support treads and risers on a stairway. Stringers are usually made of 2×12s.

3-4-5 triangle: A mathematical means of determining when a corner is square. Measure 3 feet along one side, and 4 feet along the other; if the corner is square, the diagonal distance between those two points will be 5 feet.

Tamper: A tool for compacting soil, sand, or other loose materials.

Trowel: A flat and oblong or flat and pointed metal tool used for handling or finishing concrete and mortar.

Troweling: Giving the concrete a smooth final finish with a steel trowel. This step is for interior applications, as it creates an extremely smooth and possibly slippery surface.

Toenail: To drive a nail at an angle when joining a piece where face-nailing is not possible. Screws also can be driven in this manner.

Wane: A rounded-off corner along the edge of a board, where there once was bark.

Water level: A tool composed of two clear plastic tubes that attach to a hose, used for establishing level over long distances or irregular surfaces.

Zoning requirements: Ordinances that affect deck size or location, such as set-back limits (distance from property line to structure), lot coverage (percentage that can be covered by improvements), and the deck's size and height.

INDEX

METRIC CONVERSIONS

U.S. Units to Metric Equivalents			Metric Units to U.S. Equivalents		
To convert from	Multiply by	To get	To convert from	Multiply by	To get
Inches	25.4	Millimeters	Millimeters	0.0394	Inches
Inches	2.54	Centimeters	Centimeters	0.3937	Inches
Feet	30.48	Centimeters	Centimeters	0.0328	Feet
Feet	0.3048	Meters	Meters	3.2808	Feet
Yards	0.9144	Meters	Meters	1.0936	Yards
Square inches	6.4516	Square centimeters	Square centimeters	0.1550	Square inches
Square feet	0.0929	Square meters	Square meters	10.764	Square feet
Square yards	0.8361	Square meters	Square meters	1.1960	Square yards
Acres	0.4047	Hectares	Hectares	2.4711	Acres
Cubic inches	16.387	Cubic centimeters	Cubic centimeters	0.0610	Cubic inches
Cubic feet	0.0283	Cubic meters	Cubic meters	35.315	Cubic feet
Cubic feet	28.316	Liters	Liters	0.0353	Cubic feet
Cubic yards	0.7646	Cubic meters	Cubic meters	1.308	Cubic yards
Cubic yards	764.55	Liters	Liters	0.0013	Cubic yards

To convert from degrees Fahrenheit (F) to degrees Celsius (C), first subtract 32, then multiply by ⅝.

To convert from degrees Celsius to degrees Fahrenheit, multiply by ⅝, then add 32.